Daily moments with Abba

Daily moments with Abba.

Joy Clark

XULON PRESS

Xulon Press
2301 Lucien Way #415
Maitland, FL 32751
407.339.4217
www.xulonpress.com

Cover by Bethany Michaela Clark Tecson
Illustrated by Hannah Clark
Photos by Mhiles Tecson Photography

Unless otherwise indicated, Scripture quotations taken from the King James Version (KJV) – *public domain.*

Scripture quotations taken from the English Standard Version (ESV). Copyright © 2001 by Crossway, a publishing ministry of Good News Publishers. Used by permission. All rights reserved.

Printed in the United States of America

Paperback ISBN-13: 9781662842962
Hard Cover ISBN-13: 9781662842979
Ebook ISBN-13: 9781662842986

January 1

Psalm 150:6

Let everything that hath breath praise the LORD. Praise ye the LORD.

What a fitting and perfect end to the book of Psalms. What a fitting and perfect end to each year, season, day, and to each moment in our lives. It's also a fitting and perfect way to bring in the New Year. Praise is a weapon for us against the enemy, but it's also a privilege for us too. He is so worthy of our praise; all creation praises Him, and we would do well to take example and do the same.

Praise brings victory and victory causes us to praise; it's so awesome how it works like that. Praise causes the enemy to tremble and flea, but Abba inhabits our praise, His very presence dwells with us. He takes pleasure in our praise. Praising Him will lift us out of the pit of darkness, a heavy heart, or a place of sorrow. Praising Him will lead to a joyful heart. That's why it's so important to praise Him in the midst of the struggles and hard times of life. Praising Him causes chains to fall, and praising Him brings **freedom**, **peace**, and **joy**!

Let everything that hath breath praise the Lord!

You are worthy, Abba, of **all** praise, honor, and glory; help us never to forget to praise you **always** in **all** things, in Yeshua's name, amen.

January 2

1 Thessalonians 5:21–22

21) Prove all things; hold fast that which is good. 22) Abstain from all appearance of evil.

We are to cling to things that are good. *Good* is defined as: morally right, beneficial, honorable, virtuous, pleasant, healthy, sound, kind, and having the proper qualities. *Proper* is described as: decent, appropriate, correct, and conforming to a standard, and *qualities* as: that which makes something what it is, the degree of excellence of a thing, the characteristic element. We are to hold fast to the virtuous, honorable, and sound, having the decent and appropriate characteristic elements and degree of excellence. We are instructed to prove and test everything, to have discernment so we can properly and correctly make wise decisions. We are to deeply examine all things, being extremely cautious that we have no part in evil or wrong in any way.

We are to abstain from even the appearance of evil. The definition of *evil* is morally bad, wrong, wicked, harmful, injurious, and disastrous, anything causing harm or pain. We must be wise to avoid even the looks of anything that falls under the definition of evil, fleeing as fast as we can from the slightest sight of it. We must not let it set up camp in our thoughts even for a moment but must quickly discard them. Once we have rightly distinguished what is good, we are to seize it, possess and retain it, clenching it as if it were precious jewels, or our very life because it is.

Abba, teach us how vital it is to turn and run from even the slightest appearance of evil, being wise in discerning it, for our enemy has a great way of making evil appear good. Help us to closely examine and prove all things, searching deeply into the situations and circumstances before stepping into them. Help us to seek, find good, and hold fast and cling to it, never letting go, in Yeshua's name, we ask this, amen.

January 3

Joshua 23:6

Be ye therefore very courageous to keep and to do all that is written in the book of the law of Moses, that ye turn not aside therefrom to the right hand or to the left.

Tunnel vision is like having blinders, like the ones they put on a horse, so they can't be distracted with things to the left or right of them. This is what we need daily when walking this amazing journey with the Lord. The reason for the horse wearing blinders is to keep him from seeing what's beside or behind him to prevent him from becoming distracted or panicked by what he sees. We need to put on these spiritual blinders so we can courageously walk after and keep Abba's perfect ways, without doubt or fear, not being moved by the world around us or the commotion going on to our left or right. The enemy will use whatever he can; he will cause chaos to get our eyes to turn ever so slightly from the Lord. We must keep our eyes fixed straight ahead on the Father alone and His perfect ways, pursuing and walking after Him with no distractions to trip us up or slow us down.

The Lord once taught me a very powerful lesson about setting my eyes on Him and keeping them there. In one of my morning devotion times, the sun was rising in the sky, and it was a beautiful bright ball of fire. Though looking into the sun is **not** a good thing for our eyes, and I would **never** recommend it, I believe the Lord used it this one time to teach me a valuable lesson I would **never** forget. He called me to look at the sun. It was hard, it hurt, and I kept wanting to turn to the right or left. I fought to keep my eyes on it as long as possible, then finally turned away. I heard in my spirit the Lord asking me what I saw; I said, "**sun**." I could see nothing else; all my peripheral vision was gone, and all I saw was the sun. After another moment, the same question, and the answer was still "**sun**," then after a few more moments, I slowly started getting my peripheral vision back and began to see things to the right and left of me again.

I learned a life-changing lesson here, that when my eyes are fixed straight ahead on the Lord and His ways, I can't see the distractions all around me. I see nothing but His Word, truth, perfect law, and love surrounding and guiding me. When I take my eyes off Him, then all the things of the world start coming back into sight, and I begin to look at the situation to my right or the person on my left. I become easily distracted with the winds of life and the chaos going on around me, getting tripped up and off course again.

That lesson was so powerful that it has stuck with me until this day, and I do my best now to wear spiritual blinders that keep my eyes fixed and set on Him.

Lord, help us to put on spiritual blinders so we can't be tempted to look to the left or right but only straight ahead at You, so we only see Your perfect law and all You wrote for us to walk by and do and help us to proudly and bravely keep and follow it all the days of our lives, in Yeshua's beautiful name, amen.

January 4

Ephesians 5:22–24

22) Wives, submit yourselves unto your own husbands, as unto the Lord. 23) For the husband is the head of the wife, even as Christ is the head of the church: and he is the savior of the body. 24) Therefore as the church is subject unto Christ, so let the wives be to their own husbands in everything.

As the Lord set Christ to be the head of the church, so He set the husband to be the head of the wife. As Yeshua humbles Himself and submits to the Father, so the church humbles itself and submits to Christ, and as the church humbles itself and submits to Christ, so the wife humbles herself and submits to her husband. It is a perfect order and such a perfect picture. The husband set as head protects the wife. He is her covering, defender, provider, protector, and he watches out for her and loves her as Christ does the church, His bride.

It's because of this love, protection, and provision that the wife can submit herself into his hands, believing and knowing he is going to always look out for her and have her best at heart. It's through this perfect order that God moves and shines, even in the face of difficulty. If we heed His Word and are obedient to it, He will move. If wives are humble before their husbands and submit, even in the hard times and times of disagreement, the Lord will honor the obedience of the wife, and she can sit back and watch His perfect picture unfold before her. I know in our world today, things are seen and carried out differently, but if we hold to His truth and walk it out despite the opposition the world may teach, we will be Blessed.

Abba, help us to believe and walk by every word in Your Word, to walk it out in all things as Yeshua did, and be an example for the world to see; it's in Yeshua's name we Pray this, amen.

5

January 5

Ephesians 5:25–31

25) Husbands, love your wives, even as Christ also loved the church, and gave himself for it; 26) That He might sanctify and cleanse it with the washing of water by the word, 27) That He might present it to Himself a glorious church, not having spot, or wrinkle, or any such thing; but that it should be holy and without blemish. 28) So ought men to love their wives as their own bodies. He that loveth his wife loveth himself. 29) For no man ever yet hated his own flesh; but nourisheth and cherisheth it, even as the Lord the church: 30) For we are members of His body, of His flesh, and of His bones. 31) For this cause shall a man leave his father and mother, and shall be joined unto his wife, and they two shall be one flesh.

Reading this makes it so easy to see that the husband has the greater responsibility and more difficult job than the wife. He must leave his mother and father and become one with his wife, becoming all she needs; loving and cherishing her to the point he is willing to lay his life down for her, keeping her washed and covered in the Word of Truth that he may present her without blemish, spot, or wrinkle, but holy and beautiful. He must follow Christ as Christ does the Father, so he can lead his wife. He now is not only responsible for just himself before the Lord but for his wife as well. That's a huge commitment and responsibility he has just taken on, but if he fully sets and fixes his eye on Christ and follows Him and loves Him with all his heart, there is no doubt or worry he will be all he needs to be for his wife.

Abba, help the husbands of our world to look to Yeshua and His example and strive to be like Him so they can love and lead their wives and homes as Yeshua does the church; in Yeshua's perfect name, we ask this, amen.

January 6

Ephesians 5:33

Nevertheless let every one of you in particular so love his wife even as himself; and the wife see that she reverence her husband.

We read the last couple of days how this is God's perfect will concerning the husband and wife. He knows nothing will work properly outside of it, and that's why He gives us His direction. Things will never be perfect, but they will be easier and so much better if we walk and remain in His perfect will. He knows way more than we do. He knows how He created us and what our strengths and needs are. He loves us so much more than even the concept we have of love. He set things this way, and we must believe and know it is good, perfect, and for our best.

If we can truly begin to walk as He has taught and commanded us to, I believe we will see His blessing and glory all around. We will begin to see the perfect picture He has planned from the beginning come together on this canvas of life as a masterpiece never seen before and will stand in awe of Him and His perfect ways. As husbands truly love their wives, wives genuinely reverence their husbands, and we all walk humbly in obedience before our Lord; it will be more glorious than we could ever imagine.

Abba, help us to walk out the masterpiece You have designed since the beginning, wholeheartedly submitting our hearts and lives to You and Your perfect way; in Yeshua's beautiful, powerful, and perfect name, amen!

January 7

Joel 2:28–29

28) And it shall come to pass afterward, that I will pour out my spirit upon all flesh; and your sons and your daughters shall prophesy, your old men shall dream dreams, your young men shall see visions: 29) And also upon the servants and upon the handmaids in those days will I pour out my spirit.

Paul in Acts quoted this scripture, and it's one of my other daily words, but I felt it important to share and touch on the original context of it as well. God, in Joel, gave His promise to His people that once they turned their hearts back toward Him and wept and repented that He would turn the curses into blessings and restore all and even more to them. They would no longer want to walk in sin because His spirit would be in them and would cause them to call upon Him and walk in His ways.

What a beautiful picture of God's forgiveness and mercy to His children, even after all they did to provoke Him to anger and break His heart. They just had to acknowledge their wrongs and genuinely turn from them, and God would be waiting right there to pour Himself out on them and fill them to overflowing with His spirit. He is such a good Father, definitely not worth turning from, and if you have, He is surely worth turning back to.

Abba, pour Your spirit out today upon Your children that we may dream your dreams, see Your visions, and speak Your words in a world that's becoming void of You; in Yeshua's powerful name, amen.

January 8

Micah 4:2

And many nations shall come, and say, Come, and let us go up to the mountain of the LORD, and to the house of the God of Jacob; and He will teach us of His ways, and we will walk in His paths: for the law shall go forth of Zion, and the word of the LORD from Jerusalem.

As I sat struggling to write this today, this verse brought me such comfort. Sometimes we may feel we're not enough, have nothing to give, or question what we have to give, asking, "Is it effective, can it really touch someone for Him; am I truly making a difference for His kingdom?" As I read this verse amid all the chaos of thoughts in my head, it spoke to my heart. He reminded me that if I'm coming daily before Him and up to His Holy mountain to seek Him, He will and is teaching me His ways. He is directing my words, my steps in His paths, and teaching and hiding His ways and commands in my heart, and I don't have to worry or doubt. As I typed this out today, it spoke to me again profoundly. Abba is good!

Come, let us go up to the mountain of the LORD, to the house of God. Let Him teach us of His ways and show us His paths. Let Him hide His truth and law in our hearts so we can walk in it and shine for Him. That every word coming off our tongue is seasoned by Him for the edification of others, for the building up, so they can see and hear of His goodness and come up with us to the only one who gives life, peace, joy, and love like no other.

Abba, thank You for being so faithful always, for meeting us, teaching us, and hiding Your truth in our hearts. We love You so much. Help us to always remember You're all we need, in Yeshua's name, amen.

January 9

Matthew 4:17

From that time Jesus began to preach, and to say, Repent: for the kingdom of heaven is at hand.

These words are just as meaningful and powerful today as they were almost two thousand years ago. There is no better time to repent and turn from our own ways unto the Lord and His ways than today. We no longer must sit and live in darkness, in the ways of the world, and in our own self-centered ways, but we can come before Yeshua, humble ourselves, repent, and begin to walk in the light of true life in Him.

Not one of us is promised tomorrow; we surely don't know what the future holds, but in Him, we don't have to worry or guess. We can just trust that we are held and kept, and our tomorrow and eternity is secure in Him. We can walk in a freedom today that we've never known, resting in the truth that we are His now and rejoicing in the light of His goodness and grace that now shines brightly in our lives. Wow, that is just so beautiful; it takes my breath away! Such beautiful promises, such an awesome hope of glory; no words can rightly explain it.

Thank You, Yeshua, for coming for us, for leaving the presence of the Father, the perfection of heaven to come here for us, to teach us and show us the way to new life; for laying Your life down for us so we can now have eternal life with You and Abba, We love and thank You, our Messiah, our hope of glory, amen.

January 10

Daniel 5:5

In the same hour came forth fingers of a man's hand, and wrote over against the candlestick upon the plaister of the wall of the king's palace: and the king saw the part of the hand that wrote.

I think, at that point, literally seeing only a hand and fingers writing on a wall, I may have passed out, especially knowing I had blatantly and with defiant arrogance used the sacred vessels that were taken by his father from God's temple. Even the pagans knew they were not to be touched. Then, to top it all off, by praising the gods of gold, silver, brass, iron, wood, and stone with his princes, wives, and concubines was deliberately lifting himself up against God Himself. God was not standing for it, and in verse twenty-five of this chapter, it says the Lord sent a message on the wall that said: "ME'-NE, ME'-NE, TE'-KEL, U-PHAR'-SIN."

ME'-NE, meaning: "God hath numbered thy kingdom and finished it." *TE'-KEL* meant "thou art weighed in the balances and art found wanting." *PE'-RES* was interpreted as: "thy kingdom is divided and given to the Medes and Persians, and that very night the king was slain." The last thing we ever want to do is come up against the Most High, only true God; we will **never** win. In fact, our outcome will be extremely bleak. He is God **alone** and deserves nothing less than our reverence and respect. Even if He wasn't the good, good Father that **He is**!

Abba, help us to never get so arrogant that we would even think we could do something against You, Your Word, or ways ever, but help us to humbly come before Thee always in only complete reverence of **all that You are**, in Yeshua's name, we pray, amen.

11

January 11

Isaiah 28:10

For precept must be upon precept, precept upon precept; line upon line, line upon line; here a little, and there a little.

In verse nine, Isaiah asked the people whom the Lord should teach knowledge to and whom should He make to understand doctrine, and the answer was them that were weaned from milk and drawn from the breasts. Just like we can't learn to run before learning to walk, we can't learn His Word out of proper order or timing either. My mother taught me to walk step by step, one step at a time, and we must learn His Word the same way. Just like trying to learn the back of the book without knowing the front of it, there will be errors in judgment and precepts out of line or misunderstood. Maturity will not be achieved to run with, understand, or teach the Word, let alone lead His children.

When we are babies, we live simply, but as we grow, we are weaned from the milk and go deeper into all He is, His commands, His precepts, and we learn them from the beginning and build upon them. It's like building a house and missing key elements in the foundation due to the lack of knowledge and void of understanding; not developed, learned, and matured in the building process. That house will end up falling; it might stand for a very short period but will not last. When matured and taught, one will build that house properly, with wisdom and understanding, precept upon precept, line upon line, here a little, there a little, and that house will stand and weather the strongest of storms.

Abba, help us to grow in You, hear Your Word, precept upon precept, command upon command, line upon line, and grow in the understanding of it that we may have that solid foundation from beginning to end, in Yeshua's name, amen.

January 12

Ezekiel 17:24

And all the trees of the field shall know that I the LORD have brought down the high tree, have exalted the low tree, have dried up the green tree, and have made the dry tree to flourish: I the LORD have spoken and have done it.

The Hebrew word used here for *high* is *gâbôhha*, meaning: elevated, powerful, lofty, arrogant, and haughty. The Hebrew word used here for *low* is *shâphâl*, meaning: humble, lowly, and depressed. The Lord is sovereign and just. He will bring down the lofty, proud, and arrogant and will exalt the humble and lowly. All will see it and know it was only the Lord's doing. Nothing and no one else can do what only He can do. This verse really just jumped off the page at me when I read it.

Amid all the chaos of life, this new thing called COVID-19, a presidential election unlike ever before, riots breaking out, states shutting down, and a time when we all should be coming together, it seems we are separating more. So much is going on we have no control of, but we must never forget, **God does**. He has **all** control and will right the wrong, bring down the high tree and exalt the low tree, and dry up the green tree and cause the dry tree to flourish. He is in complete control and will ultimately have His way, and we can bank on that. He is a God of His Word, and His Word stands through **all eternity**, no matter what man may think or do; God will have the final word. Find rest and be joyful in the truth of this verse.

Father, Thank You for being a just and good Father, for doing what only You can do and always watching, never sleeping, and never missing all that's going on. You, Abba, **don't miss a thing**. **We** thank You with all our hearts for that, in Yeshua's name, Amen.

January 13

Hebrews 13:5

Let your conversation be without covetousness; and be content with such things as ye have: for he hath said, I will never leave thee, nor forsake thee.

You could be the richest person in the world and still not have enough and want more; in fact, it seems the more we have and get, the more we want, and having everything still isn't enough. We are reminded here to be content with what we have, enjoy it, and be grateful; not to want what others have, whether it be material, spiritual, physical, and so on. Don't covet your neighbor's house, friend's life, favorite worship leader's gift, sibling's talents, Hollywood's looks, a rich person's wealth, **none** of it. It's the Tenth Commandment and is as important as the other nine.

Abba knows our needs and is faithful to give us exactly what we need, with our own special talents and gifts, our own beauty, inside and out, and our own precious lives that matter to Him. He will provide the food we need, shelter, clothes, and so much more. We need never worry, for His promise is true, and He will **never** leave or forsake **His** children. He will give us all we need to be joyful and content in Him if we fix our eyes on Him and not everything around us.

Abba, help us to live by this verse daily and to only look to You for all we need, inside and out, in Yeshua's Beautiful name, we ask this, amen.

January 14

Romans 12:1

I beseech you therefore, brethren, by the mercies of God, that ye present your bodies a living sacrifice, holy, acceptable unto God, which is your reasonable service.

I remember a song from when I was a young teen, by Chris Christian, titled, "Living Sacrifice." The lyrics just spoke to my heart deeply. "Take my life, a living sacrifice, knowing it's the least that I can do, make my life, a living sacrifice, holy and acceptable to you." I remembered these lyrics throughout the dark days of my life and would continue to make them my prayer, even when things appeared completely hopeless.

I know the man that wrote that song never knew how much it deeply impacted me, and others I'm sure, but God knew and I knew, and here I sit today, by the grace of God, writing this, still singing these words. What more is there with **all** that He's done for me, for every one of us, than to offer our lives to Him, presenting our bodies as a living sacrifice, holy, acceptable to the one and only true God. He sent His Son to die a horrible death so we could live, and if that alone was all He did for us, it would be more than enough and beyond what we deserve, but, oh, how He's done and continues to do so much more.

Lord, help us to present our bodies as a living sacrifice unto You, holy and acceptable, knowing You are worth and deserving of it, and it's the least we can do for You, in Yeshua's mighty and worthy name, amen.

January 15

Lamentations 3:25–26

25) The LORD is good unto them that wait for him, to the soul that seeketh him. 26) It is good that a man should both hope and quietly wait for the salvation of the LORD.

Amen. How beautiful are these words written by Jeremiah. In the midst of his questioning all that had happened: the destruction of Judah and Jerusalem, the seizing and taking captive of God's people, the feeble, poor, and broken left behind, trying to survive through battles, starvation, and disease. In the midst of his mourning and grief over all that had happened and his lamenting for all that had been lost, he spoke these beautiful, comforting, and powerful words. He had acknowledged God's justice in sending His judgment due to the sin of His people, but also acknowledged that if they waited quietly and hoped for the salvation of the Lord, He would see and be good unto them.

The LORD would not consume them because of His great mercy, and He would have compassion on them if they just turned, sought Him, and quietly hoped and waited on Him. It is the same for us today as it was for the children of Israel then. It is good for us to turn toward Him, seek Him, and both hope and quietly wait in the middle of whatever we may be facing. Whether it's trials, storms, or God's just judgment, we can find peace and rest in this hope of glory and quietly wait and see the salvation of the LORD!

Abba, give us strength in the middle to quietly wait, find our hope in You alone, and stand believing, knowing You love us, and Your mercy and compassion will meet us where we are and carry us into tomorrow, a new day. We ask this in Your son Yeshua's perfect name, amen.

January 16

Jeremiah 7:13–14

13) And now, because ye have done all these works, saith the LORD, and I spake unto you, rising early and speaking, but ye heard not; and I called you, but ye answered not; 14) Therefore will I do unto this house, which is called by my name, wherein ye trust, and unto the place which I gave to you and to your fathers, as I have done to Shiloh.

Let me give you a quick little backstory of my life. I retired back about five years ago after a couple of bad car accidents. Since then, getting up and rising early seems to get harder and harder with each day that passes. One of the things I know Abba has spoken to my heart to work on and is written in the front of every journal of mine is: "RISE EARLY." I did great for a while, but despite my best efforts, it's become increasingly difficult. Whether it be a matter of staying up too late or going to bed on time and tossing and turning all night, it is just a serious struggle lately to get up. He has spoken this to me repeatedly from everywhere I read in His word. From Moses to Joshua to the kings of Israel going to battle to Yeshua; it's always there in front of me: **rise early**.

I know it's what He wants me to work on and have victory over. A couple of months ago, I spoke to my sister, and we both wanted to rise early and spend time with Him before we started our day, so we decided she would call each morning, and we would do it. It lasted a week or so and then ended. I texted her and said we needed to do these rise-early calls again because I've been struggling. She never responded, but early this morning, she called, and when I heard the ring, I pushed silent and went back to sleep; she called again, and I did the same thing. I finally woke up for the day and felt horrible that, once again, I failed, and to add salt to injury, when I began to do my reading, these are the verses I read, **say what**? "Rising early and speaking, but ye heard not, and **I called you**, but you answered not" (Jer. 7:13). Oh, my heart, it was Abba calling me using my sister, and I answered not; I didn't rise early.

Could He ever forgive me again and give me another chance, after 1,000 chances already? I cried out and prayed, "Please Abba, Please don't let these verses come to pass in my life. Please don't do to me what you did to Shiloh. Please have mercy on me one more time." I'm sharing this with you to say, if God is dealing with your heart on a matter, just listen and do it. No matter how hard it is, don't learn the hard way like so many of us have to do so often; just listen and quickly do, knowing it's going to be for your good anyway. I know I have a long way to go to win this battle, but I **will not give up**. I will continue to strive to perfect this in my life and have the victory over it. If you find yourself like me that whatever it is Abba is working with you on is continually a struggle, **don't give up**. I am of a firm belief that if we **don't** give up and continue to try and work on whatever it may be, sincerely, with all our hearts, Abba will be there and walk through it with us. He will give us the strength to keep going until we finally conquer whatever it may be and have the victory over it.

Abba, please help us to heed quickly what You ask, to the best of our ability, knowing it is for our good, and please help and forgive us when we fail and give us the strength to continue until we have the victory and struggle no more, in Yeshua's name, we ask this, amen.

January 17

Ephesians 6:11–12

11) Put on the whole armour of God, that ye may be able to stand against the wiles of the devil. 12) For we wrestle not against flesh and blood, but against principalities, against powers, against the rulers of the darkness of this world, against spiritual wickedness in high places.

It is of utter importance to daily make sure we are completely clothed in His armor, covered from head to toe, so we can stand when the enemy wreaks havoc around us. We must be dressed in it fully to ensure we don't fall in the evil days that we **will face**. We are fighting a spiritual battle, not one of flesh and blood, but just as a soldier in the flesh will suit up in his or her armor, with weapons in hand when in battle, so we must do the same.

We must spiritually suit up each day as we rise from our bed, making sure our feet, as they hit the floor, are bound in His gospel of peace, that we strap on His truth and fasten it firmly so we can't be moved. We must put on His righteousness that protects our hearts and walk each moment by faith, extinguishing the fiery darts of the wicked, covering our mind with the salvation we have in Him, and carrying the Word of God, which is sharper than any two-edged sword (Eph. 6:14-17). There are principalities, powers, rulers of darkness, and spiritual wickedness in high places trying to wage a battle with the children of God, but they will never win if we suit up with God's armor and are daily prepared and ready. We will prevail and have the victory through our God.

Father, help us daily to rise up, apply Your armor, and be ready always so we may be victorious in the battles the enemy tries to wage against us, in Yeshua's powerful name, we ask this, amen.

January 18

Proverbs 18:21

Death and life are in the power of the tongue: and they that love it shall eat the fruit thereof.

The tongue is one powerful weapon; it can bring life or death and blessings or curses, so we must use it wisely as we would any weapon. We must think before we use it and be educated on what it can do. We will reap and eat the fruits of it, whether they are good or bad fruits, so we should be very careful when deploying words from it. Hurtful words, gossip, and backbiting can cut to the core and cause pain beyond repair. We need to make it a priority to be led by wisdom through the Holy Spirit in our speech, and we must always pray, allowing Him to fill us with His words so His words become ours. There are times when we are deeply hurt and feel justified to speak out, or when we are angry over injustices and wrongdoings, but it's at these moments we need to be especially wise and careful, seeking the Lord in prayer, asking Him to guide our tongues and hold them if need be.

Our tongues can bring life as well; they can be used to heal a hurt heart, bring joy to a sad soul, uplift and edify one who may be struggling or doubting, and speak good and blessings into another's life. They can literally change the course of somebody's day for the good or bad. Such a great power the tongue holds, and we need to be serious with the execution of each word that rolls off it.

Abba, help us to use wisdom when we speak, to always choose our words carefully and prayerfully, to not speak frivolously but with intention, and that our words be Your words, words that bring life to the hearer, in Yeshua's mighty name, we ask this, amen.

January 19

Jeremiah 9:23–24

23) Thus saith the LORD, Let not the wise man glory in his wisdom, neither let the mighty man glory in his might, let not the rich man glory in his riches: 24) But let him that glorieth glory in this, that he understandeth and knoweth me, that I am the LORD which exercise lovingkindness, judgment, and righteousness, in the earth: for in these things I delight, saith the LORD.

Abba does not delight in the wisdom of man, nor the might nor riches of man, and He says that we shouldn't glory or boast in them either. Instead, we should glory and boast in **knowing Him** and understanding Him, His Word, and His Truth.

Knowing His judgment is perfect. His righteousness is exceedingly right and perfect, and His lovingkindness is beyond comprehension and should be all we need to cause us to run after Him. It should be all we want and seek after, to know this ultimate, one and only, none other like Him God and Father and boast in Him alone. For our might, wisdom, and riches are vain and empty next to Him, His truth, and righteousness.

Abba, help us to truly come to know You and understand Your will and way. Help us to glory in You, Your law, righteousness, perfect judgment, and that beyond-conceiving love of Yours, for this truly is life, **our life**, in Yeshua's beautiful name, amen.

January 20

2 John 1:10

If there come any unto you, and bring not this doctrine, receive him not into your house, neither bid him God speed.

John was talking earlier in this chapter of the doctrine of Christ, which is God's Word, His commandments. There are just thirteen verses in this short book, but they are some profound and powerful ones. Talking about truth, His truth, and keeping His Words, His commandments, we will love Him and one another when doing so. Verse six says, "and this is love, that we walk after His commandments, this is the commandment, that as ye have heard from the beginning, ye should walk in it."

John is warning us that many deceivers and antichrists have come into the world, but we must hold fast to the truth we've learned, the same truth from the beginning that never changes so we may receive a full reward. He's instructing us to be careful and not let those who oppose this doctrine into our homes, not to bid them Godspeed, which is like giving or sending them with a blessing, with approval of their ways, to go rejoicing and being happy in their ways. In fact, he warns us that those who do are partakers in their evil deeds. **Wow**, even though we don't believe as they do or live and walk like they do, by wishing them well is like doing and being as they are. That is definitely different than what the world says today. There are few words in this book of John, but, oh, how powerful and profound they are.

Lord, help us to heed these words here, to understand truly what they imply and follow them, in Yeshua's powerful name, amen.

January 21

Hosea 10:12

Sow to yourselves in righteousness, reap in mercy; break up your fallow ground: for it is time to seek the LORD, till He come and rain righteousness upon you.

The people of Israel had a divided heart. They were no longer living for the Father but for themselves. They were found faulty (Hos. 10:2), it says, and God's judgment was coming. In verse eight, it talks about how they will cry out to the mountains to cover them and to the hills to fall on them, for it would be better than the judgment of God they will have to face. Hosea is pleading with them to seek righteousness, to break up their hardened heart and run back to the LORD.

This chapter hit me hard. How easy is it to become divided, to start seeking after our own pleasure, to follow the world, even if it's in the smallest of compromises. How easy and quickly we can turn from our first love. Many times, I've found my heart divided, running toward the wrong things, not even realizing how it was taking me further from the Father's heart and hardening mine. I've had to turn and run full force with all my might back to Him, back to seeking Him alone and His righteousness. It's not hard to find ourselves in this place amidst the world we live in; we must constantly keep our eyes fixed on the Lord. If you're finding yourself in this place that I found myself in one too many times, the place the Israelites found themselves in, say this prayer with me today:

Abba, forgive me for seeking after my own selfish ambitions and wants. Help me, Father, to turn back to You wholeheartedly and seek You with every fiber in me each day, that I will remain in Your presence always; it's in Your Son Yeshua's name, I ask this, amen.

January 22

Habakkuk 2:4

Behold, his soul which is lifted up is not upright in him: but the just shall live by his faith.

The world puts its trust in man, things, positions, money, and power, forgetting or never coming to the acknowledgment that God is **greater** than **all**. We are vulnerable to complete defeat and destruction if our faith is not in the one who is **always** victorious .

The pride of the Chaldeans was in themselves, the strong people they were, and with all the power they held. They found out quickly their faith was in the wrong place and were utterly destroyed by the one who holds **all** power and authority. Our only hope of standing in victory is when we place our faith in a victorious God, walking and living by that faith.

Abba, help us to live by an unwavering **faith** in **You** and all that You say You are, knowing we will always stand victorious if we do, for our faith is anchored in the one who wins every battle and has the ultimate victory, in Yeshua's holy name, amen.

January 23

Mark 12:29–30

29)And Jesus answered him, the first of all the commandments is, Hear, O Israel; the Lord our God is one Lord: 30)And thou shalt love the Lord thy God with all thy heart, and with all thy soul, and with all thy mind, and with all thy strength: this is the first commandment.

One God, there is no other. Anything else is false and not real. All the gods of man shall crumble like dust and perish; they have no power and can't save your soul. There is but one God, God the Father, Lord of all, who sent Yeshua, His only begotten Son, for our redemption and salvation so we may have eternity with Him.

Yeshua says we are to hear His commandment, follow it, and love Him with **all** we are; **all** our hearts, souls, minds, and might; every ounce of strength we have should be used on loving Him. He is truly worthy of all our hearts and all the love we can lavish on Him. He is worthy of being in our every thought and a part of everything we do. In fact, **all** we do should be done unto Him. He is such a perfect Father, full of grace, glory, and worthy of all we are.

Lord, You are the only God; there is no other. You alone are worthy of **all** praise, glory, honor, and all our hearts, souls, and minds. May we always love you with all we are and all our strength, in your Son Yeshua's name, we pray this, amen.

January 24

Zephaniah 3:13

The remnant of Israel shall not do iniquity, nor speak lies; neither shall a deceitful tongue be found in their mouth: for they shall feed and lie down, and none shall make them afraid.

We are part of the remnant, and we must be careful in all our words and actions. We must make sure we are representing the Lord in all we say and do and that we are representing Him correctly and in truth. We must be careful to keep ourselves set apart from the world, iniquity, and guard our tongue and not speak falsehoods or lies. We must do our best to live holy as He is holy and let His love, light, and truth shine through us in every act, deed, and word. It is going to take us picking up His Word, spending time with Him, and getting to know His heart daily.

His Word says in doing this, that nothing shall make us afraid, and we shall feed and lie down in rest and peace. It is so nice having the security and promises of His Word that we can stand on and be held by. Life is just better all-around when walking uprightly in His truth and love. Being a part of His remnant is a blessing we need to cherish and a position we need to heed.

Abba, help us as Your remnant to stay pure before You and the world we live in, to walk upright, speak truth always, and represent You correctly to the best of our ability always, in Yeshua's mighty name, amen.

January 25

Psalm 1:3

And he shall be like a tree planted by the rivers of water, that bringeth forth his fruit in his season; his leaf also shall not wither; and whatsoever he doeth shall prosper.

I know I've stated this before, but I am going to again; this is one of my **favorite** verses. Oh, that I may be like a tree, that my roots may go down deep into the Father and His heart. That I may bear fruit for Him always. That I am unmovable and unshakeable, and I stand tall and strong in the face of all things. That I'm always watered by the words of the Father, His Living Word, and I will never thirst again. That my leaves will stay green always and never wither.

When I think of a tree like this, I think about the trees in my backyard across the river; the "**biggum trees**," as hubby would call them. They are massive; they're so large it takes a few people linking hands to get around the trunk of the tree, and it seems like it is so tall, it touches the sky. Birds and squirrels find rest in their branches; they make their homes and grow their babies in them. Grass and wildflowers grow at the trunk of them, while animals and people find shade and a cool place to rest under them. The river waters them so they never lack the vital source of life that they need. They can be seen from afar off, for they stand firm and tall. Oh, how massive and beautiful they are. To be like this is my heart's desire; it's what I long for. As the song says, "This will be my song God, this will be my prayer, till the end, **till the end**!"[5]

Lord, help us to become so deeply planted and rooted in You that we truly become as this tree that Your word speaks of, in Yeshua's powerful and mighty name, amen.

January 26

Malachi 1:11

For from the rising of the sun even unto the going down of the same my name shall be great among the Gentiles; and in every place incense shall be offered unto my name, and a pure offering: for my name shall be great among the heathen, saith the LORD of hosts.

The name of the Lord is great and worthy to be praised. He will not accept and take well to His name being anything less than that. He will not be held in contempt. He is God, and there is **no** other. The whole world will see His greatness; all will hear of His great name, and His fame will continue to spread throughout time. Verse fourteen states, "But cursed be the deceiver, which hath in his flock a male, and voweth, and sacrificeth unto the Lord a corrupt thing: for I am a Great King, saith the LORD of hosts, and my name is dreadful among the heathen." There is **no** bearing false witness against Him. We shall either stand in awe and reverence of His greatness, or we will stand trembling in fear, watching from the opposing side. He alone is great, and His name will be exalted and proclaimed in **all** the earth as great and throughout **all** eternity.

The priests in Malachi weren't doing such a great job of showing the world how great and awesome He is; they weren't being good examples and were actually profaning His name and polluting His character. They were turning their nose up at Him, and He was not having it. The whole world would see one way or another that He is a great God, and His name is great to be praised.

How are we representing Him and His name today? Will the world see through our awe and reverence of Him how great He truly is? Or will they have to see through His discipline and judgment? From the rising of the sun, even unto the going down of the same, **His name shall be great**.

These were the lyrics to a song we sang in church, and the whole church would do hand movements to it. It was one of those songs that got in you and wouldn't leave. It would stay with me for days, and I would joyfully sing it, proclaiming His great name and how it is to be praised always.

I pray that, each day, I can rise and represent His greatness and wonder in the proper light, that I can honestly have a pure heart as I walk through each day as His child and that I can be a reflection of Him and His character. I pray that my actions and words can genuinely show the world how truly great He is. May this be your prayer as well. May we, daily, as His children, bring glory to His name, and may His praise always be on our tongue. May we always show how great He is in **all** we do.

The world should see and know just how great He is through the sacrifices of praise continually lifted up to Him from His children. From the rising of the sun to the going down of the same, may all we do and all we say give glory, honor, and praise to Him, for **His name is great and great to be praised**.

Lord, help us to proclaim Your great name, to lift sacrifices of praise to You continually, from the moment our eyes open to the moment we close them at night. Help us to be living examples for everyone around us of just how awesome and great You are, in Yeshua's name, amen.

January 27

1 John 2:6

He that saith he abideth in Him ought himself also so to walk, even as He walked.

For us to walk as He walked, we must know how He walked. We must draw close, become personal, and examine His steps, character, attributes, and attitudes. We must spend time getting to know Him, talking to Him, reading His words to us, and just sitting in His presence.

Once we do this, it will begin to change us and we will begin to walk as He walked. There's a saying that says, "You'll become the company you keep!" It's hard to be around someone, spending time with them, and hanging out without becoming like them, doing what they do and walking how they walk. Do we walk as Yeshua walked? Our walk will show if we are truly abiding in Him.

Yeshua, help us to draw close to You, to know You and Your heart so we can know the Father's heart; to walk as You walked so we can be pleasing to the Father as You were. It's in Your name, we ask this, amen.

January 28

Matthew 5:48

Be ye therefore perfect, even as your Father which is in heaven is perfect.

This sure seems like a high order from Yeshua to us. What exactly does it mean to be perfect? As I went to the dictionary, first, I found some great examples, such as: "making something free from faults or defects, or as close to such a condition as possible, absolute, complete, having all the required or desirable elements, qualities or characteristics, as good as it is possible to be, precisely accurate or exact."[6] Then I searched my e-Sword's Strong's Concordance for the Greek and Hebrew word for *perfect,* and the Greek was *teleios*, which translates to *tâmîym* in Hebrew, meaning, "complete, without blemish, without spot, upright, whole, undefiled." Stay with me now. The Greek word *teleios* also translates to *telos*, which is "to set out for a definite point or goal," the point aimed at. So, our point of aim is supposed to be the Father in heaven, and we are to live as He lives, being complete in Him.[7]

He is excellent, correct, and flawless, and this should be our aim. We should do all we can to be as close as possible to the Father's character and nature, becoming precise and accurate in our display of Him. We need to take on His qualities and walk in them, being upright, undefiled, whole, and pure to the best we possibly can.

Lord, help us to learn Your character so we can walk it out to the best of our ability and reflect You in all we do, to learn, take on Your qualities, and do as Yeshua has instructed us: "be ye perfect even as your Father in heaven is perfect," in Yeshua's holy name, amen.

January 29

Colossians 3:12

Put on therefore, as the elect of God, holy and beloved, bowels of mercies, kindness, humbleness of mind, meekness, longsuffering.

Paul is instructing us here as children of the Most High King, the chosen and elect, to be compassionate as the Father is, merciful and kind, AND to have the Father's heart. The Father is patient and longsuffering; look how long He waited for the Israelites. Over and over again, He had mercy and compassion on them. Look at your own life, my life, others' lives, and how He doesn't ever give up on us, never leaves or forsakes us, and how He sent His **only beloved Son** for us. This is the heart He longs for us to have, the one He wants to see in us.

We want to make sure that we, as His children, are showing a proper representation of who He is. We as the elect of God should be slow to anger, longsuffering, humble, and meek. We should be gentle and kind, showing mercy to those who don't deserve it as the Father showed us. We should easily forgive and be ready to give to those in need, putting others before ourselves. When we put on mercy, kindness, humbleness of mind, meekness, and longsuffering, we will find genuine fulfillment and peace that no one or nothing can take away.

Abba, help us as Your beloved and elect to take on ourselves these attributes so we can walk as your children and have your heart for the world around us, in Yeshua's name, amen.

January 30

Zechariah 7:12

Yea, they made their hearts as an adamant stone, lest they should hear the law, and the words which the LORD of hosts hath sent in His spirit by the former prophets: therefore came a great wrath from the LORD of hosts.

The people had come to inquire about fasting. In exile, they had fasted on certain days as a remembrance of the humiliation of being taken into exile and the destruction of the temple, but their fasts were for their own satisfaction and not for the Lord or even what He wanted. In fact, in chapter eight, He tells them to turn the fasts into cheerful feasts.

He spoke of His requirements, which have been the same and never changed, saying in verses nine and ten of chapter seven to "Execute true judgment, and shew mercy and compassion every man to his brother, and oppress not the widow, nor the father-less, the stranger, nor the poor, and let none of you imagine evil against his brother in your heart." This is what He required and had spoken through all the prophets, but the people refused to listen and just hardened their hearts more. In verse thirteen, it states that it came to pass that the LORD cried, and they would not hear Him, so when they cried, He would not hear them. Ouch, that's a dreadful day when the LORD doesn't hear our cry. Just reading this made my heart heavy and made me question why we are such a rebellious people. His laws and commands aren't that hard, and they are for our good; why wouldn't we just listen and follow them?

Lord, help us to listen and see that what You ask and require of us is beautiful and not difficult to follow. Help us to truly know that obeying it brings Your presence and the fullness of Your peace and joy, in Yeshua's glorious name, Amen.

January 31

Luke 5:26

And they were all amazed, and they glorified God, and were filled with fear, saying, We have seen strange things today.

I can only imagine by these words here how they must have really felt. Maybe they felt like the children of Israel when He parted the sea in front of them or when He brought water from a rock; maybe how those watching felt when He equipped David to take down a massive giant with one stone. We have seen some strange things today, I so **love** how they worded their experience when seeing Yeshua heal the paralyzed man.

Strange things are things that are not normal, things that are outside of our minute minds. Have you ever had a moment like this with Yeshua where you've stood speechless, saying, "I've seen some strange things today"? I know I have. I remember when the doctors told me I could never have another child, and then a year or so later, hearing my doctor on the phone say, "Joy, your test results are in, and you are pregnant." Say what? I know I had prayed and had been prayed for, and I know the word God gave me, "because of your faith, it shall be done," but the reality of it when it happens is like, **what**? Also, when my water broke, and I laid in the hospital for two weeks, trying to keep the baby in, but at twenty-seven weeks, she was coming, and the doctors and nurses told me, "if she makes it, she will be on a ventilator for quite a while," but she came out breathing on her own and was never on a vent, **say what**? Miracles unheard of, the impossible becoming possible; this is what they were seeing and experiencing—**strange things**. These are moments where the Lord just rocks your world and shows His power and glory. I Pray we all see and experience our Lord in such ways that change us forever. His mountain-moving, miracle-working power—**strange things**, as they said.

Abba, move mightily in our lives daily and cause strange things to happen that we may see Your power, glory, and stand in awe before You, giving You all the praise You are due, in Yeshua's mighty name, amen.

February 1

Deuteronomy 17:19

And it shall be with him, and he shall read therein all the days of his life: that he may learn to fear the LORD his God, to keep all the words of this law and these statutes, to do them.

This was God's instructions to the kings of Israel. It goes on to say in verse twenty, "That his heart be not lifted up above his brethren, and that he turn not aside from the commandment, to the right hand, or to the left: to the end that he may prolong his days in his kingdom, he, and his children, in the midst of Israel." How important it is to hear and follow God's instruction; to hear it and not turn to the left or right, but only follow straight ahead and do all He has commanded.

We must read His Word daily, every day of our lives, learn it and allow it to go down deep, take root, and produce good fruit, for this will show whose we are and to whom we belong. It will direct our steps and keep us safe. Following **all** the words of this law will lead to blessings and the goodness of God. We are His kings and priests who represent Him, and to do so correctly, we must know the words of this book and do them. In verse eighteen, it talks about them writing a copy of God's law in a book to be read daily and never forgotten. It is life to the hearer and doer of these laws and instructions. I've begun to sit down and not just read these words but write them on paper as well; it seems to just go down deeper when I do.

Abba, help us to spend time daily reading Your words, writing them down so they can become the very fiber of our being, the very essence of all we are and do, never to be forgotten, and followed in every step we take. It's in Your Son Yeshua's precious name we ask this, amen.

February 2

1 Corinthians 3:16

Know ye not that ye are the temple of God, and that the Spirit of God dwelleth in you?

We are the temple of the **living God**. His Holy Spirit lives within us. When we come to Yeshua and ask for forgiveness, we surrender our lives and ways and ask the Holy Spirit to come live and take up residence in us. We no longer are our own, for we become His temple, sanctuary, and dwelling place. 1 Corinthians 6:19 says: "What? Know ye not that your body is the temple of the Holy Ghost which is in you, which ye have of God and ye are not your own?" In Ephesians 2:22, we read: "In whom ye also are builded together for an habitation of God through the Spirit." See, He comes, lives, and breathes in us, and we become His, created in His image to do His good works as He works them in us.

Hebrews 3:6 tells us: "But Christ as a son over His own house; whose house are we, if we hold fast the confidence and the rejoicing of the hope firm unto the end." We are to hold fast to living and walking in His ways and truth, allowing Him to come and find a home in us and breathe His life in and through us. May our lives be like the words of the song, "Sanctuary," written by Randy Scruggs and John Thompson: "Lord prepare me, to be a sanctuary, pure and holy, tried and true, and with Thanksgiving, I'll be a living, sanctuary, for you."[8] What a miraculous and beautiful thing that He comes, lives, and dwells in us, and we become His sanctuary, His temple. Hallelujah!

Lord, prepare us to be a sanctuary for You. Wash us that we may be pure and holy, tried, and true, and that Your presence may come and dwell within us, living and breathing through us daily, so others may come to You through Your Holy Spirit they see in us, in Yeshua's holy name, amen.

February 3

Psalm 46:10

Be still, and know that I am God: I will be exalted among the heathen, I will be exalted in the earth.

Be still and just breathe.

Be still and just know.

Just be still.

If it's for an hour, a half hour, or even just five minutes today, try to stop everything and **just be still** in the presence of the **Almighty**,

Be still and just be.

The Hebrew word for *still* in this verse is *Râphâh*; which means to "let go, let alone, cease control, let drop, to release."[9] Let's try for this day to let everything go, even if just for a few moments; drop it all at the feet of the Lord, cease from the craziness, the busyness of life, give all to Abba, and **just be still**.

Lord, You long for us to just come, lay it all down, and sit at Your feet so You can wash over us with Your presence and peace. Please teach us today how to **be still** in You, in Yeshua's name, amen.

February 4

Matthew 5:8

Blessed are the pure in heart, for they shall see God.

I **love** how these are called the Beatitudes, like it's the attitude to have or be; so fitting, I think. They all are beautiful words
of guidance and encouragement from Yeshua, but this one just
seems to jump off the page to me every time I read them. This
one is my true desire and what I long for in myself; to be genuinely **pure in heart**, to have a heart that imitates the Father's. It
says in Psalm 24:2–4, "Who shall ascend into the Hill of the LORD
or stand in His Holy Place, he who hath clean hands and a pure
heart." I want to ascend into the hill of the Lord and stand in the
holy place, looking and gazing upon His beautiful and perfect
countenance and be surrounded by His magnificent and glorious
presence all the days of my life. I long for my heart to be pure with
no guile, vanity, or deceit, just pure and upright like the Father's.

If we have a pure heart, we will be merciful, humble, and meek;
we will be a peacemaker and hunger and thirst after righteousness;
we will walk in all His ways and rejoice in doing it. I know, personally,
it's not always as easy as it sounds. I struggle and try to examine my
heart daily, and garbage still grows. We need to remain conscious
daily that we are not becoming tainted or defiled in any way by the
things of this world, and we need to keep our hearts wholly and
solely for Him and Him **alone**. May this **be-attitude** be one we all
long for and seek after always, even when we hurt and it's hard.

Abba, help us to have pure hearts before You, hearts that
don't become clouded or vain from things of this world but hearts
that desire and are stayed on You continually, hearts that are after
Your very own heart; in Yeshua's perfect name, we ask this, amen.

February 5

Nahum 1:3

The LORD is slow to anger, and great in power, and will not at all acquit the wicked: the LORD hath His way in the whirlwind and in the storm, and the clouds are the dust of His feet.

How powerful is our God? To think about how we get tossed around in whirlwinds like a leaf blowing in the wind and get beaten and battered in storms, but our God **has** His way in them. **Wow**! That's some **awesome** power. It's definitely a power I want on my side.

The wicked need to fear, for the whirlwinds and storms will destroy them. He will not save or acquit them, but that is not so with His own; His children have their hope in Him and are held through it **all** by Him. To let go and let Him have His way in the whirlwinds and storms instead of fighting or fearing them is a powerful choice we may want to consider. He is a good Father, slow to anger and great in power. If we are His, we will be held.

Abba, help us learn to allow You to have Your way in whatever You choose to come our way and to trust You will hold us in it all, in Yeshua's name, amen.

February 6

Exodus 19:4–5

4) Ye have seen what I did unto the Egyptians, and how I bare you on eagles' wings, and brought you unto myself. 5) Now therefore, if ye will obey my voice indeed, and keep my covenant, then ye shall be a peculiar treasure unto me above all people: for all the earth is mine.

Oh, how I long to be a peculiar treasure unto Him, that I may be taken up on eagles' wings, protected, finding rest from the storms and destruction they bring. A peculiar treasure translates to a distinctive jewel, special like none other. How much more beautiful can it get? Abba makes us this beautiful treasure, set apart, distinctive, and precious unto Himself above all other people. This is our inheritance, our lot if we keep His covenant and obey His voice.

He will bear us up on eagles' wings so nothing can touch us; how much better can it get? I long to follow His commands, listen and obey His voice, and keep covenant with Him so He may call me a peculiar treasure of His. It sounds beyond worth it to me; the Creator of the universe, my Creator calling me His peculiar treasure, His special jewel. This is my heart's cry; may it be yours today too.

Abba, teach us daily of Your ways. Speak to us that we may hear and obey Your voice, that we may know Your covenant You made with us and keep it, that we can be set apart for You, a peculiar treasure, always kept and protected on wings of eagles until the day comes when we get to share eternity with you, in your Son Yeshua's holy name, amen.

February 7

Hebrews 12:16–17

16) Lest there be any fornicator, or profane person, as Esau, who for one morsel of meat sold his birthright. 17) For ye know how that afterward, when he would have inherited the blessing, he was rejected: for he found no place of repentance, though he sought it carefully with tears.

We studied Esau in depth a couple of months back at one of our Sabbath meetings, and it was said through my respected friend who led the meeting, **"Don't let your appetite rule you."** Those are some powerful words when truly thought about and digested. I was one who lived in the realm of instant gratification. The words *wait* and *no* were **not** part of my vocabulary and, may I say, I suffered a lot of hurt and pain in those years due to that; not being able to wait, trust God for my needs, and truly make Him the only thing I needed, the only bread I lived and walked by. I loved Him and wanted to follow Him but desired so much of everything around me, never realizing none of it would make me happy, filled, or satisfied, that only He could do that.

Sometimes we want things so bad that we don't stop to think about the outcome of our decisions, the sacrifice that may come with the acquiring of what we want or think we need. Esau was led by the flesh and only focused on how hungry he was. He gave everything away for a morsel instead of running into the arms of the Father and trusting Him. I am learning to run into those arms today, to run to the only one who can truly fill all my wants and needs in His most perfect ways, and this is my prayer that we all can always do the same.

Abba, help us to come to You, wait on You, and trust You for our every need, desire, and want, knowing only You supply all, so we never have to regret with tears what we may have lost because of not coming to You first or patiently waiting, in Yeshua's name, amen.

February 8

Proverbs 21:19

It is better to dwell in the wilderness, than with a contentious and angry woman.

It is better to live in a desert land than with a quarrelsome and fretful woman. Ouch, that's quite a harsh statement. I was a pretty hard and miserable person to live with for quite a while in my life. I would wonder how my husband put up with me during those years and times. Praise the Lord, He showed me how damaging living as such a woman could be; how contention and anger only brought discord and strife, but how humility and peace brought sweetness and honey.

It is so important not to live our lives being quarrelsome, nit-picking, and fighting over every little thing. Yes, there are times of disagreement that are valid and worth hashing through, but we must pick our battles wisely and ask ourselves, "Is this one worth it?" My mother named me Joy for a reason; she told me that God gave her that name for me so I may be joy in a world that needed it, and she prayed that I would be just that, that I would be my name.

To me, that was a huge call to live up to; if I had no other gifts or talents, my name alone would be a big enough gift in itself if lived out. This inspired me to slowly, one day at a time, allow God to work on my heart and attitude and replace it with His. I began to realize how ugly arguing sounded, how deadly anger could be, and how it destroys everything in its wake. I had enough of that in my addiction days and didn't want it a part of me for the rest of my life. A contentious and angry woman is a venomous sting that I didn't want to be associated with having anymore.

I'm not saying I'm a perfect person today and that I've totally conquered this, but I am definitely a work in progress, working toward being a peacemaker and a loving wife and mother. The old will surely still try to rear its ugly head in difficult situations, and I instantly must **stop** and **pray** and seek Daddy's heart and help in these times.

I want to point out that it's not just the women who can walk and live in this state of mind, but men must be careful as well, they are not exempt from becoming contentious, angry, and being just as venomous. Any one of us can be, and that's why it's so important to stay wrapped up in the Father, keeping His Word hidden in our hearts and becoming more like Him daily.

I can't think of anything worse than being so ugly that the people around us are better off living in a desert place than with us.

Abba, help us to run as swift as we can away from being contentious, angry, and quarrelsome, sowing discord and strife, and help us to be humble peacemakers, sharing your love with each other. It's in your Son Yeshua's perfect name, we ask this, amen.

February 9

Ephesians 2:8–9

8) For by grace are ye saved through faith; and that not of yourselves: it is the gift of God: 9) Not of works, lest any man should boast.

There is absolutely nothing we can do to earn His grace and love; it is a gift. We can't work our way into His grace or give our way into them; it is simply an act of faith. Believing He is who He says He is, and He loves us like He says He does. Believing in the depth of this **great** love He has for us, so **great** as to send His **only begotten Son** in our behalf and watch Him die the worst death possible so we may live. We don't deserve it, and nothing we do makes us deserving of it; it's only because of His **great** love for us.

Grace beyond our comprehension, given freely, we must only believe, accept, and walk in faith. Abba's favor, unmerited, given to us—there's truly no better gift. That gift has caused me to turn from everything else this world has to offer and run into those perfect unending arms of love. It has caused me to learn His ways and follow them, knowing He loves me so much and only has the best for me. Knowing all He says is good, and there's nothing better. Knowing all the instruction He gives me is beyond worth following because they all only lead to blessings and a deeper walk with my Daddy; what could possibly be better than **the best**?

Thank You, Father, for loving us so much when we don't and never have deserved it, for sending Your Son to die for us that we could be saved. Oh, how **great** Your grace is, in Yeshua's mighty name, amen.

February 10

Joel 3:10

Beat your plowshares into swords, and your pruninghooks into spears: let the weak say, I am strong.

It is time for war; the battle is about to begin. God is calling His army to prepare and get ready. It's time for God and His people to recompense judgment on the enemy's head. It's time for the weak to stand up and proclaim they are strong because God is on their side.

No need to fear and no need to doubt, but it is a time to be strong and courageous because we have the **best ally** on our side. **The Lord God Almighty, who is mighty to save! Hallelujah! Let the weak say I am strong!**

Abba Father, thank You for going before us, having our back, being our strength when we feel weak, and having the victory **always**. May our confidence be continually found in You and You alone, in Yeshua's holy name, amen.

February 11

Luke 10:2

Therefore said He unto them, The harvest truly is great, but the labourers are few: pray ye therefore the Lord of the harvest, that He would send forth labourers into His harvest.

In Luke 10:1, the Lord had just appointed seventy additional people and sent them out by twos to go into the cities and towns to prepare the way for Him before He arrived. As He was sending them, He told them the harvest was great; there were so many needing to hear the hope of the Lord, the truth of His Word and the salvation awaiting them, but yet so few to tell them and share about the goodness of the Lord. Yeshua here was urging them to pray for more laborers and more hearts to turn and be willing to go and share.

There is a vast world around us that needs the hope of Yeshua that needs to know how much they are loved, how they can be forgiven and delivered from whatever circumstance might be gripping and tormenting them, and how they can have freedom, salvation, and eternal life through our Savior Yeshua, the Messiah. It doesn't take the educated, a scholar, or a perfect person, just a sincere and willing heart that wants to share the gift he or she received with others. Will you become a laborer in His harvest? Pray this prayer with me:

Lord, call, appoint, and anoint us to become laborers in your fields of harvest; send us forth with the same hope You've given us to share with a dying world who so badly need You. Call more laborers as well, Lord. Capture and save more hearts, making them ready to labor beside us in Your fields for You, in Yeshua's name, amen.

February 12

Jeremiah 29:13

And ye shall seek me, and find me, when ye shall search for me with all your heart.

He will be found, He says, when He is searched for with our whole heart, **all of it**! When pondering what seeking Him with all our hearts should look like, a couple of scenarios came to my mind. I thought about a person with asthma in the middle of an attack, frantically searching for his or her inhaler because he or she is struggling to breathe. We should be searching for Him in such a way, knowing we could suffocate in the midst of all the worries and stresses life holds if we don't have Him who is our very breath. Then I thought of treasure hunters who will give up everything in life to search for and find that treasure. They will go down into the depths of the ocean, deep into the bellies of the earth, and to the top of the highest mountain; they will go and go, searching non-stop until they find the prize, that invaluable, precious treasure.

This is how we should search for Him. We should run after Him with **all** we have and **all** our strength, searching for the true treasure, the one that is more valuable and precious than **anything** the world has to offer, for He far exceeds all the riches of this world. He's more precious than all the rare stones hidden in the earth, more worthy and deserving of honor than all the Kings, princes, and presidents put together throughout history. He is priceless, unmatchable, invaluable, and nothing can compare to His goodness, glory, love, mercy, and authority. He is the true, genuine, utmost precious treasure, and we should run after and seek Him daily, minute by minute, with **all** our hearts, always.

Abba, help us to run after You with all our hearts and never stop, for You are the **best treasure** to be found **ever**, in Yeshua's beautiful name, Amen.

February 13

Mark 3:25

And if a house be divided against itself, that house cannot stand.

In the previous verse, Yeshua said if a kingdom be divided against itself, it cannot stand as well. Good and evil cannot coexist—it will eventually self-destruct; the division will cause its ruin. There must be unity of heart and oneness of mind for something to succeed and prosper. Conflict breads division, light has no fellowship with darkness, division causes chords to be broken, and soon after comes the destruction and fall. Whether it be a nation, church, home, or marriage, we must come together in unity on common ground.

We are His children and are of the light, His light, and we must expel and cast out the darkness. It goes personally as well—we can't have a foot in the enemy's camp and a foot in God's kingdom; we **will** fall. Division causes things to self-destruct; it brings friction, which causes things to explode. Let's seek and work to be unified in Christ, our walk with Him, our marriages, homes, places of worship, nation, and world so we can stand securely and not crumble and fall. We will prevail and have the victory when we finally do.

Abba, teach us Yeshua's words here and the truth about being divided; let them come alive to us so we can unify in You as Your body and stand victoriously with You, in Yeshua's mighty name, amen.

February 14

Zephaniah 3:17

The LORD thy God in the midst of thee is mighty; he will save, he will rejoice over thee with joy; he will rest in his love, he will joy over thee with singing.

God, the Creator of the whole universe, God over **all**, rejoices with singing over you! Take a moment and just take that in; close your eyes and just imagine that. I know it takes my breath away and seriously leaves me abandoned and speechless before Him. He is mighty to save and will save us over and over again because He loves His children with a love too deep for us to truly understand.

There is nothing more to say! Anything more would take away from the life-changing power of these world-rocking words in this verse of a mighty God rejoicing over thee with **joy**! Let those words transform your thoughts and life today as you close your eyes and breathe them in, sitting in the presence of the **Most High God**.

Wow, Abba, Your love for us is above and beyond our wildest imagination. You are just the best, and there is no better place to be than in Your presence as You dance and sing over us, your children, whom You love greater than we could ever know. Thank You, Lord, in Yeshua's precious name, amen.

February 15

Isaiah 58:11

And the LORD shall guide thee continually, and satisfy thy soul in drought, and make fat thy bones: and thou shalt be like a watered garden, and like a spring of water, whose waters fail not.

Take a moment and read the previous verses when you're able. The LORD was telling Isaiah how the fast the people were doing was not the fast He chose for them to do. The fast He chose was to set the oppressed free, to break the yokes and heavy burdens and loose the bands of wickedness, to feed the hungry, take care of the poor and clothe the naked (Isa. 58:6-7). In verse nine, it says, "Then shalt thou call, and the LORD shall answer; thou shalt cry, and He shall say, Here I AM. If thou take away from the midst of thee the yoke, the putting forth of the finger, and speaking vanity."

The LORD calls us to have His heart, care for the oppressed as He does, open our hearts and hands to the hungry, and open our homes to the poor, to help those who have nothing. He calls us to not speak vanity or be vain, unjust, unrighteous, wicked, or cause affliction. If we do this, then we will capture His attention, please Him, and He will be with us and guide and satisfy us always. We will be a well-watered garden, never lacking or wanting for anything. This is the kind of fast He desires of us.

Father, please help us to have Your heart, act as You would, pour ourselves out to those in need, help us to have Your eyes to see them, to help and love them as You would, and know this is Your will and way for us, in Yeshua's name, amen.

February 16

1 Peter 5:7

Casting all your care upon Him; for He careth for you.

Abba loves us so much and doesn't want to see us burdened, anxious, worried, or heavily ladened. He wants us to walk in His love, His peace, truly knowing He can handle whatever it is that may be distracting us, holding us back, or weighing us down. He cares for us so deeply and wants us to bring all our cares to Him. When we continue to walk in all the anxiety and stresses of our day, all the heaviness and weight of our circumstances, the world can't see Him and His true nature through our lives, our lives can't shine His light in the reality of who He is.

When we give Him all our cares and walk free from the worry and concern of it all, walking in the love of our heavenly Father, the world can't help but take notice of who He is and just how good and awesome life with Him can be. It is a dual blessing; not only does it bless us as we walk in freedom of all our cares, but it also blesses the world around us. We can truly walk in freedom daily; we just need to cast our cares on Him.

Lord, help us to cast our cares on You, who cares for us beyond our thoughts and what we could ever imagine, so we can be free to shine You in all Your goodness and glory to those around us so they can see how real and awesome You truly are, in Yeshua's name, we ask this, amen.

February 17

Daniel 3:24–25

24) Then Nebuchadnezzar the king was astonied, and rose up in haste, and spake, and said unto his counsellors, Did not we cast three men bound into the midst of the fire? They answered and said unto the king, True, O king. 25) He answered and said, Lo, I see four men loose, walking in the midst of the fire, and they have no hurt; and the form of the fourth is like the Son of God.

Most of us know this story about Shadrach, Meshach, and Abednego and how because they refused to bow and worship the statue king Nebuchadnezzar made, they were thrown into the fiery furnace. I think what amazes me most every time I read this story is their dedication to God, how they **believed** beyond a shadow of a doubt He would save them, but then taking a committed stand that even if He didn't, they still would **not** bow and worship the king's god or image he set up. **Wow**, to have such a heart toward the Father. I love a heart that is sold out completely for Abba with no reservations, distractions, hesitations, or doubts in the face of the worst possible situations. What volumes a heart like that speaks.

The Lord was not only faithful to save them in the midst of their horrifying situation, but He also showed up in the biggest way. The king called for the furnace to be heated three times hotter than normal, even the guards throwing them in died from the heat of it, but not **one** hair on Shadrach, Meshach, and Abednego was touched, and the Lord literally showed up, walking in the midst of the fire with them. Wow, I love when our God shows up in such powerful and profound ways; it takes my breath away. It astonished the king so much that he made a decree that if anyone spoke wrong of God, they would be **cut in pieces**. That tells me the effect it had on the king was very powerful.

Abba, help us have such deep and committed devotion to You amidst all things that You can be glorified, and it makes powerful and lasting impacts on the lives around us, in Yeshua's name, amen.

February 18

Luke 7:50

And He said to the woman, Thy faith hath saved thee; go in peace.

This woman was a sinner, saved by grace through faith by Yeshua, our Messiah. It's easy for me to relate to this woman and my eyes to well with tears every time I read her story. A woman with many sins, but a great faith and much love, and she came to Yeshua's feet, washed them with her tears, dried them with her hair, kissed them, and anointed them with ointment. Her heart was crying out for mercy, grace, and forgiveness in the presence of her Messiah, the only one who could save and deliver her. The utter shame and disgrace she must have felt as she brought the dirty, tattered rags of her sin-laden life before Him. Trusting and believing in Him and who He was and that He would have mercy on her, forgive her, and wash all her sins away.

This was me as I brought the devastating destruction, disgusting garbage, and filthy rags of my life before Him. Literally hanging on by a thread, shameful, and embarrassed but having faith to believe that He could wash me clean, deliver, forgive me, and give me a new hope and future, and did He ever. He is an awesome Messiah and has come to save the sinner, sick, lost, and give a new **hope of glory** for tomorrow and eternity, for this woman, you, and me.

Yeshua, help us to never be too ashamed, too afraid, or too proud to come to You in great love and faith as this woman did for help, forgiveness, and deliverance from whatever sins may be devouring us, in your powerful and awesome name, we ask this, amen.

February 19

Micah 7:8

Rejoice not against me, O mine enemy: when I fall, I shall arise; when I sit in darkness, the LORD shall be a light unto me.

In verse seven, Micah declares, "Therefore I will look unto the LORD; I will wait for the God of my salvation: my God will hear me." Micah **knew** where his help came from. It was an extremely dark time. Here in chapter seven, he talks about how the good man was perished out of the earth and there was none upright. How they all lay and waited for blood, brother hunting brother, son's dishonoring fathers, friends couldn't trust friends, and everyone was turning against each other. Sin was abounding, darkness was filling the earth, and the judgment of the Lord was coming. Micah knew there were turbulent times ahead, but he knew who to cling to in it. He knew from where his deliverance and help would come.

As I read these words, I perceived much similarity of the days we are living in, and I found great hope and comfort in Micah's words here in this verse. If our foundation is the Lord and we fix our eyes on Him, He will be the anchor that holds us in the chaos, the light that shines in the darkness, and that hand that raises us up when we fall. He will defend and deliver us in that day if our hope and trust remain in Him alone. We, as Micah, can say, "I will look to the LORD, I will wait for the God of my Salvation: my God will hear me." I can be confident, knowing I will arise after falling, and His light will brighten the darkness.

Abba, sometimes things can look pretty bleak, scary, dark, and downright hopeless, but in these times, help us to be a Micah, waiting on You, standing and declaring Your goodness and righteousness and trusting You, knowing You will fight for us, and we will see Your glory as we cling to You, our hope, in Yeshua's name, we ask this, amen.

February 20

Matthew 7:21

Not everyone that saith unto me, Lord, Lord, shall enter into the kingdom of heaven; but he that doeth the will of my Father which is in heaven.

Yeshua was giving some pretty important information here. We may call upon Him and say He is our everything and all, but unless we are doing the will of the Father, we will not enter the gates of heaven. What is the will of Yeshua's Father? Well, to know it, we have to go back to the beginning and study it. Yeshua taught us and walked it out as an example for us. He even shed His blood, making a way for us, but now it's up to us to learn the Father's will, know it, and do it.

It's a choice that each of us must make on our own. Are we willing to pick up His Word, dive in headfirst, and be submersed in the Father's heart? Are we learning who He is, hearing what His words say, and allowing them to go down deep, take root, and transform our lives so we can do His will? This is what is required if we long to see heaven and spend eternity there. These are not my words, not my stipulations, but they are Yeshua's words and the Father's stipulations. All I can say is it's so worth the journey; there is a sweetness that can't be found anywhere else, a peace beyond understanding, joy unspeakable, love incomprehensible, and a promise that is sure for eternity. Pick up His Word today, start at the beginning, and begin to find all the treasures that await inside.

Thank You, Yeshua, for these powerful and informative words You spoke. Thank for giving them to us to heed and learn from, so we can come to know the Father's will, live and walk in it, and have eternity with you and Him. It's in Your name, Yeshua, we thank and pray this, amen.

February 21

Job 1:21

And said, Naked came I out of my mother's womb, and naked shall I return thither: the LORD gave, and the LORD hath taken away; blessed be the name of the LORD.

I was reflecting on this verse this morning. This has become a somber time of year for me. I've experienced a lot of loss around this time of year: my baby girl, baby boy, uncle (who was like a second dad to me), and my mom; it kind of takes my breath away and causes me to be extremely still for a moment, reflecting on how God has called their time here to be done. My grandparents, all my aunts, uncles, and my parents are all gone now, and I am left to carry on the memory, the heritage of our Lord, so that none is forgotten.

There was purpose in each of their lives, even my babies, who only had moments and hours here on this earth. Abba is a sovereign God. He has a perfect plan, even when it hurts and we don't understand it; we must trust. We must be grateful and thankful for the moments, remember them, cherish each one and the purpose they each served, and then rest in the knowing of, **the Lord giveth** and **the Lord taketh away; blessed be the name of the Lord**.

Abba, give us rest in knowing You are sovereign, Your ways are perfect, and we can trust in them because You will hold us through it all, in Yeshua's mighty name, amen.

February 22

Deuteronomy 4:29

But if from thence thou shalt seek the LORD thy God, thou shalt find him, if thou seek Him with all thy heart and with all thy soul.

He will hear us, see us, and make Himself known. He will **not** be hidden, but we **will** find Him if we seek Him with **all** our hearts and souls. To seek means to pursue, search, run after, and if we do that with our whole heart, with all we have, with all our will and mind, searching with all our might, He will come and be present with us. We will find Him. He will become so evident in our lives that we will no longer have the ability to deny Him. We will come to know the very essence of who He is and the glory and power He holds.

It's all or nothing, though. We won't find Him if we're just halfway in, if we aren't truly serious and genuinely seeking Him with all we are. This search isn't just part-time either; it's a full-time position with every fiber of our hearts and souls. It says **all** of it. In the midst of tribulation, difficult times, even in times of turning away and getting lost, He will make Himself found to us if we search and seek for Him, pursuing Him with all we are and all our hearts and souls.

Lord, help us to pour our whole heart and soul into seeking You so we can find You in all Your glory, and You can become our one and only heart's desire all our days, for once we find You in the fullness of all You are, we will want for nothing anymore, in Yeshua's name, amen.

February 23

Isaiah 40:31

But they that wait upon the LORD shall renew their strength; they shall mount up with wings as eagles; they shall run, and not be weary; and they shall walk, and not faint.

The eagle was my dad's favorite thing. He collected them and had them all over his house. I just never understood why he liked them so much or why they became his favorite thing until the day in the midst of my distress, one flew right in front of my windshield close enough, it seemed, to reach out and touch. The Lord spoke mightily to me through that encounter, and I cried, laughed, and became encouraged to walk one more step in this journey of life. As I was driving home after this monumental experience, this verse came to my mind, and I heard the words, "I sent this for you!" I've only heard the audible voice of the Lord a few times in my life, and this was one of those times. I had to get home, read this verse, and dig deeper into all He wanted me to receive from this.

As I researched and studied, I found out the eagle is the only bird that doesn't run for shelter; they fly above the storm, flock together, and stay separate from other birds; they don't mix or mingle with them. They like to fly above all else. They are fearless in their hunting strategy; they've been known to throw a goat larger than themselves off the side of a cliff. They have excellent far-range sight, and their vision is focused. No other bird can fly as high as an eagle, and eagles test before trusting. It's worth the research to read how the female courts the male. They mate for life, and they are the most gentle and attentive parents to their young. They make their homes in high places far above where their enemies can go. The eagle is brave, majestic, beautiful, strong, and courageous, and God uses it in the Bible thirty-four times. I now know why it was my dad's beloved favorite.

Wow, did the Lord school me today with this most meaningful and precious moment. If we wait upon the Lord, our strength will be renewed, and we will mount up with wings as eagles. I know I want to mount up like an eagle and fly above the storms, be focused in my vision, and fearless in my walk.

Abba, help us to wait on You, our hope and strength, so we can run and not get weary, walk and not faint, and so we can truly soar as eagles do, in Yeshua's name, amen.

February 24

2 Timothy 2:19

Nevertheless the foundation of God standeth sure, having this seal, The Lord knoweth them that are His. And, let everyone that nameth the name of Christ depart from iniquity.

When we name the name of Christ, we become His and have a seal placed upon us, and the Father knows we are His. We become founded on His foundation, and His foundation is sure and stands forever. When we become His and name Christ as our Savior, we no longer walk in the ways of the world. We turn from sin and depart from iniquity. When we truly become His and see how beautiful, wonderful, and perfect He is, we don't want anything to do with our old life and all our old ways.

We gratefully and joyously long to follow Him and do His will. How awesome is it to know that the foundation of God is sure, and we can stand on it and not be shaken, moved by circumstances, or be blown by winds because we have a sure foundation upon which we stand. How beautiful it is to be sealed for Him, for all eternity. He knows us, and we are His; what a hope that is found nowhere else. A promise as sure as the foundation it comes from—why would we not turn from iniquity and run to Him?

Father, help us to be confident in the sure foundation we have in You, being sealed and standing firm as we name the name of our Messiah Yeshua and turn from sin and iniquity. It's in Yeshua's name, we ask this, amen.

February 25

Zechariah 9:9

Rejoice greatly, O daughter of Zion; shout, O daughter of Jerusalem: behold, thy King cometh unto thee: He is just, and having salvation; lowly, and riding upon an ass, and upon a colt the foal of an ass.

What a marvelous prophecy of hope for the future for the children of Israel. Zechariah was telling the people to **rejoice** and **be glad**, for their Messiah, their Salvation, was coming, and God would right the wrongs and smite their enemies. He was sending His Son as a lowly, humble man with great and mighty power and an everlasting peace. What a glorious day it will be. **Rejoice greatly**, for thy King is coming with His eternal kingdom, which everyone will have the chance to be a part of.

Zechariah's prophecy came to pass, and surely what a glorious day it was as Yeshua came into town humbly on the back of a colt, and all the people proclaimed, "Hosannah in the highest" and rejoiced greatly in the salvation and hope that He brought them. That day is coming again, so, today, we must listen to Zechariah and do as he instructed the children of Israel and **rejoice greatly**. Our King is coming with healing in His wings and salvation, peace, joy, and His everlasting kingdom. He is coming again to right the wrongs, once and for all, and to smite our enemies and put an end to sin and death. **Rejoice greatly**, for He is just, righteous, and His truth will stand forever!

Lord, let our hearts be glad and let us rejoice greatly, for Yeshua is coming with great power and glory to take us to our eternal home with You soon, very soon, in Yeshua's name, amen.

February 26

John 14:6

Jesus saith unto him, I am the way, the truth, and the life: no man cometh unto the Father, but by me.

Yeshua is the **only** way to the Father, period. We must believe that He is the only begotten Son of the Father, that He died and bled for us and His blood cleanses us from all sin and unrighteousness. He is our only hope, and there is absolutely no other way to the Father but through Him. Yeshua alone made the way; He is the mediator. It doesn't matter how good we are, how much we do, or what great works we may accomplish, there is no other way but through Yeshua.

He is the way, the truth, and the life, and we must come by Him to Daddy's throne. Worthy is the Lamb of God, who takes away the sins of the world. He paid the greatest sacrifice of all.

Yeshua, thank You for coming and laying Your life down for us, making a way for us to come to the Father. Show us the way and teach us the truth that we may have life everlasting with You and Abba. It's in Your precious name, we pray this, amen.

February 27

Deuteronomy 29:9

Keep therefore the words of this covenant, and do them, that ye may prosper in all that ye do.

It's actually quite simple: if we want to prosper, long to walk in peace, and have God's favor and blessing upon us, then we must simply abide in Him and walk in His covenant. I love how it spells out in verses ten to fifteen that this covenant was not just for them but for the strangers with them, and also for those that were not with them that day—the future generations, the Gentiles and foreigners who would come and choose to make Him their God, following Him, and walking in His covenant.

The blessing that comes along with making a covenant with Him and walking in His ways are immeasurable. He is such a good Father, and all He has set forth and established is for our good, so why would we fight against it?

Lord, help us to see that Your covenant is good, brings blessings and prosperity to our lives, protects and keeps us, helps us to truly comprehend the goodness of it, Abba, and see Your great love for us in the making of this covenant with us. Help us to study it and truly know it, so we may walk in it all the days of our lives, all the curses from this book do not come upon us, and our names will not be blotted out from under heaven as Your Word says, in Yeshua's name, we ask this, amen.

February 28

Mark 10:45

For even the Son of man came not to be ministered unto, but to minister, and to give His life a ransom for many.

If we want to be great, we must be a servant to all. If we are in a position of greatness or leadership, then it is our job to serve and minister to others, not to be served by others. Yeshua, our King and Savior, came in great power and might to serve and minister unto us. To be the greatest, we must humble ourselves and become the least. Matthew 19:30 tells us that the last shall be first and the first will be last. The world teaches a "me" mentality. Work hard for me, become great for me, climb the ladder of success, and become number one so others can serve me and do for me what I should be doing, so I can sit in high places and be served. It teaches that greatness comes with being served, which is completely contrary to what Yeshua said and taught.

Being the greatest means we should be a servant to all. We should be ministering to others, giving all of who we are and what we have to touch a dying world, just as Yeshua laid down His very life for us. The perfect and most beautiful picture of greatness is Yeshua, our King, coming to serve and minister to us. Let's follow His example as we seek greatness in this life; let's seek to be great as He was.

Abba, teach us that to be truly great is to become the least and humble in all, serving and giving to others over ourselves, pouring out to those around, as You pour into us, in Yeshua's mighty name, amen.

February 29

Psalm 118:29

O give thanks unto the LORD; for He is good: for His mercy endureth forever.

We serve a gracious and merciful God; there is none like Him. He is a very present help, always. He is a strong tower, a place of refuge in times of trouble. He is our defender. He fights our battles for us, and when we fall, He is there to lift us to our feet again. He is our provider and keeper, having even the very hairs of our head numbered. Our every step is ordered by Him, and He directs our paths! Oh, give thanks unto the LORD!

Psalm 107:8 says, "Oh that men would praise the LORD for His goodness, and for His wonderful works to the children of men!" He is such a good, good Father and is so worthy of our praise. Let us walk daily with hearts full of thanksgiving to Him for all He has done and is yet to do. Psalm 100 tells us to make a joyful noise to the Lord, serve Him with gladness, come before Him with singing, enter into His gates with thanksgiving and His courts with praise, and be thankful and to bless His name, **amen**! Oh, let us give thanks unto the Lord!

Abba, You are so good and Your mercy and love endure forever. May we never lack in giving You the thanks and praise You so deserve. May our hearts be full of thanksgiving **always**, in Yeshua's name, amen.

March 1

Ezra 8:21

Then I proclaimed a fast there, at the river of Ahava, that we might afflict ourselves before our God, to seek of Him a right was for us, and for our little ones, and for all our substance.

The king just released Ezra and a second group of exiles from Babylon to go back to their homeland. Ezra gathered them all together, and before they began their journey back, he proclaimed a feast before God for direction and safety. Ezra could have sought help from the king, but he knew God was his only true source of protection, provision, and direction. The people all humbled themselves before God and fasted, and God was faithful and kept them from the enemies awaiting them.

How many times are we tempted to run to others to help us? How often do we, in times of need or trouble, do what it takes and get before the LORD and fast, pray, and seek His face for answers and direction?

Ezra knew God was the only way, and he knew the challenge set before him with all the snares it held. He knew there was only one option, and that was to put his complete trust in God and take the time needed to humbly seek His face. May this be our first choice of action in the face of hurdles along our lives' paths.

Abba, thank You for the countless stories of victory in your Word when we put our faith and trust in You, in Yeshua's name, amen.

March 2

Amos 5:14

Seek good, and not evil, that ye may live: and so the LORD, the God of hosts, shall be with you, as ye have spoken.

In Amos 5:15, it goes on to say that we are to **hate** evil and **love** good. The Word of God tells us that we should turn and run from the very appearance of evil and have no part in it at all. We are instructed here to seek good, which means to pursue diligently, to search out.[10] If we want the Lord to be with us and we want to live, truly live, then we need to seek good and run after and pursue it. We must hate and depart from evil and love and seek out and cling to good.

To get a clear understanding of the words *evil* and *good* in the context of these verses, I went to my Strong's Concordance. It explains *evil* as: wretchedness, wrong, wicked, vex, trouble, adversity, calamity, distress, harm, hurt, misery, mischief, naught, sorrow and trouble,[11] **wow**! *Good* is described as better, best, cheerful, gracious, kind, pleasant, precious, sweet, favored, merry, and loving.[12] These two words embody so much; so, when it says seek good and not evil, we are to seek after pleasant, sweet, kind, and cheerful things, pursuing gracious and loving attitudes, and walking in and displaying them. As far as evil, it's not just that we shouldn't seek or be a part of bad, wrong, or wicked things, but we shouldn't seek or be a part of calamity, misery, distress, or harm; we should hate them and run the opposite way from them as quickly as possible. We are to love and cling to good.

Father, give us a true understanding of these words so we can run from evil and all its ways and cling to good and live, in Yeshua's powerful name, we ask this, amen.

68

March 3

2 Peter 1:5–7

5) And beside this, giving all diligence, add to your faith virtue; and to virtue knowledge; 6) And to knowledge temperance; and to temperance patience; and to patience godliness; 7) And to godliness brotherly kindness; and to brotherly kindness charity.

The following verses go on to say that if you possess and walk in these things, you shall not be barren or unfruitful in the knowledge of our Lord. It tells us to give diligence and make our calling and election sure, and in so doing, we shall never fall. Wow, that's quite a statement and promise, but it's true. If we diligently walk in our faith and do what's right and true, being excellent in all our actions and words, knowing Him and His truth to be real, perceiving and being sure of it, walk in self-control, not giving into our own or fleshly desires, being patient always and, in all things, cheerfully and continually persevering and enduring, knowing He holds our every moment and controls all things, being and remaining holy as He is holy, being kind and affectionate, showing His love to our brothers and sisters, and loving as He does, then we can have surety in Him from falling.

In possessing and walking in these things, we learn and know Yeshua's heart and the Father's heart. We begin to walk as Yeshua walked in love and obedience to the Father. We receive His promises while joyfully awaiting the day He returns to take us home to be with Him and the Father for all eternity.

Lord, teach us how to truly walk out each of these things, to stand firm in our faith, have virtue, knowledge, temperance, patience, godliness, brotherly kindness, and charity; let them become a very part of our nature as they are Yours and Your son Yeshua's. It's in Your Son's holy name, we ask this, amen.

March 4

Proverbs 22:6

Train up a child in the way he should go: and when he is old, he will not depart from it.

These are not just idle words in Proverbs but words of wisdom. Children are so pliable and learn so well when they are young. They long to please Mom and Dad and are so innocent when starting out. That's why it is so important for us to train them up in God's Word and truth. Deuteronomy 11:19 says, "And ye shall teach them your children, speaking of them when thou sittest in thine house, and when thou walkest by the way, when thou liest down, and when thou risest up." God knew how important it was to start teaching them while yet little children and grow and train them up in it; to teach them daily of Abba, His ways, laws, and words, and of Yeshua and how He walked it out as an example of how we should walk.

We, like Yeshua, must not just teach our children all of this, but we must also walk it all out to the best of our ability while we teach them. Actions speak so much louder than words, so we are to not just teach in word but in action as we live out His Word in our lives. We must remember also to break willfulness and self-will, knowing that discipline and correction is loving and good. Proverbs 22:15 says, "Foolishness is bound in the heart of a child; but the rod of correction shall drive it far from him." If we train them up in this manner, even when the enemy puts stumbling blocks or deceit in front of them, God's Word **will stand**. God's Word is powerful, true, and unchanging, and we can **stand** on it! When we do, our children **will too**! For when he is old, he **will not** depart from it.

Abba, help us to know Your Word, live it, and walk by it so we can be faithful to teach and train our children up in You, so they can do the same with theirs, in Yeshua's name, amen.

March 5

Micah 7:18–19

18) Who is a God like unto thee, that pardoneth iniquity, and passeth by the transgression of the remnant of His heritage? He retaineth not His anger forever, because He delighteth in mercy. 19) He will turn again, He will have compassion upon us; He will subdue our iniquities; and thou wilt cast all their sins into the depths of the sea.

I remember when the Lord delivered me out of my addiction, the last words of this verse are some of the words He spoke to me. After many years of running and hiding from Him, beating myself up, slamming into brick walls, and falling into the deepest darkest pit of addiction, I finally came to the end of myself and just wanted everything to end. When He met me that day, He told me, "I have thrown your sins as far as the east is from the west and buried them in the deepest ocean, **never** to be remembered again; now rise and walk in newness of life! **Wow**, after all the garbage I had done and the absolute awful person I had become, He saw past it all and reached out His hand, took mine, and His mercy and grace saved my soul.

Who is a God like unto thee? There is **not one**, He is the **only righteous**, **true**, **loving and merciful God; Nothing compares to Him**! There is **no other** that can do what He does, **no other** that can love as He does. We are His, and He gave the love of His life, His **only** begotten Son because He loves us so much. **Run** into those arms because there is **nothing** better than Him.

Thank You, Abba, for loving us with a love we will **never** comprehend and for having such great mercy on us when we don't deserve it, in Your precious, only begotten Son Yeshua's name, amen.

March 6

Luke 10:40–42

40) But Martha was cumbered about much serving, and came to him, and said, Lord, dost thou not care that my sister hath left me to serve alone? bid her therefore that she help me. 41) And Jesus answered and said unto her, Martha, Martha, thou art careful and troubled about many things: 42) But one thing is needful: and Mary hath chosen that good part, which shall not be taken away from her.

Sometimes I find myself in Martha's shoes, working and trying to get everything prepared and feeling anxious and stressed that I'm doing everything alone while others are off sitting, relaxing, and enjoying the day. Then there are the times where I find myself in Mary's shoes as well, where I am the one off at the feet of my Messiah, breathing in all He is, soaking up the wonder and beauty of His presence while everything else around me just fades away.

There is a time and place where we all must step up, be Marthas, and complete the jobs at hand, and it is good. Then there are the moments when we **need** to be Marys and just **let everything go** and sit at the feet of Yeshua. We must all make sure we are taking time regularly to do as Mary did, to let the world fade away and come sit at our Savior's feet and just spend time in His presence.

Lord, help us to truly value the importance of coming and sitting at Your feet, letting all else go, and just spending time with You, in Your name Yeshua, we ask this, amen.

March 7

Psalm 141:2

Let my prayer be set forth before thee as incense; and the lifting up of my hands as the evening sacrifice.

David was crying out unto the Lord, asking Him to give ear unto His voice, and asking the Lord to regard his prayer as incense and his hands lifting as a sacrifice. In the midst of the trial and temptation that faced him, he knew the only one who could help him. In verse three, he sought the Lord to set watch of his mouth and keep the door of his lips, and he goes on in verse four, asking the Lord to let his heart not turn to anything evil and keep him from falling into practicing wicked works with men who work iniquity. He knew he needed help being kept from temptation and the enemy's snares so he would not fall.

David knew where to turn his eyes and put his trust. The Lord delights in us coming to Him. He takes joy in helping us and fighting our battles. Our prayers are not burdening to Him but as incense. When we cry out to Him, it's like a sweet-smelling sacrifice lifting to His throne. He desires for us to come to Him and loves to fight on our behalf. Let us raise our prayers night and day as incense to the Father, bringing every need and trouble to Him. He is there to help and is our **only hope**.

Oh Lord, hear our cries as we come before Thee; may our prayers be as incense as we raise them to You, just as David petitioned when he cried out to You; let the crying of our hearts and lifting of our hands be as a sweet-smelling sacrifice before your throne, in Yeshua's mighty name, amen.

March 8

Matthew 5:16

Let your light so shine before men, that they may see your good works, and glorify your Father which is in heaven.

As a lighthouse is a beacon of light guiding ships to safe harbors, so our lights should shine forth, drawing others to the hope that we have found in the Lord. Yeshua is instructing us to let our light shine forth before men, and we should be doing just that. We should be bright beacons of light, illuminating the darkest corners of this world. Yeshua says in John 8:12 that He is the light of the world, so when we invite Him to come live in us, we are walking with Him, and His light will radiate through us. We will take on His nature and produce good fruit, which will glorify the Father in heaven.

Our lives will become living testimonies of the Father's goodness, and others will take notice. Like a deer in the brightness of a car's headlights, so men will be as the brilliance of Yeshua's light shines forth through us; men will stop in their tracks, take notice, and be drawn to that light. We don't need big words; we don't even need words at all, just His light beaming out of us will speak greater than a mouthful of the most profound words one can find.

Yeshua, light of the world, fill our lives with You; help us to walk uprightly as we take on Your nature and shine brightly to the world around us, so they may see and glorify the Father always. It's in Your name, Yeshua, we ask this, amen.

March 9

Isaiah 41:10

Fear thou not; for I am with thee: be not dismayed; for I am thy God: I will strengthen thee; yea, I will help the; yea, I will uphold thee with the right hand of my righteousness.

I love that Abba knew how often we would have to hear the words "**fear not**," and He put it all throughout His Word so we would be reminded of it continually. He is our very present help in times of trouble; we don't need to worry or fear. Our flesh, our humanness tends to worry and fret; we fear things seen and unseen, but when we walk in the supernatural of His Spirit, we are strengthened and encouraged, knowing He is with us and will always have our back.

We can walk, knowing He will give us strength to face the giants before us. He will keep our feet anchored on the rock when the wind and waves of the storm rage around us, and He will carry us when the waters of the flood try sweeping us away. He will be with us and won't let us go. When we walk in His Spirit, we will no longer walk in the natural, worrying and being afraid, but we will begin to walk in the supernatural, being rooted and strengthened in Him and His truth, trusting and believing **all** His Word says and promises. We will know beyond a shadow of a doubt that He is with us. He is our God and will help and uphold us.

Lord, thank You for Your consistent reminder through Your Word to us that we don't have to fear or worry ever. With You, we will be held always, in Yeshua's name, amen.

March 10

Job 37:5

God thudereth marvellously with His voice; great things doeth He, which we cannot comprehend.

Elihu spoke these words to Job in his last speech to him. He was responding to Job's questioning of God, of His unjust judgment and punishment. Who are we to question our Maker, the Maker of all creation, the Maker of the world? If He made all of creation and controls it all with such perfect precision, who are we to question Him at all? Job, in all his sorrow and loss, was trying to understand what happened, what he had done, and why God had been so harsh and allowed all this to happen to him.

Sometimes there is no understanding, it is nothing we did, or there is just no answer. God is God, and we are not. He is a sovereign God who knows the beginning from the end and, believe it or not, He always knows what's best for His creation. He knows us, created us, knows what we're made of, and our strengths and weaknesses. He will never give us more than we can handle and will always be there with us in whatever it may be we must face. Even in Job's questioning, he still knew God was good and perfect and would accept whatever it was that God allowed. Could we do that? I know at the smallest things, I tend to crumble and cry like a baby, but to learn to trust Him and cling to Him in the midst of whatever He allows is where I want to learn to be always.

Abba, help us to trust You with whatever may come our way, with whatever You may allow to touch our lives, knowing You love us so much, knowing Your ways are perfect, and You will work things perfectly out for us in the end, in Yeshua's name, amen.

March 11

John 3:14

And as Moses lifted up the serpent in the wilderness, even so must the Son of man be lifted up.

I love how the old prophecies of the new, and the new testifies of the old. Complete perfection—how much more beautiful could it get? Yeshua was speaking to Nicodemus about how one must be born again to see the kingdom of God, and Nicodemus was confused at His words and questioned, "Does one go back into his mother's womb in old age and be born a second time?" Yeshua answers and tells him one must be born of water and spirit to enter the kingdom of God. Then Nicodemus said, "How can these things be?" and Yeshua challenged him and asked him, "Nicodemus, art thou a master of Israel and knowest not these things?" (John 3:4-10).

Yeshua goes on to say one must believe to be saved, and He references the passage in Numbers 21. It talks about how the children of Israel, once again, began to murmur and cry against God, and He sent serpents to bite them, and many died. The children knew they sinned and came to Moses to pray to God for them. God told Moses to make a fiery serpent and place it on a pole, and whoever got bit, if they looked upon the pole, they would be healed and saved. This was a foreshadowing of Yeshua being hung on a tree for our salvation, having to die so we may live.

Yeshua said that just as Moses raised the serpent, so the son of man must be raised. John 3:16 says, "For God so loved the world that He gave His only begotten Son that whosoever believed in Him should not perish but have everlasting life." He basically said, "Nicodemus, all your good works to be righteous will not get you eternity with the Father; you must believe in me and be born again. I was sent from the Father and am the begotten Son who has come to take away the sin of the world.

As Moses raised the pole for the children of Israel and they looked upon it and were saved, so Abba raised His only begotten

Son on a tree before men, so if we looked upon Him and believed, we would be saved.

Abba, thank You for sending your only begotten Son for us. Help us to look to Him and believe so we can be saved, to be born again of water and spirit so we may enter Your kingdom, in your Son Yeshua's precious name, we pray, amen.

March 12

Judges 7:1

Then Jerubbaal, who is Gideon, and all the people that were with him, rose up early, and pitched beside the well of Harod: so that the host of the Midianites were on the north side of them, by the hill of Moreh, in the valley.

The first thing in this passage that captured my attention and once again spoke loud and clear to me was, "**rose up early**." The Lord has been putting this in front of me continuously; still, as I am a work in progress, this is something I am still trying to master. There is something so special about the early morning hours, the stillness in them, the awakening of life at the rising of the sun, and the excitement of another day being unwrapped for us by Abba with all His beautiful blessings and awesome adventures awaiting.

The second thing is how God delivered the Israelites from the Midianites. The Midianites had oppressed God's people for seven years, and it was time for their deliverance. Gideon rose early with thirty thousand men to go to battle against them, and the Lord said, "Nope, hold up, there are too many of you, Gideon." By the time Gideon was done doing all the Lord commanded, there were only 300 men left to fight the vast army of the Midianites. That may have been the point where some fear would have risen in me, causing me to doubt the outcome. God wanted it to be known by all that it was only by Him this victory would take place. The power and victory lie in God alone and is another lesson vital for our walk with Him. Gideon trusted and believed God and was obedient to all God said and saw God move in an awesome and mighty way as He gave him the victory that day. Oh, how I love that His Word never grows old, He never changes, and He will do the same for us if we will listen and obey. Rise early. Trust me, I have the perfect plan, with the perfect answers that will always bring victory.

Abba, thank You for giving us clear guidelines, for fighting the battles, and always being victorious. You are a good, good Father and always worthy of all praise and honor, in Yeshua's name, amen.

March 13

Jeremiah 35:18–19

18) And Jeremiah said unto the house of the Rechabites, Thus saith the LORD of hosts, the God of Israel; Because ye have obeyed the commandment of Jonadab your father, and kept all his precepts, and done according unto all that he hath commanded you: 19) Therefore thus saith the LORD of hosts, the God of Israel; Jonadab the son of Rechab shall not want a man to stand before me forever.

I think this has to be by far my favorite Old Testament story. The Rechabites, who are they? Whoever heard of them? I know I never had, and the first time I did, it was so profound it became branded into my mind and heart that day. This is a group of people who faithfully followed all they were commanded by their ancestor Rechab, the father of the Rechabites, and were completely obedient. From abstaining from wine to not building houses, sewing seed, or planting vineyards to never becoming involved in Baal worship, they were fully obedient in all that was commanded. See, Rechab knew the LORD was the one true God. He knew what God said to be true, and he followed it, commanding his children and people to do the same.

The LORD had Jeremiah bring them to the Temple to use it as an example before His own people who were constantly rebellious and wouldn't listen to or heed anything the Lord said. Then He had Jeremiah tell the men of Judah and Jerusalem that because they had not listened, all the evil He had pronounced against them would come to pass, but as for the Rechabites, not a man of them would lack standing before the LORD and beholding His face forever. Wow, that is absolutely life-changing; it is possible to be completely obedient and not constantly rebellious.

Abba, help us to be like the Rechabites, following and keeping Your commands and always walking in Your ways, in Yeshua's name, amen.

March 14

Luke 6:31

And as ye would that men should do to you, do ye also to them likewise.

If I know nothing else in my life, I know this one thing for sure, that I want to be treated right by others. I desire for others to be kind to me, not to be rude, mean, offensive, or hurtful, but kind and considerate, holding a door for me, or just smiling and saying "Hi." What a difference that makes in my day. No matter how bad things get or how hard life may be, a smile, kind word, or gesture of goodness can turn the whole day around.

I know I'm not alone in this desire; we all want to be treated fairly and justly with kindness and compassion. If this is how we long to be treated, then how much more should we treat others the same? Even if others fail to treat us right, we still should treat them with love and respect. It just might make such an impact on them, causing them to treat the next person with love and respect. We should always, no matter how others may act, do our best to treat them as we desire to be treated.

Lord, fill our hearts with Your love, teach us to act right and do unto others as we would have them act and do to us. Show us the true blessings that come with it as we do, Lord, in Yeshua's name, amen.

March 15

2 Chronicles 7:14

If my people, which are called by my name, shall humble themselves, and pray, and seek my face, and turn from their wicked ways; then will I hear from heaven, and will forgive their sin, and will heal their land.

For the first time in my life, we are in some uncharted waters in this world. The whole world went on a lockdown, and almost everything closed. Life, as we knew it, was coming to an abrupt halt. Fear, craziness running rapid, the death toll is continuing to rise amidst the cases of infection, and the health system is overwhelmed, on top of the election we faced with all the division it brought. If we ever needed the Father, it is **now**! He is the **only** answer.

I pray that it all has shaken us so deeply to our very core that we cry out, turn from everything that has led us away, and turn back to our only hope. I pray our hearts and minds turn and run toward Him with all the might we hold. **He seriously is our only hope**. I wish it didn't take things like this for us to see and realize how bad we need Him, but I pray in the midst of this all, we **truly** learn just how much we do and **never forget** it. I pray we all learn to reverence, hear, and follow Him in a deeper way and seriously drown out all the distractions and things that take us away from Him and all His goodness.

Please, Abba, help us all to humble ourselves before You, seek Your face more than we ever have, turn from our wicked ways, all of them, and turn back to You, our **only hope**. Root and ground us in You that we don't turn from Your will and ways ever again, in Yeshua's powerful name, amen.

March 16

Romans 8:31

What shall we then say to these things? If God be for us, who can be against us?

I don't claim to know everything, but one thing I know beyond a shadow of a doubt is that God's Word is **true** and can be believed and stood upon. I don't know why most things happen. He's God, and I'm not. I don't know the beginning from the end or why He allows certain things, but I do know He is **perfect**, **good**, and He **loves** His children.

I also know that in His perfection, His justice and judgment must come. I know all the enemy tries to do and use for evil God can turn and use for good. Genesis 50:20 says, "But as for you, ye thought evil against me; but God meant it unto good, to bring to pass, as it is this day, to save much people alive." I know as well that whatever the reason may be, things happen like they do. Abba will hold, keep, and protect His children. He will **never** leave or forsake us. He will be with us through whatever it is, hold our every moment, and fight for us. We can always find rest and peace in that. If God is for us, who can be against us?

Is He your Daddy? Is Yeshua your Savior? Have you surrendered your life to Him? Are you doing your best to walk as His child would? Then you can find rest and peace in the words of this verse.

Abba, help us to set our eyes on You, wrap our hearts in Yours, and walk as Your child, believing You for us because when we are Yours, You are for us, in Yeshua's name, amen.

March 17

Psalm 91:1–16

1) I who dwelleth in the Secret Place of the Most High shall abide under the shadow of You, Almighty God. 2) I will say of You LORD, You are my refuge and my fortress: my God; in You will I trust. 3) Surely You will deliver me from the snare of the fowler, and from the noisome pestilence. 4) You shall cover me with Your feathers, and under Your wings shalt I trust: Your truth shall be my shield and buckler. 5) I shall NOT be afraid for the terror by night; nor for the arrow that flieth by day; 6) Nor for the pestilence that walketh in darkness; nor for the destruction that wasteth at noonday. 7) A thousand shall fall at my side, and ten thousand at my right hand; but it shall not come nigh me. 8) Only with my eyes shall I behold and see the reward of the wicked. 9) Because I have made You LORD my refuge, even You most High, my habitation; 10) There shall no evil befall me, neither shall **any plague** come nigh my dwelling. 11) For You will give your Angels charge over me, to keep me in all my ways. 12) They shall bear me up in their hands, lest I dash my foot against a stone. 13) I shall tread upon the lion and adder: the young lion and the dragon shalt I trample under feet. 14) Because you hath set your love upon me, therefore I will deliver you: I will set you on high, because you hath known my name. 15) You shall call upon me, and I will answer you, I will be with you in trouble, I will deliver you, and honor you. 16) With long life will I satisfy you and show you my salvation.

I delivered today's verses in a personalized way; as I was reading this one day, I felt the Lord tell me to personalize it because He was saying it to us, His children, and it's just as much for us today as it was for His children back then.

Father, You are such a good, good Father, and I thank You for these words, every one of them that we can stand on. Thank You for Your faithfulness, love, protection, keeping power, and **all** that you are, in Yeshua's name, amen.

March 18

Mark 6:6

And He marveled because of their unbelief. And He went round about the villages, teaching.

If we saw Yeshua today, here in our time, would we recognize Him? Would He look like the vision we hold of Him? If He walked beside us today, would we know it is Him, or do we have Him in a box of our own making with certain expectations? The children of Israel were looking for a king to come and save them, but maybe their vision of Him was that of a well-suited man with full armor, riding in on a horse, defeating the Romans, all the heathens, and delivering them from bondage. Maybe their vision of Him was that He would come as a mighty warrior, like a Goliath walking in and just desolating their enemies. One thing is apparent and true, they did not see Him as an ordinary, humble, lowly man coming with great power and authority. His own town and people could not wrap their heads around the fact that this could be their Messiah, this could be their deliverer. They instantly questioned the works He had done, who He was, who His mother was, the brother and sisters He had, and dismissed Him as just another man. Yeshua marveled at their unbelief.

Will we know Him when He returns? We need to spend time with our Messiah now, daily walk with Him, and grow in our relationship with Him, so when the day of His return comes, we know it's Him. Even if He returns in a way we're not expecting, we will know Him so well that there won't be a question or doubt; He won't marvel at our unbelief because He doesn't appear to us in the way we may have envisioned Him.

Abba, help us to know You and Your Son, our Savior, deeper every day, so when You send Him back for us, we don't miss Him, but we will know Him no matter how He appears because Your Spirit in Him will witness to Your Spirit in us, in Yeshua's precious name, we ask this, amen.

March 19

Zechariah 8:16–17

16) These are the things that ye shall do; Speak ye every man the truth to his neighbor; execute the judgment of truth and peace in your gates: 17) And let none of you imagine evil in your hearts against his neighbor; and love no false oath: for all these are things that I hate, saith the LORD.

Live, breathe, and walk out His Word; it shouldn't be so difficult, but the flesh loves to war against us when doing so. That's why His Word tells us in Galatians 5:24 that they who are Christ have crucified the flesh. We must die to our flesh daily, to ourselves, our wants, desires, and take up our cross, follow, and be obedient to His will and way.

We need to speak the truth, live righteously, and execute the judgment of truth and peace in our homes and our lives. We must keep our hearts from imagining evil against our neighbors, despise the wrong, and don't like or associate with falsehoods or false oaths. We are to be separate, holy, set apart, dedicated, and hallowed so our lives may be pleasing before the Father. Let's do our best to die to the flesh daily so we may be vessels of righteousness for Him, refraining from the things He hates and walking in the ways He sets before us, truly resembling a child of His.

Abba, strengthen and equip us to live, breathe, and always walk out Your Word that we may glorify You in all we do, in Yeshua's name, amen.

March 20

Ezekiel 20:12

Moreover also I gave them my Sabbaths, to be a sign between me and them, that they might know that I am the LORD that sanctify them.

What a beautiful gift He gave us when He gave us these days to just dive into all He is, rest in His love for us, and grow in the knowledge of His truth He has given us. Just to know that He loved us so much He set these days aside for us, for our good, as a sign to show we are His, to know He is our Creator, Father, God who sanctifies us, what a beautiful picture, perfect plan, and beyond a special day.

I've only come to know, understand, and keep His Sabbaths in the last five years or so of my life and, **wow**, what I was missing out on all those years prior. Like Yeshua said in Mark 2:27, "The Sabbath was made for man, and not man for the Sabbath." Abba set this day aside special for us to bless and give us much-needed rest, lavish us with His love, Word, and presence, and to grow us in His will and way and gather us with the body of Christ, so we could fellowship and grow together as His family, having each other and not being alone. He set the example for us as He Himself kept the first Sabbath, and on the seventh day rested, reflected on all He did and saw that it was good. Oh, what a blessing and gift it's been for me to learn, experience, and keep His Sabbaths, to sit back and reflect on just how good and perfect He is, falling more and more in love with Him the deeper I go into His heart. May we all come to know the true gift of these days and how awesome His perfect plan from the beginning still is.

Abba, thank You for loving us so much that You set a special day aside for us and you, a special date we can go on and be lavished with Your love and lavish our love on You. There is nothing better than being with You, in Yeshua's name, amen.

March 21

John 4:14

But whosoever drinketh of the water that I shall give him shall never thirst; but the water that I shall give him shall be in him a well of water springing up into everlasting life.

When Yeshua gives us a drink of His living water, we will **never** thirst again. There is no other drink that can quench the thirst of a human soul but the drink Yeshua gives. The drink He gives sprigs up into everlasting life, satisfies our every need, and fulfills our every desire. Just one drink from His well, and we will thirst **no more**.

Have you ever been so thirsty your lips are just dry and cracked, you don't even have enough saliva in your mouth to swallow, but then you're given a glass of cool water that just moistens your lips and wets your mouth, allowing you to swallow those life-giving qualities it holds? A human body cannot live without water. Well, it's the same with our souls; they need that life-giving water only Yeshua can give to live. When your soul is thirsting from the barrenness of the desert place and your heart is cracking from the hard, dry hurts of life, Yeshua can give you a drink that will be as a well springing up into everlasting life, and you will **never** thirst again. Doesn't that sound like the **best** drink ever?

Yeshua, please give us a drink of Your water that we will never thirst again, Your life-giving water that will satisfy and fill our soul with everlasting life. We want a drink from You, in Your powerful name, we ask this, Yeshua, amen.

March 22

1 Kings 2:3

And keep the charge of the LORD thy God, to walk in His ways, to keep His statutes, and His commandments, and His judgments, and His testimonies, as it is written in the law of Moses, that thou mayest prosper in all that thou doest, and whithersoever thou turnest thyself.

It's quite simple, if we keep His ways, command, statutes, and testimonies, as Moses gave to us, then we will prosper in all we do. He will be with us, fight for us, protect and keep us, and will bless us in all our ways.

It's **not** complicated, so let's not allow our minds or flesh to complicate it on us.

Abba, help us to walk in all Your ways, keep Your charge, and do what's right, that in all our words and steps, may we simply follow You and do all You say; in so doing, we will be blessed in the drought, the storm, the hurt, and loss. You will be there and never leave; that in itself is the biggest blessing of all, in Yeshua's name, we pray, amen.

March 23

Habakkuk 3:18–19

18) Yet I will rejoice in the LORD, I will joy in the God of my salvation. 19) The LORD God is my strength, and He will make my feet like hinds' feet, and He will make me to walk upon mine high places.

Though Habakkuk saw terror, destruction, and desolation all around him and even trembled and quivered in the flesh, he was able to go to that place of rest in Abba, knowing his salvation was of God. He could rejoice in the middle of it all because his faith was in God, who was his very strength. God would cause his feet to be like deer's feet that prance across the troubles, and they would not trip or fall.

Oh, the beautiful imagery as I just picture that deer gliding through the forest, not being affected by the thorns and cracks under his small but strong and sure hooves. Deer seldom slip or fall; their little hooves are a wonder, and they make all their running and jumping possible. As I researched more about them, I found out they jump, run, and walk on their third and fourth phalanges; their hooves are made of keratin, the material that our fingernails are formed with, and each toe is capped with a hard nail that forms the hoof. The black outer edge of the hoof provides traction on wet and soft surfaces and also absorbs the shock of each stride. The inside provides traction and a cushion on hard surfaces. They are strong and can be a powerful weapon in a bad situation. Wow, how perfect our God is and how perfect He made everything. It blows my mind when I study the details of some of the things He compares us to; it really brings it to light and reveals a much deeper significance. "He will make my feet like hinds' feet" sheds a whole new light on how He will take care of us and sustain us in times of trouble. We can truly rejoice and find joy in the God of our salvation as Habakkuk did, knowing He will do all this for us.

Abba, may we find joy and rejoice in times of trouble, sing and dance rather than fret or worry as we come to know You more deeply and place all our confidence and faith completely in You, in Yeshua's mighty name, amen.

March 24

1 Timothy 6:20

O Timothy, keep that which is committed to thy trust, avoiding profane and vain babblings, and oppositions of science falsely so called.

We are not to argue over the Word of God; it can prove itself and will **never** return void. If we just walk and stand in what it says, it will speak louder than any debating we can do. The Strong's Concordance definition for the word *babblings* is "empty sounding, fruitless discussion."[13] The truth of God's spoken Word will go on to produce much fruit, but the vain babblings and arguments will be empty and fruitless. He doesn't need us to prove His Word; it proves itself. He just needs us to speak it and walk it out.

When studying the Strong's definition of the oppositions of science, it defines it as conflicts of theories and knowledge.[14] Timothy is instructed here to stand in what he's been given and taught and to not have the need to fight and debate those that may oppose him. We were all created differently; no two of us are the same. We are all works in progress and are on a continual path of learning; not one of us has arrived. So, let's live out what God has taught and given us, witness when He opens the door for us to do so, allow Him to shine through us always, and pray without ceasing but cease empty and fruitless debates and conflicts.

Lord, help us to just live and walk out your word and will in peace and love, shining you as we do and to avoid unnecessary babblings knowing the truth of your word will stand always and never return void, in Yeshua's name, Amen.

March 25

Luke 9:23–25

23) And He said to them all, if any man will come after me, let him deny himself, and take up his cross daily, and follow me. 24) For whosoever will save his life shall lose it: but whosoever will lose his life for my sake, the same shall save it. 25) For what is a man advantaged, if he gain the whole world, and lose himself, or be cast away?

Truly, what does it benefit us if we gain the whole world but lose our soul? We may have riches, popularity, and status, but we are desolate inside. None of that can fill like Yeshua can; we will always come up empty and wanting. He says here that if any want to follow Him and have what He has, he or she must lose his or her own life, lay it down, and take up his or her cross, then will he or she have all he or she needs and find true fulfillment.

Apart from Him, we are but dust; we are nothing, with no hope for completeness, true happiness, and eternal life. All the world can give will disintegrate and dissolve; it will utterly perish. It's like trying to hold water in your hands. It just seeps through and is gone, leaving nothing but emptiness. Yeshua says if we, instead, lay our lives down, lose our lives for His sake, we will surely find it. We will find real life, true life, life everlasting, full of joy unspeakable, a peace beyond understanding, genuine fulfillment, and true purpose in Him. The greatest riches in the world don't compare to knowing and following Him.

Lord, teach us how to take up our cross daily, to deny ourselves and lose our lives so we can truly find it in You, the only reality worth knowing and living, our hope, our rock, in Yeshua's name, we ask this, amen.

March 26

Daniel 6:21–22

21) Then said Daniel unto the king, O king, live forever. 22) My God hath sent His angel, and hath shut the lions' mouths, that they have not hurt me: forasmuch as before Him innoceny was found in me; and also before thee, O king, have I done no hurt.

Praise the Lord, He shuts the lions' mouths. When we are sealed in Him, He does things that will simply amaze us, leaving us in awe and wonder. Daniel had nothing to fear, for He knew who was on His side and who had His back. He knew He did nothing wrong and didn't deliberately do any hurt to the king. He just faithfully continued to bow before the Lord and pray to make his petitions known to God alone.

If we trust God when things get hard and refuse to bow our knee to anything but Him and walk by His commands and decrees, then we can rest in knowing He will keep us in all our ways. He will set a hedge of protection around us and close the lion's mouth. **Praise the Lord, we serve a mighty and awesome God**.

Father, may we never stop coming to You, bowing our knee before You, and laying our petitions at your feet, for You and You alone are God; you are worthy and are our present help always, in Yeshua's name, amen.

March 27

Isaiah 58:13–14

13) If thou turn away thy foot from the sabbath, from doing thy pleasure on my holy day; and call the sabbath a delight, the holy of the LORD, honourable; and shalt honour Him, not doing thine own ways, nor finding thine own pleasure, nor speaking thine own words: 14) Then shalt thou delight thyself in the LORD; and I will cause thee to ride upon the high places of the earth, and feed thee with the heritage of Jacob thy father: for the mouth of the LORD hath spoken it.

I have learned in my later years to call the Sabbath a delight. I just wish I would have learned sooner. What a gift to have a day set apart holy to the LORD, a day to just totally die to self, desires, own pleasures, worries, wants, and the weight of the world, a day to just totally be consumed with the Father, glorifying and honoring Him and bathing in all His goodness and love. It's the most delightful thing I can think of, a taste of eternity here on earth. I just wish I would have come to the knowledge and truth of this sooner.

The blessing in setting this day aside is such a treasure in and of itself, but then Abba just multiplies it all and puts a cherry on top. He promises from His own mouth that if you do this, He will cause you to ride upon the high places of the earth and feed us with the heritage of Jacob. **Wow**, I think that's called blessing upon blessing.

Abba, thank You for showing and teaching me the truth and beauty of Your Sabbath. It is such a delight and blessing, and there truly is no better place to be. It's so blessed already as it is, but you just make it sweeter and sweeter. Thank You so much for this oh so special day You set aside for Your children, in Yeshua's name, amen.

March 28

Proverbs 3:5–6

5) Trust in the LORD with all thine heart; and lean not unto thine own understanding. 6) In all thy ways acknowledge Him, and He shall direct thy paths.

If we are fully putting all our trust in the Lord and acknowledging Him in all we do, not reasoning our own thoughts and ways into the picture, then we have no reason to worry or fret. It's when we start rationalizing our own knowledge and wisdom for our own wants and desires toward a planned outcome for the future that we must worry. Then when things don't turn out how we planned or how we thought they should be, we're discouraged, angry, confused, empty, and lost.

It's when we stop trusting in our own understanding and give everything to Him, trusting Him for the next step, the next breath, tomorrow, and the future that we actually will arrive at the perfect destination He has appointed just for us. As I am writing this, He is speaking to me as well. The world tells us to make a plan, go after it with all your might, and become all you can be. The Word says to wait upon the Lord, trust in Him, and He will direct your every step and make you all He's purposed you to be since before you took your first breath. His outcome, the end destination with Him, will be so much better than anything we could think or plan.

Abba, we lay all our own ways and understanding at Your feet and acknowledge You in all, trusting You to direct our paths to the perfect destination You established long ago for us, in Yeshua's precious name, amen.

March 29

1 Corinthians 5:6

Your glorying is not good. Know ye not that a little leaven leaveneth the whole lump?

Leaven puffs up, spreads, and makes everything it touches grow bigger. There are many different leavening agents out there, from yeast to baking soda to any agent that causes a substance to rise, grow, and puff up. We are warned in Scripture to be careful of the leaven. We are instructed during the Feast of Unleavened Bread to put all leaven out of our houses in Exodus 12:14–20. Yeshua warns us in Luke 12:1 to be careful of the leaven of the Pharisees. Here, Paul is warning us again to be careful; boasting in wrongful things is not good. He says we should be cleaning out all the old leaven so we can be a new lump, for just a little bit of leaven will affect the whole loaf; it will grow, expand, and puff up.

Just a little glorying in the wrong thing, a little acceptance of anything contradictory to the Word of God, a little compromise with the world can grow out of control quickly in a life and destroy it. Paul is warning us in this passage to be careful not of those of the world but of associating with those who bear the name of brother. Those being part of our godly family and practicing sexual immorality, greed, idolatry, reviling, drinking, or swindling, we should not even eat with such, for a little leaven leaventh the whole lump. We need to be mindful, watchful, and careful of what we allow and have association with.

Abba, help us to be aware and discerning of anything that may come close to the crossing of any line but to stand firm in the wisdom and knowledge of the truth You have given us, not wavering in any way but doing our best to remain obedient, righteous, and holy as You have called us to be, in Yeshua's mighty name, amen.

March 30

Exodus 33:14

And He said, My presence shall go with thee, and I will give thee rest.

Amen, the presence of Almighty God, the great I Am, our Creator, our heavenly Father with us always, wherever we go, holding and keeping us, giving us rest; is there anything more promising or better? Nothing compares to the presence of God Almighty in our lives, walking with us, guiding and directing us, and keeping us in His perfect peace. The Lord was telling Moses here that he had found favor in His sight and that He knew him by name.

I don't know about you, but I long to find favor in His sight. I long for Abba to say that about me and know me, and I know Him in such a way that I never have to doubt or worry again. I long that He would show me His glory in such a way that my countenance would glow as Moses did when he came down from that meeting. He is not untouchable to us today, and we can encounter Him in such a way that it will change us forever.

He will walk with us, and His presence will surround us. He will give us rest from the weariness and struggles of life, and I believe He will show us His glory as He did Moses if we genuinely and sincerely seek Him with our whole hearts. He loves us and desires to know us by name. He desires to be Lord of our lives to have favor on us and bestow us with His goodness and promises. We just must seek and desire Him.

Lord, we long to have Your favor as Moses did; we want nothing more than for Your presence to always go with us in all our days and give us rest. Please hear our prayers as we cry out and seek You, Lord, and please show us Your glory in this world today and surround us with Your presence that we are changed forever, in Yeshua's powerful name, amen.

March 31

Mark 10:27

And Jesus looking upon them saith, With men it is impossible, but not with God: for with God all things are possible.

Sometimes things can seem really bleak; our situations or circumstances can just look impossible, and we get frustrated or lose hope. I love it here where Yeshua tells us that what is impossible with man is not with God. He brings hope into the hopeless and tells us that with God, **all** things are possible. Mountains are moved, battles are won, storms cease, sickness is healed, and the impossible becomes possible with God.

We must believe He can handle anything and everything and trust that what He chooses the end result to be is His perfect plan and for our best. We don't have to walk around weary, hopeless, or beaten because our God can do above all we could ask or think and makes all things possible through Him. It's time to make our impossibilities God's possibilities.

Lord, help us to bring the impossible situations, the impossible circumstances we face in our lives to Your throne and lay them at Your feet, knowing You alone are the God of the possible, and we can trust and find rest in You, our hope of glory, in Yeshua's name, amen.

April 1

Jeremiah 33:3

Call unto me, and I will answer thee, and shew thee great and mighty things, which thou knowest not.

Have you ever wondered, like I have, if God has heard your call, if He's there and if He's ever going to answer? Well, we don't have to wonder anymore. We can rest in knowing He **will** answer because His Word here says if we call unto Him, He **will** answer, and His Word is true, for He cannot lie. I believe this word is just as much for us today as it was when He spoke it to Jeremiah. If we love Him above all else and seek and call out to Him today, He will hear and will not ignore us. If we set our eyes on Him and watch, wait, and listen, He will show us great and mighty things that we have not known. He will take us deeper into all He is and reveal His heart and truth to us.

As we seek and call upon Him, I believe He will open our eyes to things to come, to future plans He has for us. He longs to show us so we can accomplish His will and the purposes He has ordained for us since before we were a thought in our mothers' minds. He wants to be our only hope, to use us and wants us to be His hands and feet so He can shine through us to a world that is lost and has no hope. "Call unto me and I **will answer,**" He said. It's not hard, just call, then watch, wait, and listen. He will answer.

Lord, we call unto You today. Please hear our prayers and answer as Your Word says You will. Show us Your heart, teach us Your ways, draw us closer than ever to You, and show us great and mighty things we have not known. We long to know more and go deeper into all You are, in Yeshua's holy and precious name, we ask this, amen.

April 2

Psalm 23:1–6

1) The LORD is my shepherd; I shall not want. 2) He maketh me to lie down in green pastures: he leadeth me beside the still waters. 3) He restoreth my soul: he leadeth me in the paths of righteousness for his name's sake. 4) Yea, though I walk through the valley of the shadow of death, I will fear no evil: for thou art with me; thy rod and thy staff they comfort me. 5)Thou preparest a table before me in the presence of mine enemies: thou anointest my head with oil; my cup runneth over. 6) Surely goodness and mercy shall follow me all the days of my life: and I will dwell in the house of the LORD forever.

I want to challenge you today to take time out of your schedule and just sit and meditate on this passage. No matter how well you may or may not know it, I'm asking you to just take a few moments to dig deeper into every word and truly meditate on all it is saying. This passage holds so much encouragement, peace, and power to enable you to face the day ahead without worry or fear, but with strength, hope, and a sound mind.

It helps us to know we are truly the Lord's, that He orders every step of ours and walks each one with us. No matter what the day ahead may hold, we can face it and not fear because He holds our every moment. We can sit amidst our enemies and not fret. We can walk along still waters and find rest and peace for our souls. Just meditate on this for a while and then let it empower you as you walk through your day. Let it fill you with hope, peace, and joy, knowing you will dwell in His house forever, and His mercy and goodness shall follow you **all** the days of your life, amen!

Abba, let each and every word of this passage wash over us as we take time to meditate on it, allowing it to sink deep into our hearts and minds as it equips and empowers us to face the day ahead, in Yeshua's beautiful name, amen.

April 3

Matthew 5:17–18

17) Think not that I am come to destroy the law, or the prophets: I am not come to destroy, but to fulfill. 18) For verily I say unto you, Till heaven and earth pass, one jot or one tittle shall in no wise pass from the law, till all be fulfilled.

How can we mess it up and confuse it when Yeshua clearly states it here? He never came to do away with the Law; the Law is good, as the prophets and their messages are too. He didn't come to destroy any of it, but as He said, He came to fulfill it, and He did just that and said the whole way, "**Follow Me**." In looking up the Greek word used for *follow*, its definition explained it as: "properly to be in the same way with, a particle of union"[15]; in other words, to be like something or someone. We are called to be like Yeshua, to walk, love, and be obedient to the Father as He did.

Not one iota or least particle, as defined in the Greek,[16] shall pass from the law until **all** is fulfilled. Maybe walking as Yeshua did to the best of our ability, following the Father's set-in-place perfect law and plan, taking up our cross and dying to our own flesh, and following Yeshua's example until He comes to take us to our eternal home with Him and the Father is part of the fulfilling. I know when the enemy is thrown into the lake of fire and sin and death are gone forever, all will be fulfilled. So, let's follow Yeshua, walking as He did in obedience to His Father's law and will until that day because He knew His Daddy's ways were perfect.

Abba, thank You for Your Son to walk out Your will and be the perfect example for us to follow to Your heart and eternal fulfillment, in Yeshua's powerful name, amen.

April 4

Proverbs 15:15

All the days of the afflicted are evil: but he that is of a merry heart hath a continual feast.

I've read this verse before, but it never seemed to stand out to me until a few months ago when the Lord put it before me and, once again, rocked my world like He is so good at doing. I had been struggling for quite some time since I lost my mom, which has been over a year ago. There was about a six-month span around losing her where I lost quite a few other close people in my life as well. It was a very dark and gloomy time, it was winter, it seemed the sun never shone, and I spent a good majority of many days crying.

Then so many other changes began happening way too fast all around me. It was doing something to me, but I couldn't figure out what. I couldn't put my finger on what exactly was wrong and why I would wake up every morning crying. I just wanted so bad to wake up happy and be my name again. I had moments of Joy and many times of happiness and excitement, but it didn't seem to take away or end this lingering heaviness, this overwhelming sadness. Then one morning I woke up sobbing again and cried out to Abba begging Him to help me, telling Him I can't wake up like this anymore, asking Him what was happening with me? Then I heard the words: Evil Forebodings.

I had no clue what that meant, and I instantly started researching it. I was led by the Lord to this verse. The Amplified Bible Classic Edition says it this way: "All the days of the desponding and afflicted are made evil (by anxious thoughts and forebodings), but he who has a glad heart has a continual feast (regardless of circumstances)." WOW, some powerful eye-opening words the Lord put before me that morning. I made a decision that day to begin a journey of walking in freedom of affliction and to fill my heart and life once again with a merry heart, a heart full of

Thankfulness. I made a choice to walk full of joy (my name) which was given to me for a reason.

I am a work in progress and am still learning to deflect those anxious thoughts and the evil forebodings the enemy tries to afflict me with. The good news is, I now know what it is, what's going on, what the answer is and how I can overcome through a merry and joyful heart all because of the Lord bringing me to this verse and teaching me that day.

If you find yourself struggling, sad, lonely, anxious, and fearful, this verse provides an answer, it is a merry heart. It is a choice only each of us individually can make. We don't have to live with the daunting, relentless affliction the enemy wants to drown us in. We can choose to turn and run to the arms of a loving Father, where there is fullness of joy and mercies new each morning. I'm continually remembering and working on this, but **today, I choose joy**!

Abba, help us to recognize the fiery darts the enemy tries to continually wound us with and learn to deflect them with Your Word, Truth, and Joy, in Yeshua's powerful name, amen.

April 5

John 8:31–32

31) Then said Jesus to those Jews which believed on him, If ye continue in my word, then are ye my disciples indeed; 32) And ye shall know the truth, and the truth shall make you free.

If we want to be disciples of Yeshua, then we must continue to know and walk in His Word. His words are not His own words but the words of the Father. He says it in John 14:10 and John 12:49. In John 6:38, He says He's not here to do His own will but the will of the Father in heaven. This is the truth that will set you free. We read about this just the other day in one of the daily words. If we believe in Yeshua and continue in the words from the Father He is speaking, following Him in all we do, then we are His and will know the truth of the Father's will and ways, and it will truly make us free.

John 8:47 says: "He that is of God heareth God's words." Yeshua is the Son and hears and speaks what the Father says, so when we hear His words, and follow Him we don't have to worry about being tricked or deceived by false doctrines, lies, or the wrong way because we know He speaks the truth from the Father, and following Him will lead us to the Father's heart. Yeshua is our goal, our aim; His words bring life and freedom because they are the Father's words. They are truth and will stand for all eternity. It just makes perfect sense that we are to walk as He walked, continue in His words, follow Him, and do as He did. Knowing the truth of this will **set us free! Amen**! I know I long to be free. I am so done with all the years of bondage to the wrong things.

Abba, thank You again for loving us so greatly to send Your heart, Your only begotten Son to speak and walk out Your heart for us. Yeshua, thank You for being obedient until the end and being the perfect example, knowing your Father's ways are perfect and nothing compares, and teaching us that the truth of that will set us free. It's in Your name, Yeshua, we pray, amen.

April 6

Hosea 13:4

Yet I am the LORD thy God from the land of Egypt, and thou shalt know no god but me: for there is no savior beside me.

God wanted His children to realize and know that all their idols would never save them. He alone had the power to save or destroy them. Their only hope was in knowing Him. There is only one God, the true God, the God of heaven and earth, the star breather, and the **only** answer.

The world may try to sell its idols or teach there are other gods, but it doesn't change the fact that there is **only one true God**, **one true** mountain mover, storm calmer, miracle worker, and **one great I Am** that can save the human soul and grant eternal life. That's the **only God** worth knowing.

Abba, help us know You alone as Your Word says here, as our God and Savior, for all else is fake and powerless. You **alone** hold **all power** and **authority**, in Yeshua's name, amen.

April 7

Mark 14:3

And being in Bethany in the house of Simon the leper, as he sat at meat, there came a woman having an alabaster box of ointment of spikenard very precious; and she brake the box, and poured it on His head.

Yeshua said that wherever throughout the whole world the gospel is preached, this woman and what she did is to be spoken of and remembered. This was such a great act and sacrifice that Yeshua never wanted it forgotten. Though at the time nobody still knew or understood what was about to happen shortly from this moment, He did. He knew He was going to be delivered up and would be beaten and scourged and hung on a cross for us all, and the Spirit of the living God moved this woman to do such a great and beautiful act of anointing His body for His suffering and death.

This ointment was a prized possession, I'm sure; very precious and expensive, for all there contested it for the value, but she saw the value of Yeshua and had only one vision of pouring it all out on Him, Yeshua, our Messiah, who shed His blood and died for us. What are we willing to bring and give to Him? The wise men brought frankincense, gold, and myrrh; the poor widow brought her most precious possession of her last two mites; and this woman, her alabaster box. What prized possession are we willing to give up and bring to the King of kings? Are we willing to give our best to Him, our all to Him? Are we willing to give our lives as a living sacrifice? Is He worthy? **Yes, He is**! He died for us so we may live. He is worthy of **all** I have and **all** I am. Let's bring our **all** to Him, our prized possessions, all of our hearts, and our lives.

Abba Father, Your Son came to bring us Your truth to teach us how to walk it out, live it, and how to give all we are for You, Your truth and Kingdom, and then He laid His life down so we could do it. Help us to never take that in vain or for granted and dedicate our lives to being living sacrifices to You, holy and acceptable as Yeshua did. It's in Your Son's precious name, we ask this, amen.

April 8

Zephaniah 3:15–16

15) The LORD hath taken away thy judgments, He hath cast out thine enemy: the king of Israel, even the LORD, is in the midst of thee: thou shalt not see evil anymore. 16) In that day it shall be said to Jerusalem, Fear thou not: and to Zion, Let not thine hands be slack.

Once again, the LORD is going to have mercy on His wayward children. He's going to take away His judgments pronounced against them, forgive them, and a remnant will be spared. Verse thirteen says: "The remnant of Israel shall not do iniquity, nor speak lies; neither shall a deceitful tongue be found in their mouth: for they shall feed and lie down, and none shall make them afraid." Their hearts will be turned toward their first love, the Father's heart. They won't see evil anymore and will no longer have to fear, for the Lord God Almighty will be with them in their very midst, fighting for them.

No wonder Zephaniah tells the people to sing and shout, be glad and rejoice with all their hearts because the one and only true God, the one who made and holds all things is sparing them from judgment. He is protecting and keeping them, and they are reminded once again to **fear not**. Oh, we can be such hard headed people; there does not seem to be much change in us throughout the generations, but one thing is constant, and that's our God. He stays faithful throughout history and will continue to **now**. As bleak as things may seem to get, when darkness seems to cover the face of the land, He **never** changes and will, in His ultimate love and mercy, spare us again. So, rejoice and be glad, shout and sing out loud, and fear **not**, for our God will be in our very midst and will deliver us, **amen**.

Abba, thank You for Your unfailing, never-ending love and mercy given to Your children, to us; when we don't deserve it. You are such a good, good Father, and we love and praise You, in Yeshua's name, amen.

April 9

Colossians 3:23

And whatsoever ye do, do it heartily, as to the Lord, and
not unto men.

    I used to live my life pleasing man. I thought if I could do what
they wanted and needed of me, if I could make them happy, then
I would be accepted and wanted. I knew I had a gift for loving
people, and that was good and a blessing, but my downfall was
doing it to seek their approval and acceptance. I would do all I
did to fit in, to be accepted.

    The Lord taught me through some seriously painful and hard
lessons that if I continued to do all I did unto man, I would consistently be let down, left feeling empty and abandoned, but if
I began to do all I do unto Him, He would bless it, be there, and
would never fail me or let me down. He even taught me to take it
a step further, and when I do all that I do unto Him, to do it quietly, without a show, and He will bless it openly; not to do anything to be seen and rewarded by man, but to do all unto the Lord,
knowing He will issue a reward beyond anything man could give.

    Acceptance, approval, or a pat on the back from man does
not compare to the reward the Lord gives when we do all to
the best of our ability, with a grateful and joyful heart unto Him
alone. If you find yourself working hard doing all you can to the
best of your ability, feeling looked over, and taken advantage of
or forgotten, keep doing it; do it unto the Lord with a grateful and
joyous attitude, knowing the Lord sees and your reward **will** in
surety come from Him in His perfect timing.

    Lord, help us do all we do unto You, not to please or seek
approval or acceptance from man, but to rest in knowing You see
all and hold our reward in Your hand, in Yeshua's name, amen.

April 10

Psalm 147:3

He healeth the broken in heart, and bindeth up their wounds.

I walked through many years with such heaviness and bro-kenness in my heart. It became commonplace to just put a Band-Aid on it and keep walking. I just kept adding Band-Aid after Band-Aid, trying to hide and protect all the cuts and wounds. As I sat one morning, trying to apply yet another Band-Aid to a new cut, I began to sob, realizing that these temporary fixes were not working. I realized it was becoming harder to walk with all the heaviness of the hurt and Band-Aids building up.

I saw how my heart was becoming callus from all the repeated friction, irritation, and constant pressure, never truly healing from the beginning, and how it would only become more difficult if I did not find and get help immediately. Continuing to walk through the rest of my life like this would eventually become impossible. Feeling hopeless and in complete despair, the Lord brought this verse to me. He said He would take my heart with all the broken-ness, wounds, and hurts, bind it up and heal it properly forever; not temporarily, not just some quick fix Band-Aids, but a perma-nent binding up and healing, making it new—a heart of flesh so I can live and love again. He can and will for you too, just trust and believe Him when He says it.

Thank You, Abba, for Your perfect healing, for loving me, us, so much that You are willing to bind up all our wounds, take all our brokenness, replace it with beauty, and fill our lives and hearts with a love beyond comprehension. You truly are an awesome and loving Father, in Yeshua's beautiful name, we pray, amen.

April 11

Luke 12:7

But even the very hairs of your head are all numbered. Fear not therefore: ye are of more value than many sparrows.

If we have any doubt, worry, or fear at all, this verse alone should reassure us of His awesome love and mindfulness of our every moment. Only our Creator can have each one of the hairs on our heads numbered. It surely scales down the grandeur of man, knowing not one could have such knowledge and greatness as our God. It surely causes me to take a step back, catch my breath, and say, **wow**; though my life is but a vapor, it is so valuable and important to You, Lord, that You have the very hairs of my head numbered. He loves us so much and is so intimately involved with every single detail of our lives, down to the very hairs on our head. Ponder that thought seriously for just a moment, **wow**.

We need not fear, worry, or doubt, knowing our God is so deeply and intimately involved in each detail of our lives. **Fear not**, for not one sparrow falls to the ground without the Father seeing and knowing. He created all things, and all His creation is good. He is pleased with it and loves and cares for it, and we are worth more value to Him, **wow** again. His love and mindfulness for us and His mercy and grace are beyond our understanding. What blessed children we are to have a God and Father who loves and cares for His children like no one or nothing else could come close to ever doing. Find comfort and encouragement in knowing that today.

Abba, thank You for being so deeply and intimately involved in every part of our lives and beings. You are great and mighty, awesome and amazing, and mere words don't describe how good and loving You are. You are worthy of it all, and we love You with all we are, in Yeshua's name, amen.

April 12

Revelation 3:15–16

15) I know thy works, that thou art neither cold nor hot: I would thou were cold or hot. 16) So then because thou art lukewarm, and neither cold nor hot, I will spue thee out of my mouth.

A lukewarm person is one of the most dangerous kinds of persons to be. I believe more people fall and are led astray by the life of a lukewarm person more so than that of one who does not believe or follow the Lord at all. There is great danger in believing one can compromise even a little. When one makes that first compromise to follow and do as a lukewarm person does, the very foundation under them begins to shake. It does not take many compromises for it to begin to crumble. The Lord hates one being lukewarm so much that He will spew them out of His mouth, literally vomit them up. The Strong's definition states: "to vomit, come forth in a flood or gush, to expel rapidly and forcibly."[17]

It is not a place I would want to find myself in. I remember a friend of mine doing a skit one time as we spoke to the twelfth graders before they graduated. To make a long story short, the person on fire for the Lord, the hot person, was trying to get to the person who did not know the Lord at all, the cold person, but the lukewarm person was right in the middle blocking the way, causing distractions and confusion. The progress is not good until the lukewarm person is taken out of the equation. Make a choice today to be **hot** for our Lord, being on fire and making a difference for Him, so we don't find ourselves spued out of our Creator's mouth.

Abba, help us and fill us with Your fire so we can burn hot for You in all we do and say, so on that day, we will hear from You, "Well done, my good and faithful servant," in Yeshua's powerful name, we ask this, amen.

April 13

Zechariah 13:9

And I will bring the third part through the fire, and will refine them as silver is refined, and will try them as gold is tried: they shall call on my name, and I will hear them: I will say, It is my people: and they shall say, The LORD is my God.

Ouch, two parts were cut off and died, but this third part was left, verse eight said. The third part, the remnant, would be saved, but not without incident. They would have to face the fire and be purified, tried, and refined. Nobody likes being in the fire; it's hot and suffocates, where one can barely breathe. You cannot see through the smoke, and it's just simply a hard place to be.

The one reassuring thing with being in the fire, though, is God is there with us. When it gets too hot to where we may be burned, He is there with us, and His Word says we will not be. Being in the fire has a purpose, for sure, but it is not to destroy us; it is to cleanse, purify, and refine us, to melt away all the impurities so we can stand cleaned, changed, and anew before the Lord. The fire will also strengthen us and teach us. We need not fear, as we can do all things through Christ who strengthens us. Do you long to be His remnant always, even with the fires you may face and have to go through? I know I do because through them, though it may not be fun, may hurt, and be hard, I know He will be with me, and I will come out of it new, purified, and refined, and so will you!

Thank You, Lord, for always sparing a remnant, even with the fire we may have to walk through. We know with You, we will be kept, in Yeshua's mighty name, amen.

April 14

Nehemiah 1:9 (ESV)

But if you return to me and keep my commandments and do them, though your outcasts are in the uttermost parts of heaven, from there I will gather them and bring them to the place that I have chosen, to make my name dwell there.

Nehemiah was petitioning the Lord to give ear to his prayer. He knew how far God's children had fallen, how corrupt they had become, and how they were not keeping His commands and statutes anymore. He was reminding the Lord of His Word that said if they were unfaithful, He would scatter them among the nations, but if they returned, He would, once again, gather them. Verse four says when He heard the great affliction that his people were in, he sat down and wept, mourned, fasted, and prayed before the God of heaven.

God heard Nehemiah's prayer. He saw his sincere heart and gave him favor with the king, who allowed him to go repair and rebuild the wall in Jerusalem so the city and God's people could be restored. We can be Nehemiahs and have a part to play in the rebuilding of our nation, the renewing of the family of God, and the restoring of His Word in this place we call home. It just takes a genuine and sincere heart, prayer, and a willingness to be used by Abba. I know I long to see a place that seeks God's face, reverences His words, and walks by His commands once again, a place that lifts His name high and rejoices in His goodness, a place that is filled with His glory and is blanketed with His love.

Lord, thank You for hearts and men like Nehemiah that are broken for Your people and seek Your face for healing and answers. Help us to be genuine like him, deeply loving Your children and this place You have given us and allowing You to use us to make a difference here, in Yeshua's name, amen.

April 15

Acts 2:39

For the promise is unto you, and to your children, and to all that are afar off, even as many as the Lord our God shall call.

I love this verse; all the promises God gave are just as much for us as they were for the children back from the beginning; not only just for us but for our children, our children's children, their children, and forever throughout all our generation to those who keep and walk by His Word—those who look to Him, hear, and listen to all He says and follow it, being baptized in Yeshua's name for the remission of sins, leaving the old man dead in the water and beginning this amazing new journey with the Lord, who now will send His Holy Spirit to make His abode inside us, making us now His temple.

He will walk with us daily, teach us of Abba's ways, and equip us to become all the Father created us to be. We will now be called children of God, having full access to all the inherited blessings and promises. We will now be grafted in and become like a natural born child of His, His very own, bought and paid for by the precious blood Yeshua shed for our salvation. We are now heirs of the kingdom, and that very Spirit that raised our Savior from the dead will come and dwell in us. What a gift, blessing, and awesome promise that we inherit.

Thank You, Lord, for not forgetting or ever looking past us who are sinners, leaving us hopeless, but making your promises available for us, our children, their children, and all the generations to come. You **truly** have not missed a thing. We love You more than words and thank You for coming and making Your home in us, in Yeshua's name, amen

April 16

Deuteronomy 30:19

I call heaven and earth to record this day against you, that I have set before you life and death, blessing and cursing: therefore choose life, that both thou and thy seed may live.

It is a choice, and it is our choice. God is a gentleman and will not force us to do what is right, good, and true. He will, however, bless us over abundantly, above, and beyond when we do choose Him. He will give us life everlasting in paradise with Him, Yeshua, and all the rest of the family of God who choose Him as well. He will give us protection daily, promises we can stand on, our every need met and taken care of, so we never have to worry or fear.

We will never beg for bread as it says in Psalm 37:25. All the promises and blessings listed here in Deuteronomy 30 will be ours. It seems like a no brainer what choice is the best. If we are truly not seeing and getting it all as being good and a blessing, then there is always the other choice we have the freedom to make. We can choose death. We can choose to accept the fate of all the curses mentioned here as well: not having protection, our every need met, our every moment held, not having the surety of storms being calmed, the promise of never walking alone, and the greatest gift of all, everlasting Life. To me, there is only **one** option, only **one** choice, **choose ye this day**!

Abba, help us to see always, truly deep down see how Your way is good and perfect. Help us to choose it and the life it brings with all the blessings it holds, in Yeshua's powerful name, we pray, amen.

April 17

Psalm 128:1–6

1) Blessed is everyone that feareth the LORD; that walketh in his ways. 2) For thou shalt eat the labor of thine hands: happy shalt thou be, and it shall be well with thee. 3) Thy wife shall be as a fruitful vine by the sides of thine house: thy children like olive plants round about thy table. 4) Behold, that thus shall the man be blessed that feareth the LORD. 5) The LORD shall bless thee out of Zion: and thou shalt see the good of Jerusalem all the days of thy life. 6) Yea, thou shalt see thy children's children, and peace upon Israel.

We need only to walk in His ways and in reverence before Him, then happy and blessed we will be. **What more is to be said**? Does it get any better than this?

Abba, help us to always fear and reverence You and never stray from Your ways. We pray this in Your Son Yeshua's mighty name, amen.

April 18

Matthew 8:26

And He saith unto them, Why are ye fearful, O ye of little faith? Then He arose, and rebuked the winds and the sea; and there was a great calm.

I'm pretty sure the disciples were beside themselves watching Yeshua calm the seas. Verse twenty-nine says they marveled, wondering what kind of man this was that even the sea and winds obeyed Him. I marvel myself at all He can do, why I would ever worry or fear, and why my faith ever falters. I just don't know and can't understand, especially when I know the one who has ultimate authority over all things. He can speak just one word, and everything changes. I know He holds my every moment and will keep me through every storm.

This is true for all of His children. We need **not** fear, doubt, or be ones of little faith. It says here there was a great calm. He speaks **great calms** to the **worst storms**. We need only to stand, believe, and watch Him move on our behalf. He is the great physician, miracle worker, and wind and sea commander; darkness trembles at His name. With Yeshua for us, **nothing** can be against us.

Yeshua, thank You for speaking to the great tempest that arises in our lives. Thank You for rebuking them and calming the winds and seas like You do. You are worthy, adored, and Your name is **great**. It is in Your name, Yeshua, we always pray, amen.

April 19

Malachi 4:4

Remember ye the law of Moses my servant, which I commanded unto him in Horeb for all Israel, with the statutes and judgments.

Webster Dictionary describes *remember* as: "to keep in mind, to think of." Strong's Concordance describes it as: "to be mindful, record, keep, think on."[18] I love how it uses the word *record*, like a song, movie, or special moments we put on tape, to have them always so we can play them and remember them. This is what the Lord is telling us here: record it on the pages of your heart, the lines of your mind. Engraft it there so it will be thought of always, so we can put it on repeat and play it over again, never forgetting it.

We need to think on and remember it to the point it becomes a part of us, our very being, so it becomes ingrained in our every fiber, so we **truly** know it; His law, statutes, commands, judgments, every word He has spoken, each instruction He has given, and not just so we know it, but so we walk by it **always**. Remembering it is knowing it, and knowing it is walking by it, and in turn, to walk by it, we **must** know it, and to know it, we **must** remember it. His words are and have always been the most important thing throughout time and will be throughout eternity; it is probably best if we know, remember, and walk by them now.

Father, help us to know how important it is to remember, think on, record, and walk by Your Word. Saturate us with it, Abba, so Your words become part of the very essence of who we are, and we walk by them all the days of our lives, in Yeshua's name, amen.

April 20

John 14:27

Peace I leave with you, my peace I give unto you: not as the world giveth, give I unto you. Let not your heart be troubled, neither let it be afraid.

Struggles, hardships, troubles, and hurts are some of the natural occurrences of life here on earth that all of us are sure to encounter. His Word tells us we will face tribulations and persecutions. He never promised things would be easy and perfect; He just promised to be with us through it all. He promised He would never leave or forsake us. He told us to be of good cheer, for He has overcome it all, and He gave us His peace to keep us in the middle of the struggles and pain, a beautiful and perfect peace that passes all understanding; one that we cannot comprehend, but it will just soothe our souls in the worst of circumstances.

Nothing the world can give can come close to comparing to His perfect peace. It is a gift from Him that all we have to do is accept and rest in. We don't have to worry, fret, or fear, for in the midst of trouble, we can just seek His peace, that beautiful gift, and rest in it. My life has had and still has its share of struggles and troubles. It seems like they search me out some days, and I must willingly work to choose that peace He says He has given. It may take time to learn how to accept that peace of His and rest in it, truly knowing He has and holds all things and will work all things out, but when we learn and do it, it's beyond worth it. It truly is a peace beyond understanding, a place we cannot comprehend.

Lord, please teach our hearts to not be troubled or afraid but to trust in You, knowing You're in complete control, and to rest in that perfect peace You give. It's in Your name, Yeshua, we pray, amen.

April 21

Isaiah 43:1–2

1) But now thus saith the LORD that created thee, O Jacob, and He that formed thee, O Israel, Fear not: for I have redeemed thee, I have called thee by thy name; thou art mine. 2) When thou passest through the waters, I will be with thee; and through the rivers, they shall not overflow thee: when thou walkest through the fire, thou shalt not be burned; neither shall the flame kindle upon thee.

So many times, I have to call to remembrance this verse and speak the words of it over my life. His Word was not meant to just be read but to be believed and spoken. It is the **spoken Word** that brings life, and we need to take these verses that speak life and speak them over ourselves and a lost world that so desperately needs to hear them. We all so desperately need to hear them; they truly are our only hope.

Don't be afraid. I have redeemed you. I have called you by name. You are Mine. Speaking these words daily will cause us to see everything in a different light, and they will actually bring life into our beings. When we know we are His, when we truly believe it beyond a shadow of a doubt, knowing when we walk through the waters, they **will not** sweep us away or take us under, or when we are in the midst of the fire, we **will not** be touched by the flame and will come out without a burn on us, we can then truly live and walk differently. We walk with hope, knowing we are held. Let us do our best to not just read His Word but to know it and speak it over ourselves and into a dying world.

Abba, help us to know Your Word is true and sure and to believe it will change our very being and our circumstances when we begin to speak it out, in Yeshua's powerful name, amen.

April 22

Philippians 4:19

But my God shall supply all your need according to His riches in glory by Christ Jesus.

I love how it does not say some of our needs or only certain needs, but our Father in heaven will supply **all** our needs; not only all our physical needs but our emotional, mental, and spiritual—**all** of our needs. He is a good Father and loves us so much and knows what we need and is already handling it all before we even ask. He is involved in every second and mindful of every moment of our lives.

Not only does He supply our every need but He gives us good and perfect gifts when we ask. In Matthew 7:11, Yeshua says, "If ye then, being evil, know how to give good gifts unto your children, how much more shall your Father which is in heaven give good things to them that ask him?" **Wow**, He loves His children so much He wants to give good gifts and blessings along with supplying our every need. David says in Psalm 37:25 that in His lifetime, he has never seen the righteous forsaken or God's children begging for bread. That surely tells me that being a child of the Most High King, having Him for our Daddy, we will want for **nothing**. He is not only God, Creator of **all**, but He is our Father, our Abba; we are part of the best family ever and are called His own. What a heritage we have because Yeshua made a way for us.

Thank You, Abba, for supplying all our needs, giving us good and perfect gifts, and the **best** one of all, Your Son, Yeshua, who laid His life down for us so we can be a part of the best family ever. It is in His name we pray, amen.

April 23

Ezekiel 12:28

Therefore say unto them, Thus saith the Lord GOD; There shall none of my words be prolonged any more, but the word which I have spoken shall be done, saith the Lord GOD.

The children of Israel had heard Abba's warnings for a long time through many prophets. They chose to either not believe them, thinking God would never destroy them, or some thought it is not for now but for future days, times far off. They all were wrong when God's judgment fell and every word He spoke was fulfilled.

We must be cautious to ever think God's words are idle and cautious not to play games with time, thinking there is plenty of it. **Now is the time** to believe and walk by His every word.

Abba, help us to take You at Your word, always knowing You will always accomplish what You say, whether for discipline and destruction or for good and blessing, in Yeshua's name, amen.

April 24

Zechariah 8:23

Thus saith the LORD of hosts; In those days it shall come to pass, that ten men shall take hold out of all languages of the nations, even shall take hold of the skirt of him that is a Jew, saying, We will go with you: for we have heard that God is with you.

All the nations will hear that the one and only true God is with Israel, His children, from the beginning. They will know that He has set up His kingdom among them and will see that His truth and way from the beginning is the only way. They will long to go with them and live and serve the true God and walk in all His ways.

Those who have given their lives to Christ see now, and they see they are grafted in and have become one of His children, one of His own, but not all see yet, and we must pray for their eyes to be opened. For there is one God, one truth, one way, one family, and we must humble and accept that truth if we want to be a part of Him.

Abba, help us to see Your way, truth, and law so that we may live and walk by it and become part of Your family, in Yeshua's powerful name, amen.

April 25

1 Corinthians 15:33

Be not deceived: evil communications corrupt good manners. It's simple, you hang around with the wrong people or hang out in wrong places, it will ruin and defile you. To break it down, *evil* is bad or wicked, anything that is not of God.[19] *Communications* is described as companionship, association with.[20] *Corrupt* actually states to shrivel or wither away, **ouch**, to spoil, ruin, defile, or destroy.[21] *Good* is useful, better, kind, and gracious,[22] and *manners* is morals, a person's standards of behavior or beliefs.[23] So don't be seduced or err, bad and wicked people and places will shrivel, wither, and destroy kind, gracious, and useful standards of your behavior and beliefs.

The Bible tells us to be separate from the world and its ways for a reason. There is a famous saying that states, "you become the company you keep." My mother used to drill this into my head. I didn't listen and had to learn the truth of it the hard way; definitely **not** a way of learning I would encourage. The better and more simple way is to believe His Word and be not deceived.

Abba, help us to choose our associations carefully, to give thought to who we surround ourselves with, where we go, and what we do, knowing those decisions and choices could ultimately destroy what You have taught us to know, believe, and stand on, and in the long run, separate us from You, in Yeshua's mighty name, we ask this, amen.

April 26

Isaiah 30:21

And thine ears shall hear a word behind thee, saying, This is the way, walk ye in it, when ye turn to the right hand, and when ye turn to the left.

Wow, I remember when I was being called out from where I was hearing these words from the Lord. Although I was still being shaken and stirred because I've always been such a literal person; I still needed something literal to happen so I would know for sure. I can't advise this as being wise, as it can really hurt some-times, but I do advise to spend time with Abba, drawing closer to Him and His heart. Daily press in and learn His voice, so when you hear a word behind you, like His Word says you will, when He speaks the words, "This is the way, walk ye in it," you will know it's your heavenly Daddy because you know His voice from spending so much time in His presence, and you will walk in that way.

He will speak to you, and He will direct your steps on the right path, the perfect path because all His ways are **perfect**; we just must listen, obey, and follow the steps He lays out before us.

Help us, Abba, to always draw close to You and spend time in Your presence so we will know Your voice and walk in Your way, in Yeshua's name, amen.

April 27

Deuteronomy 4:7–8

7) For what nation is there so great, who hath God so nigh unto them, as the LORD our God is in all things that we call upon him for? 8) And what nation is there so great, that hath statutes and judgments so righteous as all this law, which I set before you this day?

How could the Law be bad and burdensome? It is an established set of principles given by God Himself for our good, a set of instructions laid out before us for our success. **Burdensome? I think not!** The Father who created us in His image and loves us more than our human minds can conceive cared enough to place guard rails at the edge of the cliffs for us so we wouldn't plummet to our death. He loved us enough to set up righteous truth and decrees that would protect us and keep us from falling away from His loving arms. It became easier to understand when I became a parent and established rules and safeguards for my own children that would keep them from harm and wrong, just as Abba did for us, His children. They are good and for our benefit and safety.

He established and set before us upright ways that would keep us from skinning our knees or banging our heads into a brick wall. He issued statutes and judgments that would keep and hold us in His loving arms, in perfect freedom, free from the bondage of the world and its ways, free from sin and the enemy's grasp. Surely, we are a blessed people to have an Almighty Abba that loves us so much. I know I thank Him for His righteous law He has given for my protection and good.

Thank You, Father, for loving us so much as to give us such righteous laws, perfect direction, and wise instructions to keep us from harm and death. Thank You for wrapping us in Your arms of love that will carry us safely to eternity with You through Your son, our Savior. It is in His name we pray this, amen.

April 28

James 2:26

For as the body without the spirit is dead, so faith without works is dead also.

In verse twenty-four, James says, "ye see then how that by works a man is justified, and not by faith only." If we truly believe, our actions will show it. We will, by our works, prove our faith. Doing good works is a byproduct of faith. If we truly believe God is who He says He is, a good and loving Father, we will do our best to be good and loving children. We will become a willing vessel, doing our best to be His hands and feet, allowing Him to use us and work through us as Yeshua did.

Let me be clear, works alone **won't** get us to heaven. We cannot work our way there, but our faith in God takes us into His heart, causing us to want to walk in love and mercy, to want to do good works that will glorify Him. We must be willing and obedient to walk out all He calls us to, whatever it may be, so through our works of obedience, our faith will be made perfect. Just as with Abraham when, by his obedience, he toiled to gather the wood, his son, and headed up the mountain to sacrifice him; through his works, his faith was made perfect, and Isaac was spared. **Yes**, the just shall live by faith, and that faith will cause us to walk out all the Lord asks of us. It will cause us to be humble enough to lay down our lives, as Yeshua did, to take up our cross and become His hands and feet, that He may be glorified through our works, and our faith will be made perfect by them. Our faith is dead without works just as the body is dead without the Spirit.

Lord, help us to be faithful like Abraham, being obedient to whatever job or task You call us to do, no matter how hard it may be, believing that in so doing, righteousness may be imputed to us, and we may be called a friend of Yours, like Abraham, and that our faith may be made perfect by it, in Yeshua's powerful name, amen.

April 29

1 Samuel 15:23

For rebellion is as the sin of witchcraft, and stubbornness is as iniquity and idolatry. Because thou has rejected the word of the LORD, he hath also rejected thee from being king.

Wow, Saul paid a high price for rejecting the Lord. Saul's rebellion against God was compared to witchcraft, ouch. The Lord, in Leviticus 20:6, says He will set His face against and cut off anyone who has anything to do with witchcraft. Saul's stubbornness was iniquity and idolatry. We must think hard about having a rebellious spirit and consider the steep cost we will pay if we rebel against Almighty God. I was rebellious in my younger years, and it led me straight to the door of death, not something I would advise for anyone.

How many times does the Lord call us to something or ask something of us, and we dig our heels in, fight, and struggle with Him over it for whatever the excuse? I used to be one of the most stubborn people I knew, hardheaded and stubborn, thinking it was a good thing, and I was justified in it. I would have to be drugged with heels dug in and smoking to get me to do something I didn't want to do, things that were good with benefits, but I had to be stubborn and learn the hard way. The price paid for those actions and behaviors was always high and never worth the cost. Saul's rebellion and stubbornness came at a detrimental cost: God rejected him from being king. If there tends to be even the smallest amount of these in your heart, it might be time to bring them before the throne of our King and lay them down. I know it is something I've had to do and something I have to continually check my heart for and ask for Abba's help to keep them far from me.

Father, shine a floodlight into our hearts and expose any rebellion or stubbornness that may be dwelling in them. If there is any there, help us lay it at Your feet and surrender it to You so we can find your forgiveness and freedom from it, in Yeshua's powerful name, amen.

April 30

Acts 4:12

Neither is there salvation in any other: for there is none other name under heaven given among men, whereby we must be saved.

Yeshua alone is where our salvation comes from. There is no other name for man to be saved by. At the name of Yeshua, every knee shall bow and tongue confess, it states in Philippians 2:10–11; there is such power in His name. Luke 10:17 says, "And the seventy returned again with joy, saying, Lord, even the devils are subject unto us through thy name." Many times, Yeshua rebuked the devils out of men, and they had to flee, they knew He had authority over them. That is why when we pray, we are to pray in Yeshua's name. In John 15:16, Yeshua says, "That whatsoever ye shall ask of the Father in my name, He may give it you," and He says it again in John 16:23–24. In John 14:6, Yeshua says, "I am the way, the truth, and the life: no man cometh unto the Father, but by me."

Romans 10:9 tells us that if we confess with our mouths the Lord Jesus and shall believe in our hearts that God raised Him from the dead, we **will** be saved. Yeshua is the **only name** under heaven that gives us hope for an eternal salvation with Him and the Father. Oh, what a **beautiful** name—the true meaning of His name says it all: to rescue, deliver, save, and is salvation! Amen, He is our salvation, for there is no salvation in any other but **Him alone**.

Thank You, Yeshua, for laying Your life down to save us, that we may find salvation, deliverance, healing, and power in Your name. What a **wonderful** name it is, and it's in Your name, we pray, amen.

May 1

Mark 7:7–8

7) Howbeit in vain do they worship me, teaching for doctrines the commandments of men. 8) For laying aside the commandment of God, ye hold the tradition of men, as the washing of pots and cups: and many other such like things ye do.

The commandments of man became more important than the commandments of God. The Pharisees were calling out the disciples to Yeshua when He answered them, telling them how it really was, making it fully clear to them that they rejected God's commands to honor and kept man's. Their traditions had surpassed God's commands; they cared more about keeping, teaching, and enforcing them than what God had instructed.

I see this still happening today. We care more about holding to the traditions of men, what they say, and their holidays and views rather than Abba's perfect ways, His appointed times, and His commands. Man's traditions should never trump God's perfect ways. If it doesn't line up with what He says, then it should be discarded and not even considered. We must be careful to examine what we do and say, making sure none of it goes against what the Father says or makes what He says of no effect. His commands protect us and are for our good. His ways and appointed times are perfect and need no adding to or changing. It's time to lay aside the ways of man and fully learn the ways of the Lord.

Father, please teach us Your ways once again; help us to value and hold to Your commands, appointed times, and perfect ways and never reject them, and help us to never put man's traditions in place of Yours, in Yeshua's name, amen.

May 2

Amos 8:11

Behold, the days come, saith the Lord GOD, that I will send a famine in the land, not a famine of bread, nor a thirst for water, but of hearing the words of the LORD.

To not be able to hear the words of the Lord is a scary place to be, a lonely and empty place, a hopeless place. Verse twelve says: "And they shall wander from sea to sea, and from the north even to the east, they shall run to and fro to seek the word of the LORD, and **shall not find it**." There's been desert seasons in my life where I've wondered, "Have you taken Your presence from this country? From me? I can't hear Your words that are my life; this deafening silence is taking my breath away and withering my spirit. Lord, please don't take Your presence from me, this country, and this world." I don't ever want that day to come that I'm not in His presence.

Psalm 16:11 says: "Thou wilt shew me the path of life: in thy presence is fulness of joy; at thy right hand there are pleasures for evermore." I want to be in the presence of the Lord all the days of my life. I want His fullness of joy in my life. I don't ever want to live even one day **not hearing the words of the Lord**. Matthew 4:4 says: "Man shall not live by bread alone, but by every word that proceedeth out of the mouth of God." His words are life, and without them, there is emptiness, hopelessness, and death.

Abba, please don't let us see the day where Your words are muted; please don't send a famine of Your words. They are life, and we need them to live. We need You, Lord, more than ever, in Yeshua's name, we ask this, amen.

May 3

Isaiah 6:8

Also I heard the voice of the Lord, saying, Whom shall I send, and who will go for us? Then said I, Here am I; send me.

Isaiah was willing to go and do the work of the Lord. He was willing to go and be His mouthpiece, hands, and feet, knowing it would be hard and might not end well for him. He was willing, stepped up, and volunteered to go. Unlike Jonah, who ran when called, Moses, who said he couldn't because he was not eloquent and was slow of speech and tongue, or Jeremiah, who said he was too young, Isaiah said, "Send me, I'll go!"

What about us? What will we do or say? Will we find excuses? Will we run the other direction? Or will we be as Isaiah, with a willing heart, saying, "Here I am, Abba, send me, use me, I'll go. I'll tell them of Your goodness and truth. I'm not much—I am a sinner, but Your will cleanses me, enables, and equips me to do whatever You need." Will this be our answer? I know, I pray to have that willing heart.

Abba, help this to be our answer and heart, to go and do for You always, no matter what the cost, in Yeshua's mighty name, amen.

May 4

Luke 6:38

Give, and it shall be given unto you; good measure, pressed down, and shaken together, and running over, shall men give into your bosom. For with the same measure that ye mete withal it shall be measured to you again.

It seems to me this verse goes hand in hand with the verse in Galatians 6:7 that says, "What a man soweth that shall he also reap. If you give it will be given back to you." I am an avid believer in tithing or giving wherever God leads. Nothing we have is truly ours anyway; all we have has been given by the hand of God. Romans 11:36 says: "For of Him, and through Him, and to Him, are all things: to whom be glory forever. Amen."

God gave all to us when He sent His only begotten Son so we could have a hope of salvation and eternity with Him. Yeshua gave all for us when He laid His life down and shed His innocent precious blood for us. Abba continues to meet our every need so we are never found wanting. I think giving back wherever we can, helping wherever He would have us to would result in nothing less than abundant blessings, good measure, pressed down, shaken together, and running over, amen! What you give in all areas of your life, from finances to hard work to a shoulder or ear, all of what you do and give will be measured and given back to you. Let's never be stingy or tight-handed with **anything** God has given and blessed us with! Acquiring that heart condition now is just building up treasures that will be awaiting you in heaven.

Abba, thank You for every single thing You have given and gifted us with. Help us to know all we have is from Your hand and it's only because of You. Help us to have that heart of giving like Yours with all You've given us, in Yeshua's name, amen.

May 5

Nehemiah 9:17 (ESV)

They refused to obey and were not mindful of the wonders that you performed among them, but they stiffened their neck and appointed a leader to return to their slavery in Egypt. But you are a God ready to forgive, gracious and merciful, slow to anger and abounding in steadfast love, and did not forsake them.

What an awesome God He is, faithful, forgiving, merciful, and full of love; how He patiently waits on us to come to our senses again and humble ourselves before His throne with repented hearts. How often do we stop and truly take notice of all the miraculous and awesome wonders of His all around us? How He quenches the thirst of the dry ground, clothes and feeds the birds throughout harsh winter days, grows trees to great heights and covers the earth with an array of beautiful colored flowers, or how He's breathed His breath of life into each of us, giving us all the gift of enjoying His prized creations.

How often are we genuinely mindful of all His goodness and treasures, or do we as His children, back in Nehemiah's day, become stiff-necked, forgetting all He's done and neglecting to take notice of all His awesome wonders all around? I know I am so grateful that even when we do forget, when we do become hard-headed and neglectful, He never changes. He remains constant in His love toward us. He is patient, merciful, and never forsakes us.

Abba, help us to constantly remain mindful of all the wonders You perform around us daily, from just waking us each morning to filling our lungs with Your breath and always providing our every need; help us to never search for or want any other **king** but **You**, in Yeshua's mighty name, amen.

May 6

Acts 28:26–27

26) Saying, Go unto this people, and say, Hearing ye shall hear, and shall not understand; and seeing ye shall see, and not perceive: 27) For the heart of this people is waxed gross, and their ears are dull of hearing, and their eyes have they closed; lest they should see with their eyes, and hear with their ears, and understand with their heart, and should be converted, and I should heal them.

I wrote on this from the Isaiah scripture but felt it deserved being touched on again, seeing Paul here did as well as Yeshua did in Matthew. Paul here was speaking to the Jews in Rome. Acts 28:23 says: "to whom he expounded and testified the kingdom of God, persuading them concerning Jesus, both out of the law of Moses, and out of the prophets, from morning till evening." There arose a division among them, as some believed his words and some did not. He then began to quote the words here in this verse out of Isaiah. They were acting again as the children in Isaiah's day, with no understanding and not perceiving all God was showing them because their hearts were hardened.

History is just repeating itself again, like His word says, and instead of learning from Moses and the prophets, they were walking in their own unwise understandings. Paul wasn't teaching anything new or different; he lined up with the teaching of Moses, the prophets, and Yeshua. Man just chooses to walk in his own understanding instead of the one laid out by the Father in clarity in front of him. We have a choice today as well; will we walk in believing, perceiving, seeing, and hearing what the Lord has given and said, having our own understanding enlightened by the Holy Spirit and the Word? Or will we choose to walk in our own understanding, in our hard-headedness not believing, perceiving, seeing, or hearing all the words of the law of Moses sent from Abba and all the confirmations of it confirmed over again through the prophets and our Messiah Yeshua? I know I'm tired of learning the hard way and want to see and truly perceive, hear, and really understand, having my heart changed forever. Are you with me? Join me in this prayer!

Abba, help me to lay down all my own understandings and ways and hear and follow all You have commanded, for it is good and the way to life everlasting, in Yeshua's holy name, we pray, amen.

May 7

Jonah 1:4

But the LORD sent out a great wind into the sea, and there was a mighty tempest in the sea, so that the ship was like to be broken.

Sometimes, when we're not doing what we know to be doing or we go the opposite direction of His calling, storms arise. Sometimes they are earth-shattering storms, depending on just how stubborn we choose to be. We can end up in some literally horrifying situations until we stop, turnabout, heed, and be obedient to what He's saying.

We may try to run from what He's asked of us, but we can never hide from the Lord. He knows where we're headed before we even get there. We must find assurance in knowing He will go before us, walk beside us, and always have our backs wherever He sends us, so we need not ever be afraid or doubt. It's smart to save ourselves the headache, storm, and pain from running and just listen and follow from the start.

Abba, help us to run toward You and not away when we're given an assignment from You. Help us to not be afraid but be assured of Your ever-present help and presence, in Yeshua's name, we ask this, amen.

May 8

Matthew 5:19

Whosoever therefore shall break one of these least commandments, and shall teach men so, he shall be called the least in the
kingdom of heaven: but whosoever shall do and teach them, the
same shall be called great in the kingdom of heaven.

Do you want to be known and called the least or greatest in
the kingdom of heaven? To be known and called great in heaven,
we just need to do and follow God's words, walking them out and
teaching them by our lifestyles to the world around us, keeping
His commands and teaching our children and our children's children to do the same.

His commands are not burdensome, 1 John 5:3 says. They
are perfect as the Father is, and they are for our good. They bring
wisdom, understanding, and life for those who listen and follow
them. We are blessed that Abba gave us such righteous and perfect decrees, setting us apart by them from the nations and safe-
guarding us with them from the enemy's ploys and snares he tries
to entangle us with.

Oh Abba, thank You for loving us enough to give us such a
beautiful set of instructions and commands that keep us safe
within Your care and arms that bring wisdom and life to those
who follow and walk by them. We are truly blessed to have a
Father that cares and loves us so much. Thank You. We love You,
and it's in Your Son Yeshua's name, we pray this, amen.

May 9

Isaiah 40:8

The grass withereth, the flower fadeth: but the word of our God shall stand for ever.

Despite what things may look like and how dark and hard things may get, God's Word is true and will stand forever. People may try to silence it and the world may try to get rid of and do away with it, but His Word will stand the test of time and will **never** return void. This world may pass away, but God's Word shall **always remain**.

That's why it is so important to dive in and submerse ourselves in His Word, to read it, learn it, know it, and walk by it. It is the only thing in this life that will remain constant. It is the only foundation that will stand sure against any storm, lie, doubt, or whatever the enemy may try to use to destroy it with. James 2:19 says even the devils tremble because they believe and know He is the one and only true God, and His Word will stand forever. Amen! The grass and flower may wither and die and the earth may pass away, but God's sovereign, awesome, and perfect Word will stand and remain **forever**. Now that's something I want my hope and trust to be found in.

Abba, help us to fill our lives with Your Word. May it be our solid foundation, so we will never be shaken, and may it carry us into everlasting life with you, into Your perfect and beautiful, eternal kingdom, where it shall stand forever, throughout all eternity, in Yeshua's mighty name, we ask this, amen.

May 10

Zechariah 14:16

And it shall come to pass, that every one that is left of all the nations which came against Jerusalem shall even go up from year to year to worship the King, the LORD of hosts, and to keep the feast of tabernacles.

I am so grateful that after fifty years of my life, somebody finally taught me about God's appointed feast days. I grew up in the church and never learned about these beautiful, holy, set-apart, appointed by God Himself, special feasts. These are His appointed times, His special days, and what a blessing it is that we are chosen to be a part of them. To know that He has called us to come and be a part of these amazing, anointed, and set-apart times with Him, our Abba, our Father, is such a gift. He calls us to come tabernacle with Him. What could be better?

Zechariah here is talking about the final days. Zechariah 14:9 says: "And the Lord shall be King over all the earth: in that day shall there be one LORD, and His name One." Amen, how beautiful will that day be! Everyone in that day will go and keep the Feast of Tabernacles, to worship the Lord, tabernacle with Him, and those who don't will have no rain, and the Lord will smite the heathen and those who don't come. Wow, I am so glad He has opened my eyes and ears and has taught me how to practice tabernacling with Him, getting me ready for that day. What a great day of worship and rejoicing it will be! If you are new to His feast and special dates and don't know much about them as I was, I implore you to dig into His Word and search them out. He will show and teach them to you.

Abba, thank You. We are beyond grateful for these special appointed times commanded by You to draw nearer to You and all You are. We love You so much. Help us to come to know Your appointed times more and in a deeper way with every special feast we keep, in Yeshua's name, amen.

142

May 11

John 10:28

And I give unto them eternal life; and they shall never perish, neither shall any man pluck them out of my hand.

When we come to Yeshua, confess our sins, ask Him to forgive us, and give our hearts to Him, we become His. We are bought and paid for by His precious blood that He shed for us at Calvary, and we are held and kept. **No one** can steal us from Him, **no one** can take us from the palm of His hand. He will fight for us, protect, hold, and keep us, always. We will spend eternity with Him and the Father, forever rejoicing before the Throne.

We can choose to walk away, but why would we, knowing He loves and cares for us more than anyone else in the entire world and He is the greatest and best gift ever given? **No one** and **nothing** can take us away from Him against our will. He **will** keep us safe and guarded in the palm of His hand, carrying us into an eternal life with Him and Abba. What a treasured and priceless gift we've been given.

Yeshua, thank You for paying for and buying us with Your very blood, that precious blood that washes and covers us. Thank You for giving us the best gift of all, Your life, so we may live, for holding us in the palm of Your hand, so none can pluck us from You. We love You so much, in Your precious and powerful name, Yeshua, amen.

May 12

Micah 4:12

But they know not the thoughts of the LORD, neither understand they His counsel: for He shall gather them as the sheaves into the floor.

Once again, as in so many times past, the Lord will save and deliver a remnant. He will gather them from the place of captivity, from the far-off places, and He shall reign over them in Mount Zion forever, it says. It's so awesome to see how every time it seemed hopeless and a loss cause for God's children, He gathered the remnant and raised them up, giving them victory and dominion once again over their enemies.

In verse thirteen, they are told, "Arise and thresh, O daughter of Zion: for I will make thine horn iron, and I will make thy hoofs brass: and thou shalt beat in pieces many people:" Once again, He would redeem His people from the hands of the enemy. Though their enemy and the nations would gather against them, they knew not the plans of the Lord, that He alone would rule from Zion as King with His children that He redeemed and saved. **Wow**, over and over again, our God has defeated the enemy, saved, and spared His children that look to Him, and set their eyes on Him, and He **will** do it again. We need not worry or fear; we serve a mighty and awesome God that will never leave or forsake His own. Arise and thresh God's children. He **will** save us and have the victory, **always**.

Abba, thank You for saving us and sparing us over again, for Your faithfulness and hand of redemption when it looks hopeless. It's because of Your constant, unfailing love we can be reassured You will keep us and reign victorious always, throughout all eternity. We thank You and praise You for the awesome, unchanging King that You are, in Your Son Yeshua's name, amen.

May 13

Romans 1:16

For I am not ashamed of the gospel of Christ: for it is the power of God unto salvation to every one that believeth; to the Jew first, and also to the Greek.

First off, Yeshua tells us in Luke 9:26 that if anyone is ashamed of Him or His words, of that one will He be ashamed before His Father. That's a scary place to be and a place I know I never want to find myself. I don't ever want to find myself being shy about my Savior. It is a gift to know Him, a gift that Yeshua came and saved my life. He is our hope of glory; how can it be possible to be ashamed of that?

We should want to shout it from the rooftops and tell everyone of this amazing gift we've been given that we surely didn't deserve. We should beam like beacons of light, shining the gospel of our Savior and how He came, bled, died, and rose again, defeating death and the grave, canceling our sins by His shed blood, opening all the blessings and promises to us if we just believe, repent, and turn to Him; granting us new life and life everlasting with Him and the Father. May we all stand grateful and strong, proudly declaring the gospel of Christ, the gift from God the Father for us, His children, who He loves so much.

Abba, help us to declare loud and clear the gospel of Your Son Yeshua, for You sent Him so we could live, and He walked out Your will perfectly, being the example for us, and then gave His life so we could have this hope. Help us to **never** be ashamed of that, for it would be a sad and dreadful day if Yeshua had to be ashamed of us to You. May we joyfully show Your goodness and wonders always, gratefully with all our hearts, proclaiming You and Your Son to the world. It's in Your Son Yeshua's precious name, we ask this, amen.

May 14

2 Samuel 22:2-3

2) And he said, the LORD is my rock, and my fortress, and my deliverer; 3) The God of my rock; in Him will I trust: He is my shield, and the horn of my salvation, my high tower, and my refuge, my saviour; thou savest me from violence.

The Strong's definition of *violence* is: "false, injustice, oppressor and unrighteous."[24] What a freedom it is knowing that He has my back and is my defender. It's like having a 10,000-pound weight lifted off my shoulders, knowing that I don't have to worry about tomorrow, fear my enemy, or have the answers to my problems. I don't have to worry about what others might say or do to me because I have a strong, high tower I can run into, a safe haven I can find rest and peace in always, a deliverer who holds all the answers.

Oh, to remember and always walk in this would make life so much sweeter. So many times, though, I struggle with the weight of things, fight the endless battle of the flesh, and all the doubting, to, once again, realize the truth of these words in this verse. I need to stop and remember where my help comes from, who fights my battles, and walk in knowing He defeats my enemies and works all things out for me. I then surrender once again and lay everything at His feet. We don't have to carry the weight of worry, fear, or doubt; we have a strong tower, a fortress and deliverer we can trust. These words are true, and if we will remember them and walk by them, letting Him fight our battles and defeat our enemies for us, we can then experience true freedom, peace, and a joy beyond our understanding. He is our refuge, our savior and deliverer. He will rescue and save us from whatever tries to hurt or destroy us. Find freedom and joy in knowing and believing that today.

Abba, You are all we need, You are our everything, our answer to every situation and circumstance. You always have our backs and will fight for us; hold and keep us in the safety of Your care. Help us to live our lives knowing this sincerely, in Yeshua's name, amen.

May 15

2 Timothy 3:16

All scripture is given by inspiration of God, and is profitable for doctrine, for reproof, for correction, for instruction in righteousness:

Nothing can stand up against the spoken Word of the Lord God Almighty. The scriptures are our breathed-by-God instruction manual. They are our answer key to the questions of life, the tests of life, and they hold all authority. They are His spoken Word given to direct our paths. They are life and absolute truth. As I was writing this, the Lord brought to mind our kitty, Blossom. Blossom is a unique cat, to say the least. Cats, for the most part, are known to not really be water lovers, but we have this special cat that can be on the complete opposite side of the house, sleeping in a bedroom, or out in the sun porch, and as soon as you run water out of any faucet in the house, she is instantly there. Something about the sound of running water and getting a drink from the freshness of that running stream will wake her from her sleep, stop her in her tracks in the middle of whatever it is she is doing, and cause her to come running.

I began to think about His spoken Word, His words that are living water to our souls, so much so that if we have one drink from Him, we will **never** thirst again. I believe this is how Abba wants us to be with His Word, constantly having our ears open, running after the slightest sound of the living water flowing from it. It is for our teaching, correction, conviction, and training in righteousness, breathed by God Almighty for us. It is perfect, good, and the only thing that will satisfy a thirsting soul!

Abba, may Your words cause us, no matter where we are, to come running as fast as we can to get a drink from Your living water. May we know and understand they are our help and answer in every circumstance life holds, in Yeshua's powerful name, we ask this, amen.

May 16

Psalm 31:15

My times are in thy hand: deliver me from the hand of mine enemies, and from them that persecute me.

David placed his whole life in the hands of the only one who could keep it. He knew there was only one true God, and that God not only held the whole world but He held his every moment as well. He found everything he needed to live in, knowing his times were in the hands of the great I AM. Only God alone could save him from his enemies, rescue him from despair, defeat and protect him in times of trouble, and deliver him from the faces of those who sought his life. What a surety to know and have, a lesson and example for us today.

Our times are in the Father's hand, the one and only true God who holds our every moment. We can trust Him and not be moved in the face of adversity, knowing He alone can rescue us if we let go and let Him. If we surrender all we are and wholly give our lives to Him, we can have this same assurance David had. We can find our shelter and safety in the Father's bosom, being held and protected by His arms of love.

Abba, help us to fully know You hold our every moment. Help us to surrender to You all we are so You can direct our every step, fight our every battle, and victoriously bring us to Your eternal shores when it's our time. Thank You for being our all in all, always. We love and adore You, and it's in Your precious Son, Yeshua's perfect name, we pray, amen.

May 17

Revelation 1:3

Blessed is he that readeth, and they that hear the words of this prophecy, and keep those things which are written therein: for the time is at hand.

What a truth this is, time is at hand, and we never know when He is going to require His breath back from us, so we must live each day, each moment as if it were our last. We should be walking in constant mindfulness of His words, being obedient to all He has said because of how much we love Him; loving Him with all we are because He first loved us, fully believing His ways are perfect and true and that we will, at that moment, account before Him for every word and deed we've said and done.

That's why John called those blessed who read, hear, and keep all the words of this book because in so doing, on that required day, that no man knoweth when it is, we will be found washed and covered, blessed and favored, being welcomed into Abba's eternal kingdom. This is a serious matter, for it holds our eternal outcome.

Lord, help us to heed John's words here spoken through Him to us by Your Holy Spirit. Help us not to take them lightly but to heed them with all diligence as they are life, and not just this life here on earth, but eternal life in Your kingdom. Thank You for loving us so much to give us such powerful, perfect, and beautiful commands and instructions that we are truly blessed when we read, hear, and keep them, in Yeshua's name, amen.

May 18

James 1:19–20

19) Wherefore, my beloved brethren, let every man be swift to hear, slow to speak, slow to wrath: 20) For the wrath of man worketh not the righteousness of God.

This is definitely a behavior that takes much practice. Our human nature wants to usually speak before we think. I believe that's why we're given specific instruction on it. Our human nature tends to get angry when wronged; it wants instant gratification and to see immediate results. It's not always quick to hear either, to truly hear: **unreserved, impartial hearing**. There may be some who are naturally quiet and humble and don't struggle with this or some who, through much work, have the victory in this area and no longer struggle, or there are those who, like myself, are a constant work in progress and must often reflect on and remember these words.

I am determined to work hard to engrain them into my very fibers so I can work the righteousness of God in and through my life, being humble in the face of adversity, merciful in the face of persecution, quick and genuine in my listening, and patient and mindful in my every word. If you, like me, are a work in progress in this area, meditate on the words of this verse and allow them to become grafted in you and change you into the reflection of the Father.

Abba, we love You so much and want to work Your righteousness in all we do and say. Help us to meditate on these words that they go down deep and begin to change us into Your image, causing us to have Your heart so the world will see You through our words, humility, patience, and love, in Yeshua's name, amen.

May 19

Malachi 2:17

Ye have wearied the LORD with your words. Yet ye say, Wherein have we wearied Him? When ye say, Every one that doeth evil is good in the sight of the LORD, and He delighteth in them; or, Where is the God of judgment?

The law of the Lord was a good thing and was given not only to guide and direct us but to protect us as well. It was like a guard rail keeping us from danger, the things we didn't know about and couldn't see. The priests were messengers of God to the people and were expected to know, keep, and walk out the Law and all the goodness of it. They were expected to obey it so the people would see how good and perfect it was and follow it as well.

The Lord was upset with the priests earlier in verses eight and nine. He said they departed out of the ways and had caused many to stumble at the Law, and they have been partial in the Law. They were degrading the good of the Law that God set and made to guide, direct, and protect His people, and the people no longer had a proper and true example of the righteous law. They became morally confused as we are today. They, as we, have drifted so far from the instructive, good, and perfect law of God. We must get back to knowing the true righteousness of it and begin walking in it once again.

Abba, teach and show us that Your perfect law is for our good and protection, and help us to walk in it, follow, and obey it once again, in our world and personal lives, for it is vital for our survival, in Yeshua's mighty name, amen.

May 20

Mark 10:14–15

14) But when Jesus saw it, He was much displeased, and said unto them, Suffer the little children to come unto me, and forbid then not: for of such is the kingdom of God. 15) Verily I say unto you, Whosoever shall not receive the kingdom of God as a little child, he shall not enter therein.

That childlike faith is a faith like no other; the yearning in their eyes for love, the excitement in their eyes to learn and experience new things, and the complete trust in their eyes as they see a world through the innocence of that childlike faith, where everything is good, kind, pure, and loving. You can give a child an empty box and watch him or her turn it into his or her prize possession as he or she plays for hours, using only his or her imagination, transforming it into an array of things. It is the simplicity of a child's mind to find joy in the little things in his or her tiny world.

Then comes life: the growing up, weights of the world, and reality of people and things around us, like sin, imperfection, and heartbreak, and slowly, walls are built. If we are to receive the kingdom of God, we **must** do it as a child. We **must** come with that childlike faith from before the tainting of the world. We **must** shake off all the weights, doubts, lies, and come in the innocence of that childlike faith, that childlike excitement for all Abba has awaiting us. That childlike trust is knowing He loves us beyond everything and will never abandon us but has good awaiting us.

Abba, we come before You and ask that You take all the grown-up garbage away so we can once again come to You in that childlike faith, seeing You with that excitement in our eyes, like we've received the **best gift ever**, fully letting go, trusting and believing You, in Yeshua's name, we ask this, amen.

May 21

3 John 1:4

I have no greater joy than to hear that my children walk in truth.

Amen, John was so happy to hear that his beloved were walking in truth. Imagine the great joy it brings the Father when we do the same when we walk in the truth of His Word. I know watching my children grow in the knowledge of His truth makes my heart sing and causes me a big smile. When I see God's children walking in His truth and standing firm on His Word in the craziness of this work, it brings me such **great joy**!

Imagine the Father's heart when He sees His children being set apart for Him and sees their desire and strive to live, follow, and walk by His truth. Oh, the exceeding joy He must feel! He loves us so much and only wants what He knows is best for us, and that is the truth of His Word. He gave it for our instruction and protection. May we walk and grow in it all the days of our lives.

Abba, if it brings John great joy to see his beloved walking in Your truth, if it makes my heart sing and rejoice when I see my own children walking in Your ways, how much more does it make Your heart exceedingly happy when You see all Your children walking in it? Help us, strengthen us, and direct us that we always will walk pleasing to You, in Yeshua's name, amen.

May 22

Jonah 1:5

Then the mariners were afraid, and cried every man unto his god, and cast forth the wares that were in the ship into the sea, to lighten it of them. But Jonah was gone down into the sides of the ship; and he lay, and was fast asleep.

How many times do we, like Jonah, think we can run from the command of God? How many times do we, like Jonah, turn the opposite way, find somewhere, and go to sleep as if everything is going to be ok and God doesn't see or care? I don't know why we don't constantly watch for the lightning bolt, the discipline that's about to come for our disobedience. Do we not think about or realize the lives we may put at risk from deliberately disobeying and then arrogantly falling off to sleep as if we've done nothing wrong?

I know I've been in this place when the Lord has called me to do something, and I continue to let my flesh be disobedient and dictate what I do. Over and over again, the Lord calls me to "Rise early," and I still fight this battle of getting up each morning. The plus in Jonah's situation was that it called the men on that boat to see God as the **one** and **only true God**; it caused them to fear Him, sacrifice unto Him, and make vows unto Him when they saw His great power. Jonah did end up repenting and going to Nineveh but not before suffering in the pit first. My goal, hope, and prayer is that we can learn from this, and when God calls us to a task, we won't run the opposite direction and go to sleep, but we will instantly heed it.

Abba, please help us to learn from these mighty and powerful examples You have set before us in Your Word. Help us to slay the flesh so we can be obedient to You without hesitation, in Yeshua's mighty name, we pray, amen.

May 23

Luke 18:19

And Jesus said unto him, Why callest thou me good? None is good, save one, that is, God.

Yeshua was telling them here that it is all about His Father, the God of the universe. He is good, the giver of life, and Creator of all things. He is the only one good. He was telling them, "Don't call me good; it's not me, it's my Father in heaven," and "Give credit where credit is due, to the one and only good one." Think about it, there is so much good Yeshua did. Just look at how He laid His life down for us and how good He was to do that. What we must remember, though, is that He was being obedient to a good Father, a Father He knew was absolutely perfect and was the explicit image and definition of **good**.

Yes, I believe being obedient to the Father made Him good, but He was saying in complete humility, "**Don't** call me good; there is **none** good, not even Myself, but just one, and that is Abba." Yeshua knew how good Abba was because He intimately knew Him, making obedience to Him so much more a pleasure and joy for Him and a perfect example to us. It's so important for us to capture and understand Yeshua's message in these few words of His here. He wants all to know it's all because of the Father.

Thank You, Yeshua, for pointing us to Daddy, for teaching us how to walk before Him, pray to Him, and give all glory to Him as You do, for He is a **good, good Father**, and You have paved our way to Him through You, in Your beautiful name, Yeshua. We thank You, amen.

May 24

Haggai 1:6

Ye have sown much, and bring in little; ye eat, but ye have not enough; ye drink, but ye are not filled with drink; ye clothe you, but there is none warm; and he that earneth wages earneth wages to put it into a bag with holes.

Ouch, everything they do is in vain the Lord is telling them. They continue to take care of all of their own needs and necessities while they allow God's house to sit in ruins. How often do we work our lives away to provide for our wants and desires, to have nice homes and cars, and in so doing, are not mindful at all of the things of the Lord? He was telling the people here that He was going to cause a drought on everything until they began to become mindful of His things and start rebuilding His house. When they did, He would stop the drought, take pleasure in them, and be glorified in it.

So many times, life happens, and we get so busy and lost in doing this life that He, somewhere along the line, gets left behind and forgotten about; He, His kingdom, and what He requires of us start to take second place. This should never be and can't be because things will quickly come to a halt, and drought will come. We must, in all things, throughout our entire lives, in all we do, be mindful of Him first, His ways, His master plan, and think first on these things. He must always be and remain first in our lives. We must give Him the wheel and follow and do what He is asking us to. He will take care of our lives and our needs when we do.

Abba, help us to always do what You call us to, being more concerned with what You ask than our own desires and needs, knowing You will always provide us and our needs when we are obedient, in Your Son Yeshua's name, we ask this, amen.

May 25

John 14:21

He that hath my commandments, and keepeth them, he it is that loveth me: and he that loveth me shall be loved of my Father, and I will love him, and will manifest myself to him.

It is truly that simple. If we love Him, we **will** keep His commandments, and if we keep them, then we will be loved by the Father and Yeshua, and Yeshua will shew Himself to us. His commands are **not burdensome** but **beautiful**. Deuteronomy 30:11 tells us what He commands are **not** hidden from us or too far off. Deuteronomy 30:14 says, "But the Word is very nigh unto thee, in thy mouth and in thy heart, that thou mayest do it."

When we give our lives to Christ, the Holy Spirit comes in and writes the commands on our hearts, so we will know them and walk by them. When we begin to, Yeshua will shew Himself to us in such beautiful ways, ways we couldn't imagine or comprehend.

Yeshua, help us to walk by all You've said and done here on this earth, to follow Your example and keep Your commands, knowing that all You've said and done has been the Father's perfect will, and all He's said You've followed and walked out perfectly for us.

Thank You, Abba, for loving us so much to let Your beloved Son go from Your presence to walk it all out, suffer greatly, and die that we may know You, Your perfect will, and have an eternity praising You, in Your Son Yeshua's powerful and precious name, amen!

May 26

Esther 1:22

For he sent letters into all the king's provinces, into every province according to the writing thereof, and to every people after their language, that every man should bear rule in his own house, and that it should be published according to the language of every people.

The king's wife, Queen Vashti, didn't adhere to the king's calling and disobeyed his request for her to come to his feast. It made him look like he had no authority in his own house and with his own wife in front of princes of the other nations. They all feared that their wives would do the same. Esther 1:20 says, "And when the king's decree which he shall make shall be published throughout all his empire, (for it is great,) all the wives shall give to their husbands honour, both to great and small." It was important to establish a president to show that he was the head of his home just as he was the kingdom he served.

If he allowed his wife to blatantly disobey him, what would come next? His children? His kingdom? The princes of the other kingdoms? See, God has set and established a perfect order, and we truly need to take notice and respect it. It's not to say the king should lord over the queen, but there should be honor and respect both ways. God did bring good out of Queen Vashti's disobedience and made a way for the nation of His children to be saved through Esther becoming queen, but it doesn't give us the right to do the same. Women should always have respect for their husbands and submit to the authority God has given them over their homes and families. They should honor them and respect them as they have been called to do, for the husband is the head of the wife as Christ is the head of the church, Galatians 5:23 states.

Abba, help us women to heed the lesson here with Queen Vashti and not become self-centered and disobedient to our husbands. Give us strength to love them as you have called us to, even when it's hard. Help us husbands to love and honor our wives as Christ does the church and to lay our lives down for them, and even those of us who aren't married, help us to learn from and cherish this valuable and important lesson of love and honor, in Yeshua's name, amen.

May 27

Matthew 7:6

Give not that which is holy unto the dogs, neither cast ye your pearls before swine, lest they trample them under their feet, and turn again and rend you.

Yeshua, here, in His own words, is warning us to be careful, not to be nonchalant with what He has given us but to be wise, using it effectively. He warns us not to give His holy things to the dogs, the gifts He's given us, the pearls of spiritual wealth to the swine. They don't care about the value of any of it, the sacredness of it; they don't desire it for anything, only to trample on it and then turn and rend you with it. Strong's definition of *rend* is "to break, wreck or crack, to shatter into minute fragments."[25] Wow, that seriously can be devastating, and that is why it is so important to heed Yeshua's words and be wise, using caution when distributing the precious gifts and talents Abba has blessed us with.

We should always be led by the Spirit in all things. The Lord knows the good ground He has prepared and made ready, and we should be led by Him so the holy things of His are not trampled and disregarded. If we are cautious and wise, allowing His Spirit to lead us, we can be sure we're casting where it will benefit and grow and not be trampled under feet.

Abba, help us to always seek You and be led by Your Spirit with all we do, with Your Holy things and the pearls You've given. Help us to always cast them according to Your leading, in Yeshua's perfect name, we ask this, amen.

May 28

Galatians 6:7

Be not deceived; God is not mocked: for whatsoever a man soweth, that shall he also reap.

It's a biblical law you will reap what you sow, what goes around comes around, and what you give is what you will get. How often do we consider our every action? Our every word? Do we think about what they might feel like on the receiving end as we are delivering them? We surely need to because God is **not mocked**, and it will all surely return upon our heads, be it a blessing, love and good, curses, meanness, or evil. I sowed a lot of garbage and junk in my lifetime, and let me tell you, I ended up reaping a ton of horrific pain because of it. Sometimes I did things unconsciously, not even thinking about the repercussions that would come from it, and then suffered greatly after. That is why I try to think about, remember, regard, and reverence this verse in all my actions and words today. It took me a little while to realize the truth of it, but since I have, I do my best to allow it to effectively govern everything I do.

This is a truth: **be not deceived, God is not mocked**. Whatsoever we sow, we shall reap; if we sow division, our lives will reap dividing, somewhere, somehow, in our own relationships, circumstances, or situations. If we sow anger, we'll reap fury and rage. If we sow meanness, we will reap the pain of it ourselves. If we sow happiness, we will reap joy, kindness, good will, and blessing. If we sow love, we will reap a harvest of warmth, caring, adoration, and compassion. The choice is ours; what will we choose?

Abba, help us to take You and Your Word seriously, that it may govern our every word and action so we can reap good and blessed harvests from You, in Yeshua's name, we pray, amen.

May 29

Job 38:3–4

3) Gird up now thy loins like a man; for I will demand of thee, and answer thou me. 4) Where wast thou when I laid the foundations of the earth? declare, if thou hast understanding.

Wow, that was quite a profound question God put before Job. The seriousness of His statement alone, "Gird up thy loins like a man," makes you know God was not in the slightest bit enthused by Job's questioning of Him, and then His, "For I will **demand,**" yes, He was not having it by any means. In Job's defense, though, he had just lost everything. I think I might ask why too. No, I don't think, I know I would. I'd cry like a baby, probably scream aloud, fall on my face, beat the ground, and ask, "Why, what have I done, Lord? Why me?" As with Job, though, who am I to question the God of the universe, the God of all creation? As God sternly answered Job, "Where were you when I laid the foundation of the earth? Do you have understanding?" Ouch! Do we think we have the right to question His motives and what He allows? Do we think we know better than Him? Who are we to instruct Him? His ways and thoughts are far above ours and are perfect.

I'm sure I'm not alone in saying that many times, I've found myself doing the same thing as Job and asking why, not even coming close to experiencing half of what Job had. I don't know why I would feel entitled to an answer instead of just trusting the God who created me and breathed His breath into my lungs, instead of just believing He is in control and knows what He is doing. Who am I to question my Maker? Who is the clay to question the potter that formed him? Yeshua, the Son of God, did not even question His own Father but was just obedient in all things. Who are we? Let us be careful in questioning what the Father allows and learn to trust that whatever it is, we are and will be helped by Him, no matter what.

Father, not one of us were there when You laid the foundation of the earth or have the understanding of Your thoughts and ways; they are so far above us. Help us to never question You and Your ways. Help us find true rest and peace in knowing they are perfect and You will be with us and hold us in and through whatever You allow, in your Son Yeshua's precious name, we ask this, amen.

May 30

Romans, 4:21

And being fully persuaded that, what He had promised, He was able also to perform.

Paul was talking about Abraham here and how Abraham believed God, and it was counted unto him for righteousness. He goes on to say in verses twenty-three and twenty-four that this was not given for just Abraham alone but for us as well. If we also believe in Him who raised Yeshua, our Messiah, from the dead, righteousness will be imputed to us as well. Abraham believed and was fully persuaded that God was able to do all He had promised. Ephesians 3:20 says, "Now to Him that is able to do exceedingly abundantly above all that we could ask or think, according to the power that worketh in us." He can do more than our minds could ever comprehend or imagine.

He is the mountain mover, storm calmer, star breather, miracle worker, great physician, sea splitter, marriage healer, and life giver. He is the Great I AM, Alpha and Omega, Beginning and the End, and He **always keeps His promises**! We can stand, fully persuaded, and know as Abraham that He will do the same for us. What a sweet peace and serene rest, knowing what that brings.

Abba, help us to truly know down deep that You are all these things and more, and may we, as Abraham, have such a genuine faith, believing, knowing, and being fully persuaded that You **will** be all these things to us as well, and You can perform **all** You have promised, for You are the promise keeper, in Yeshua's wonderful name, we pray, amen.

May 31

Obadiah 1:4

Though thou exalt thyself as the eagle, and though thou set thy nest among the stars, thence will I bring thee down, saith the LORD.

Woe to those who think they're out of reach; the Lord sees everything and will bring down those who exalt themselves on high. No one is ever untouchable to God. He will abase those who exalt themselves against Him. I think about the prime example, Lucifer, the anointed cherub, perfect in his ways, Ezekiel 28:14–15 says. He was filled with every precious stone, Ezekiel 28:13 says. He thought himself so beautiful, as He was, but used it to try to exalt himself above God. God was not having it, and though he was beautiful and cherished, God cast him out of heaven into eternal darkness.

Here in Obadiah, the Lord was speaking to the people of Edom. Obadiah 1:3 says, "The pride of thine heart hath deceived thee, thou that dwellest in the clefts of the rock, whose habitation is high; that saith in his heart, Who shall bring me down to the ground?" They had exalted themselves a little too high, and the Lord was telling them He was going to bring them down; they were not untouchable. There is a powerful lesson to learn here about staying humble and never thinking more of ourselves than we ought. 1 Corinthians 10:12 says, "Wherefore let him that thinketh he standeth take heed lest he fall."

Lord, help us to always be mindful and careful of ever exalting ourselves to a place we have no business being, knowing if we do, we will be brought down by You. Help us to remain humble in all our ways so we don't have to worry. It's in Your Son Yeshua's holy name, we ask this, amen.

June 1

Deuteronomy 31:6

Be strong and of a good courage, fear not, nor be afraid of them: for the LORD thy God, He it is that doth go with thee; He will not fail thee, nor forsake thee.

The Lord was promising His children that He would be with them. He would go before them and prepare the way, go with them and keep their every step, and be behind them so they didn't have to fear at all. He promised them that His mighty and powerful presence would surround them always, and they had learned that He was a God of His word. His promises could be stood on forever.

I believe His words to His children then are just as relevant to His children today. That's why it is called the Living Word; it's alive and transcends time. He will be with His children today just as He was with them thousands of years ago. He will never leave us or forsake us. There will be times in life we must face and encounter trials, storms, sickness, or losses that will shake the ground we stand on. It's so reassuring at those times to know there is an almighty, faithful God that promises to go before us, walk beside us, and have our backs through it all when we feel beaten and defeated. It's so nice to have the constant reminder of His Living Word over and over again throughout all the pages of it that we need **not** fear or worry. We can be strong and stand secure because we know the promise keeper who will not fail or forsake us. We must set our eyes on Him and put our trust in all He says, for all He says is true and will outstand time. Now that's a surety I don't want to be without.

Abba, thank You for Your Living Word that spans time, for all the promises You've given to Your children, for holding us always and keeping us in and through all things. There is nothing that compares to You and Your love, in Yeshua's name, amen.

June 2

Luke 17:17–18

17) And Jesus answering said, Were there not ten cleansed? but where are the nine? 18) There are not found that returned to give glory to God, save this stranger.

What happened to the nine? Yeshua entered the village, and when they saw Him, verse thirteen says "they lifted their voice and said, Jesus, Master, have mercy on us," which goes to say they knew Him as master; they were part of the faith. Yet it was the stranger, Yeshua called him, the one who didn't know Him, who wasn't part of the faith, who turned back. The Greek word for *stranger* here means: foreign, not Jew.[26] Not only did he turn back, but it says that with a **loud** voice, he **glorified God**, and he fell down on his face at Yeshua's feet, giving Him thanks.

Wow, why did the other nine not do the same? Were they too busy going and doing all they couldn't do as lepers? Did they go back to their families first? Was that more important? Did they feel entitled to the healing? Did they just not think about thanking Him? Were they not grateful? This wasn't just a little thing that happened to them; this was huge—they were healed from leprosy. Have there been times in our lives where we were one of the nine and, for some reason, didn't stop and give glory to the Lord when He had done something for us? Maybe He cleared the traffic for you this morning, gave you the front parking spot, or healed your sickness; big or little, we should stop and give glory to the one who did it for us. May we always be the one who turns back and with a **loud** voice, and **glorify God**!

Lord, help us to never forget to give You glory for the things You do in our lives. Help us to not be nonchalant, even in the little things you do because even the little things are **huge**, in Yeshua's name, amen.

June 3

1 Corinthians 2:9

But as it is written, Eye hath not seen, nor ear heard, neither have entered into the heart of man, the things which God hath prepared for them that love Him.

Abba's ways are so far beyond what we could ever ask or think. His ways are so far above what we could imagine, but in His ultimate love and mercy for us, He bestowed His Spirit upon us to come and dwell within us, showing and teaching us of His great mysteries and all the things that are freely given to us from Him. He is such a good Father and loves us so much that He sent His very Spirit, His Holy Spirit, to dwell in us that we may be filled with His wisdom and know those spiritual things.

1 Corinthians 2:10 says: "But God hath revealed them unto us by His Spirit: for the Spirit searcheth all things, yea, the deep things of God." The Spirit searches out the things we could never know, perceive, or understand on our own and then witnesses those things to us. His Spirit fills us with godly wisdom so we can know His heart and navigate through this life.

Abba, wow, the things that You have prepared for those that love You are so beautiful and perfect beyond what our minds can comprehend, but praise be to You that You hath sent Your Spirit to live and dwell in us, revealing and giving us glimpses of Your goodness and glory. Thank You, Daddy, in Your Son Yeshua's name, we pray, amen.

June 4

Isaiah 61:3

To appoint unto them that mourn in Zion, to give unto them beauty for ashes, the oil of joy for mourning, the garment of praise for the spirit of heaviness; that they might be called trees of righteousness, the planting of the LORD, that he might be glorified.

This is such a **glorious and life-changing verse**. If this doesn't encourage someone and put a smile on his or her face and new joy in his or her heart, I don't know what will. He is going to give **beauty** in return for the ashes of our lives and take all the mourning and turn it to joy. **Yes**, so **beautiful**, and a garment of praise to break that spirit of heaviness. These aren't just mere words; these are spoken by the mouth of God, the one and only Most High God, who doesn't speak frivolously or waste His breath. **Not one** of His most powerful words He has spoken returns unto Him **void**, for it is spoken out of His mouth and goes and accomplishes all it is set forth to accomplish.

This is a promise from Abba we can trust and walk by. He is a good, true, and faithful Daddy who loves us more than anything, and He will keep His word, every one He has spoken. Through the keeping of it, **all** glory is given to Him, the only one deserving of it. Do you want beauty for your ashes? The oil of joy for mourning? A garment of praise for the spirit of heaviness? He is ready and waiting to give it to those who come to Him. I know firsthand because He did it for me, and I had a massive amount of ashes, mourning, and heaviness. If He did it for me, an addict from the streets of Detroit. He will do it for you! His words are true, His promises sure, and you can count on every one of them.

Oh Father, let this ignite **joy** in us that will hold and carry us through the trials and pain this life has a way of bringing. Help us to come to You and trust and believe Your words, accept, and walk in them that we may be called trees of righteousness, and have beauty, joy and a garment of praise, in Yeshua's name, amen!

June 5

Psalm 1:1–2

1) Blessed is the man that walketh not in the counsel of the ungodly, nor standeth in the way of sinners, nor sitteth in the seat of the scornful. 2) But his delight is in the law of the LORD; and in His law doth he meditate day and night.

We are to meditate, study, think on, and ponder His Word, commands, and laws, day and night. We should desire, delight, and find pleasure in doing so. It is life to us and will keep us from walking in wrong counsel, being deceived or ensnared by sin, and sitting or associating with mockers and arrogant people.

The **law** of the LORD is **good**. It protects and keeps us from falling off a cliff, getting burnt by the fire, or being devoured by our enemy. The wages of sin are **death**.

LAW OR LAWLESSNESS (SIN)?

LIFE OR DEATH?

I will choose to delight in and meditate on His **perfect law** set up for my good; how about you?

Thank You, Abba, for Your beautiful, magnificent, good, and perfect law that keeps and protects us always. We are a blessed people to have such righteous decrees to walk and live by, in Yeshua's name, amen.

June 6

Mark 6:11

And whosoever shall not receive you, nor hear you, when ye depart thence, shake off the dust under your feet for a testimony against them. Verily I say unto you, It shall be more tolerable for Sodom and Gomorrha in the day of judgment, than for that city.

If the message of our Lord that we walk in and live by is not received or is not heard, then we are instructed to literally depart, shaking the dust off from under our feet as a testimony against them and let God be God and handle the rest. We're not to hang around, compromising, begging, and trying to make them see; we're not to turn around or go back. Yeshua says we are to depart, wiping the very dust off our feet.

So much has changed in our world today; we coddle grown adults the way only babies were meant to be coddled. We hang around and spin our wheels on things we weren't meant to, wasting precious moments we can't get back. There are those in this world who are **not** going to hear and receive us, no matter how hard we try. That is a fact, and we must listen to Yeshua here and let God be God and do what only He can do. If we're not received, we must just **depart**; no ifs, ands, or buts about it. His Word isn't open for debate, only for obedience. If we stay, they might not get the judgment they need from Him to turn to Him, or we might get caught up in that judgment because we weren't obedient to His Word and compromised and didn't depart. It's not up to us to change any one. We walk and are His living testimony, and those who receive us we leave our peace with, and those who don't, we depart, shaking off the very dust from our feet as a testimony against them and leaving God to do the rest.

Abba, help us to do as Your Word says in the hard situations, when we're not received and not heard, to depart, Lord, and leave it in Your hands for You to do what only you can, in Yeshua's name, we ask this, amen.

June 7

Nehemiah 8:14

And they found written in the law which the LORD had commanded by Moses, that the children of Israel should dwell in booths in the feast of the seventh month.

I love this passage in Nehemiah, where Ezra brought the book of the Law before the people after the wall of Jerusalem was built and completed. They all gathered, and Ezra began to read the book of the law of Moses, and he helped the people understand all the words of it. It was in the seventh month this took place, and he began to read how God commanded His children to build booths and dwell in them. It all just lined up so perfectly; such perfect timing Abba has.

It was a special feast, a celebration they were to keep once a year to commemorate the temporary dwellings of their forefathers. It was to also remind them, and us as well, that this is not our home; we are just sojourners, and this is only our temporary home. For this feast, they were to gather olive, pine, myrtle, and palm branches and build a temporary dwelling, booths, and dwell in them for the days of the feast. So, the children of God did just that, and Ezra read to them from the Law every day, and they rejoiced and worshiped the Lord; what a blessed and beautiful time it must have been. We also are to keep this feast yearly as a command from the Lord, and why would we not? For it is truly such a joyous and beautiful time!

Abba, thank You for giving us such a beautiful and amazing feast to not only remember how You rescued and saved Your children from their slavery in Egypt but how You kept them safely in the wilderness in temporary dwellings, just as You do to us now until we arrive at our forever home, our eternal home with you. What a beautiful celebration of remembrance of your faithfulness and a reminder of what is still yet to come; it is just so perfect, Abba. Thank You, in Yeshua's name, amen.

June 8

Malachi 4:2–3

2) But unto you that fear my name shall the Sun of righteousness arise with healing in His wings; and ye shall go forth, and grow up as calves of the stall. 3) And ye shall tread down the wicked; for they shall be ashes under the soles of your feet in the day that I shall do this, saith the LORD of hosts.

For those who fear the Lord, who reverence Him, giving Him all respect and honor, He will arise, defend, and keep them in that day. Malachi 4:1 says: "For, behold, the day cometh, that shall burn as an oven: and all the proud, yea, and all that do wickedly, shall be stubble: and the day that cometh shall burn them up, saith the LORD of hosts, that it shall leave them neither root nor branch." Human nature tends to walk in a prideful way; our feet tend to run toward things of this world, as if we're missing out on something. I don't want to go there; I don't want to be found among the proud or wicked. I want to be found on the side that treads down the wicked, the side that fears and reverences the Creator of all things, my Creator, my Abba and King.

I so desire the Son of righteousness to arise in my life with healing in His wings. To be that calf growing up in a stall, protected, and kept, and the wicked being ashes under my feet, not being swayed, touched, or moved by them in any way. The Lord is good, faithful, and true, and He will fight for us, stand for us, and hold and keep us. He is beyond worthy of our reverence and respect, and I count it a privilege to stand before Him in awe and wonder, with fear and trembling.

Abba, teach us to fear and reverence You, Creator of all things, to stand in awe and wonder before You, knowing that all things are by You and all things are from You, and it's You alone who will hold, keep, and carry us into eternity with You and Your Son Yeshua. It is in His name we pray, amen.

June 9

Acts 5:41

And they departed from the presence of the council, rejoicing that they were counted worthy to suffer shame for His name.

Imagine that, they just got finished being beaten for the sake of Yeshua and walked away rejoicing, counting it a blessing to be worthy to suffer for His name. I can't say I would have reacted the same. I know I would love to be strong enough to do that, but I wonder if I would have broken down and cried, or ran away and hid after, or maybe just walked away quietly, not saying a word, but to walk away rejoicing and being glad, hmm, I'm just not sure I could have had that response.

How incredibly awesome their reaction was; a beautiful example for us to follow. They definitely walked out and were an example of 1 Thessalonians 5:18, giving God thanks in all things, in every circumstance, an example I surely desire to be like and walk out in my own life. Like David, who said in Psalm 34: 1, "I will Bless the LORD at all times: His praise shall continually be in my mouth." He had already set in His mind He would praise the Lord, no matter what the situation or circumstance would be. That's true love and devotion, a heart completely surrendered and sold out to the Lord, a heart I so desire to possess and have.

Lord, help our hearts to be so completely sold out and devoted to You that we can, in all circumstances, even if being beaten and scourged for Your name, rejoice and be glad, sing Your praises from our lips and count it a blessing that we are worthy enough to suffer for You, for You are **truly worthy** of it all, in Yeshua's name, amen.

175

June 10

Leviticus 26:2–4

2) Ye shall keep my sabbaths, and reverence my sanctuary: I am the LORD. 3) If ye walk in my statutes, and keep my commandments, and do them; 4) Then I will give you rain in due season, and the land shall yield her increase, and the trees of the field shall yield their fruit.

It's quite simple: if we walk in reverence and respect for the Father, hearing His words and doing them, He will be our God, and we will be His people. He will take care of us, defend, and keep us in and through all things. If we keep reading in Leviticus 26, verses eleven and twelve say, "11) And I will set my tabernacle among you: and my soul shall not abhor you. 12) And I will walk among you, and will be your God, and ye shall be my people." We will be His very own, the God of all things, the highest King and authority. We will have a seal on us and will be His. He will give rain in due season and increase the yield of our land and the fruit of our trees if we just hear and follow.

2 Corinthians 6:16 states: "And what agreement hath the temple of God with idols? For ye are the temple of the living God; as God hath said, I will dwell in them, and walk in them, and I will be their God, and they shall be my people." Oh, I just love how the Word confirms itself. We are the temple of the Living God; He walks with us, and we are His. His perfect ways will leave us speechless and in awe and wonder when we walk in them. Ezekiel 37:27 tells us again, "My tabernacle also shall be with them: I will be their God, and they shall be my people." His words are true, for He **cannot** lie. His ways are perfect, and there are none better. If we listen and walk in them, we will be blessed beyond measure. We will have the one and only true God dwelling in us. He will be our God, holding our every moment.

Father, teach us Your Word, statutes, and commands that we may know them and walk by them all our days, not just for the rain and yield You will bring, but because they are good and perfect, given to protect and keep us. You love us greater than we can ever comprehend, so may we love You enough to trust, believe, and follow Your perfect ways, that we may be Your people, and You will be our God, in Yeshua's holy name, we pray, amen.

June 11

John 4:36

And he that reapeth receiveth wages, and gathereth fruit unto life eternal: that both he that soweth and he that reapeth may rejoice together.

What a joyous and glorious day it was when I reaped what had been sown for me, when I worked and gathered all the fruit, knowing it was sown for my eternal salvation with Abba. It's an even greater, joyous, and glorious day now that I can sow, in hopes that others may reap as I have. I pray that you reap what has been sown in the pages of this book. I pray that as you read the words of the Lord in these pages, you reap a bountiful harvest, fruits that lead to eternal life, and that those fruits cause you, in turn, to sow as well, that others may reap from all you sow.

Others labored so we may reap a bountiful blessing, and we must now labor so others may reap as we did. It is beautiful and glorious to rejoice together in the fields of harvest for the Lord. His fruit is good and leadeth to life eternal.

Abba, thank You for those who have labored and sown so we may reap fruits unto life eternal and help us to labor and sow so others may reap as well, in Yeshua's powerful name, amen.

June 12

Zechariah 4:7

Who art thou, O great mountain? before Zerubbabel thou shalt become a plain: and he shall bring forth the headstone thereof with shoutings, crying, Grace, grace unto it.

It was time for the Temple, God's house, to be rebuilt, and as always, there was some kind of opposition happening. The Lord was making it clear to them in the prior verse that it wouldn't be by their might or power, but only by the Spirit of the Living God would it be done. Then He tells them that the mountain that stands before Zerubbabel would become a plain; the Lord, by His might and power, would flatten it.

So often, we try to accomplish things by our own might. We exert all our power and strength trying to make things happen or make mountains move, and while trying to fight against the opposition, we wear ourselves out. There have been days that I've sat and tried with all my might to write these words, to no avail. I can't find the words; my own words are just vain and empty and have no power, and I feel this block until I remember to stop, let go, and wait on Him. We must remember in these times to hold to these words and believe He will meet us and make a way. If we trust Him and just let Him be God, He will flatten the mountains, fight the battles, and supply us with whatever we need for the task set before us. We just need to stand ready to move when He does.

Abba, help us to know and remember it's never by our own doing, strength, or power as we do what You've called us to do, but only by Your Spirit does it happen, in Yeshua's mighty name, amen.

June 13

Romans 10:17

So then faith cometh by hearing, and hearing by the word of God.

If we want our faith to grow to be strong and unwavering, then we must spend time with the Lord and in His word. Faith comes through hearing the Word of God, through taking time daily and submerging ourselves in it. It holds so much instruction, truth, treasures, miracle after miracle, and abundant promises, and it's a personal letter from the Father Himself. It holds Yeshua's words, proclaiming and confirming all the Father has said. Every word is so beautiful and powerful; they are life-giving and edifying for the soul. It can't help but to build our faith.

Even if we don't understand some of it, if we spend time in it and pray, the Holy Spirit will quicken it to us, but we must be diligent with a genuine heart, truly desiring just to know Him more. Jeremiah 29:13 says, "And ye shall seek me, and find me, when ye shall search for me with all your heart." If we just continue in those times to seek Him, even when we can't understand what His Word may be saying—if we will just continue to faithfully dig in and listen, He will come and reveal things to us, grow our faith, and take us deeper into His heart and all He is.

Abba, Your word is true, for it cannot lie and will not be broken or return void, so help us to dig into it that our faith may be grown, that we may become unwavering, being rooted and held in You always, in Your Son Yeshua's precious name, we ask this, amen.

June 14

Haggai 1:13

Then spake Haggai the LORD'S messenger in the LORD'S message unto the people, saying, I am with you, saith the LORD.

I wrote on this story once before; the message is so powerful in this book I had to touch on more. God called the people to rebuild His temple. His temple was lying in waste as the people went about their own lives and business, taking care of their own homes and not even concerned with God's place that lay in ruins. He sent a drought upon them, the heavens held its dew, and the earth didn't produce fruit, it says; a drought upon the cattle and upon the labor of their hands. When Haggai spoke the Word of the Lord to the people concerning all this, they feared before the Lord, turned from their own ways, obeyed the voice of the Lord, and began to rebuild the Temple. The Lord then spoke through Haggai, reassuring them all that He would be with them.

Sometimes we can get so busy doing life that we may put the things of the Lord on the back burner or, like the people in Haggai's day, think it's just not time. We must be careful to not get so involved in living our lives that we leave Him or His ways on the sidelines. We must remain constant in staying wrapped in His ways, thoughts, and desires for us, being mindful of the things of Abba that far exceed the things of this world. When we are mindful of the things He is calling us to do and obedient in doing them, as His Word says, "I am with you saith the Lord," no matter how large or hard the task may seem.

Abba, help us to always be on Your page, to be ready and waiting to do all You've called us to, to not get distracted by things of this life but to be constant and attentive, with a willing heart to run after all You ask, in Yeshua's name, we ask this, amen.

June 15

Matthew 6:21

For where your treasure is, there will your heart be also.

One way to see and know what your heart is really set on, what's really in it is to look at what is most important to you, what you value most. From the beginning, it's always been about our hearts. Abba wants our hearts, He's a jealous God and wants our affections, attention, and intentions to be set and focused on Him. He's given us a precise path to see where our hearts really are by telling us to take a look at what we treasure and value because whatever that may be is where our hearts are. Is our treasure and value in our job, home, possessions, family, or children? Maybe even our ministry? Ministry is just an extension of our relationship with Him, so if we treasure our ministry and put more attention into our ministry than we do Him, there is still a heart issue. We mustn't ever treasure the gift more than the Giver.

He must be the treasure we seek, He alone must be our desire, focus, and what we value and cherish. When it is, then we can rest, knowing our hearts are in the right place. There is no better treasure to be found than the one who created, owns, and holds all things. He is the ultimate treasure and prize. We need to continually examine ourselves to see where our treasure is; it will show us who or what sits on the throne of our hearts.

Lord, may You be the King of our hearts. May we love and value You above all things. May our hearts be found wrapped in You, and may You alone be the treasure we seek, in Yeshua's name, amen.

June 16

Psalm 92:12

The righteous shall flourish like the palm tree: he shall grow like a cedar in Lebanon.

I love how Abba uses literal things to compare His children, like Jeremiah 17:8, saying, "You will be like a tree planted by the waters," or in Isaiah 40:31, "They that wait upon the LORD shall renew their strength; they shall mount up with wings as eagles," or here in this verse, how the righteous shall flourish like a palm tree and grow like a cedar of Lebanon. To stop and research the qualities of each of the things identified is definitely worth the time and study. We talked about this verse and the palm tree at one of our Sabbath fellowships, which caused me to go home and research it more. They are one of the few trees that can grow and thrive in harsh, dry, desert valleys. Their leaves have flexible spines that keep them safe as they fold up in rough weather. They have these cylinder-like rings around their trunks that allow them to bend up to fifty degrees without breaking; they create like a super strength in them. They are known for their symbol of victory and triumph. The wind from storms actually strengthens their roots, so they come out of a storm stronger, say what? I **love** that.

The palm tree holds some amazing qualities as with the majestic and beautiful cedars of Lebanon that Abba compares the righteous to. The righteous will come out of a storm stronger, be victorious, and thrive in desert situations because their thirst will be quenched by Abba, their roots will be deep into Him. They may bend hard but they won't break because Abba is their strength. When we truly look at the qualities of the things He compares His righteous children to, it will give us encouragement, knowing these qualities are within us if we are His and walking in righteousness as well. It will strengthen and inspire us to walk victoriously as the children of the Most High. He compared His children, the righteous, to things like this so we could learn and glean from the examples, seeking and desiring to walk and live by them.

Abba, help us to truly learn and see the qualities You equip Your righteous with and help us to walk in those strengths so we can live victorious lives for You, in Yeshua's powerful name, amen.

June 17

3 John 1:11

Beloved, follow not that which is evil, but that which is good. He that doeth good is of God: but he that doeth evil hath not seen God.

God Himself is the definition of **good**, and there is **no** evil in Him. All He created is good. He gives good gifts, works all things for good to those who love Him and are called according to His purpose, and is a good, good Father. Those who love Him and follow Him will take on His nature; they will have His heart, be good as He is, and do good like He does. We are to follow after that goodness and be examples of it for others.

We are not to follow evil, which means we turn and go in the opposite direction. Those who do evil don't know God; they aren't about Him, His business, or purposes, and we have no business following them or contemplating any of it. We are His children, children of the light, and should follow His goodness and light. For the Lord is light and good, and there is no darkness or evil in Him at all.

Lord, help us to follow that which is good, You and Your ways, to walk in Your light, teach us to walk as the King's kids, and shine You and Your goodness in all we do. Help us to always turn and **run** from the evil the enemy may set before us and to have **no** part in it. You alone are **good**, and may we follow and submerge ourselves in You and Your goodness always, in Your Son Yeshua's beautiful name, we ask this, amen.

June 18

2 Corinthians 1:20

For all the promises of God in him are yea, and in Him are Amen, unto the glory of God by us.

The Lord's promises will never be broken. They are forever **yes** and **amen**. They are promises we can stand on and rest in. His words are sure and true, and if He's promised it, He will do it, not just for His children back in the wilderness but for His children throughout time, for His children today. If you are His child, you can rest and be assured that you can stand on the promises of an amazing Father.

Have you ever experienced a situation where someone had made a promise to you; you were excited beyond words for it and couldn't wait for it to come to pass, only to be let down and broken when it never did? The promise was broken for whatever reason—maybe it was accidently forgotten about, but it surely makes it hard to take the word of that person again or believe his or her promises in the future. We are let down and are not as confident in trusting or believing him or her the next time. This is not so with our heavenly Father. He will **never** let us down. He will **never** leave us or forsake us. We can remain confident always that He will be with us, keeping every word He's ever spoken and fulfilling every promise He's ever made. We don't have to worry or be afraid of being let down or disappointed from broken promises with the Lord. His promises are **yes** and **amen always**.

Abba, thank You for always being faithful, Your kept promises, and Your Word that we can stand on and trust in because You will **never** fail us, leave us, or forsake us, in Yeshua's name, amen.

June 19

Psalm 145:14

The LORD upholdeth all that fall, and raiseth up all those that be bowed down.

I love how when you continue reading onto verse sixteen, it says, "He opens His hand and satisfies the desire of **every living thing**." He catches and upholds us when we fall; when we humble ourselves and bow before Him, He raises us up. He loves to care for His people. He loves when we surrender ourselves to Him, allowing Him to direct our steps, hold our moments, take us on new and exciting adventures, use us in ways we could never imagine, and satisfy our desires.

He has caught me with two hands when I have fallen more times than I can count. Verse eighteen says, "He is nigh unto all that call upon Him in truth," and verse nineteen says, "He hears their cry and WILL save them." **Amen**, it's **true**. I can testify of it firsthand. He has saved me from trouble over and over again, spared me from the ploys of the enemy, and rescued me and lifted me up out of the midst of so many storms. He wants nothing more than to be everything to you and me. He delights in being our **all** and meeting our every need and desire. He is an amazing Abba.

Thank You, Lord, for catching us when we fall, always being right there and upholding us, and for raising us up when we're bowed down. You are such a loving, caring, and **always faithful Father**, worthy to be praised forever, in Yeshua's name, we pray, amen.

June 20

Joshua 3:13

And it shall come to pass, as soon as the soles of the feet of the priest's that bear the ark of the LORD, the Lord of all the earth, shall rest in the waters of Jordan, that the waters of Jordan shall be cut off from the waters that come down from above; and they shall stand upon an heap.

Sometimes the Lord will part the waters while we are standing on the shore watching, then sometimes He won't part them until we, in faith, step out, take the first step, and place the soles of our feet in the water. The Lord told Joshua that **as soon** as the soles of their feet were in the water, the waters would be cut off. They had to step out in faith and step into the water fully; their feet had to rest in the water before the Lord moved.

It must have been a little scary, I would think, for the priests carrying the ark, seeing down. In verse fifteen, it talks about how the Jordan overflows all its banks at the time of harvest. I live on a river, and every spring when all the snow melts, all the water causes the river to overflow. What usually is about a four-foot bank raises over the bank to the point my backyard will suddenly look like a lake, and the flow of that river becomes so powerful it will take trees down and sweep away whatever may lie in its path. For me, to step into it would surely frighten me, and I don't know if I would have the courage to do it. The thing the Lord is calling us to might be extremely scary, like stepping into that overflowing river. If we trust Him and take that first step, believing He will be there waiting for us, we will see His amazing power and witness His miracles firsthand.

Abba, help us to walk by faith and not by sight, to step out, no matter how scary or impossible it may look, to trust You and take the first step, believing and knowing You will be there to part the waters and lead us to the Promised Land You have awaiting us, in Yeshua's powerful name, amen.

June 21

Luke 6:45

A good man out of the good treasure of his heart bringeth forth that which is good; and an evil man out of the evil treasure of his heart bringeth forth that which is evil: for of the abundance of the heart his mouth speaketh.

We must keep, protect, and guard our hearts with all diligence, for the issues of life flow from it, Proverbs 4:23 tells us. Our mouths speak what is in our hearts, so we need to bring our hearts before the Lord and ask Him to clean out whatever garbage may be there, make them pure, and then set a hedge about them. We must be careful what we take in and allow to set up residence and keep our minds and thoughts on what's honest, true, of good report, just, lovely, and pure, as Philippians 4:8 tells us.

Physically, what we consume affects our hearts, and it is the same spiritually. We must be careful and wise with what we watch, listen to, and take in. We must ask the Father to make our hearts pure before Him and wrap our hearts up in His, so we can know Daddy's heart and speak goodness and life in this world and to those around us.

Abba, we pray and ask today, as David did, that You would create in us a clean heart and renew a right spirit within us so when we speak, it is good and edifying to the hearer and pleasing to You, in Yeshua's holy name, amen.

June 22

2 Corinthians 5:17

Therefore if any man be in Christ, he is a new creature: old things are passed away; behold, all things are become new.

This is what God assured me of when He delivered me from my years of addiction. He told me that He had thrown it as far as the east is from the west and buried it in the deepest ocean, **never** to be remembered again. All the old Joy had passed away, and I was rising to walk in newness of life; **all** things have become new. **Hallelujah, amen**! What a miracle, what a gift, all the garbage from our lives taken to the dumpster by the Most High God, to be disposed of **forever, never** to be thought about or remembered again.

The Lord loves us so much that when we come to Him with the brokenness of our lives, He desires nothing more than to save us from it, take it away, and give us a brand-new life and identity in Him. We are no longer defined by the old, by the sin that beset us, but we are now defined by a God that saved us. His **great** love for us has done away with all the old and garbage the enemy tried to fill our lives with. Abba sent His Son to surrender His life, go to a cross, and shed His precious, perfect blood for our redemption so we could become a new creature. His blood would wash away the old, all the sin, and we would walk in newness of life in Him. Amen, the gift of all gifts, grace beyond comprehension.

Thank You, Lord, for making a way for us to become new, walk free from the old, sin, and garbage that tried to destroy and devour us, and for giving us beauty for our ashes, in Yeshua's mighty name, amen.

June 23

Proverbs 2:6

For the LORD giveth wisdom: out of His mouth cometh knowledge and understanding.

The Lord longs for us to desire and be filled with His wisdom. James 1:5 tells us, "If any of you lack wisdom, let him ask of God, that giveth to all men liberally, and upbraideth not; and it shall be given him." His wisdom is so far beyond the wisdom of man. Earlier in Proverbs 2:1–5, it tells us that if we will receive His words and hide His commandments in us, if we will incline our ears unto wisdom and our hearts to understanding, if we will cry after knowledge and raise our voices for understanding, if we will seek it as silver and search for it as hidden treasure, **then** we will understand the fear of the LORD and find the knowledge of God.

I long to have godly wisdom, knowledge, and understanding; to see through His eyes, understand through His heart, His mind, and operate in His purposes and ways. His ways are perfect, and His wisdom and knowledge exceeds man's. His thoughts and ways are so far above ours. I believe it's time to take Proverbs 2:1–5 to heart and listen to and follow its instructions so we can understand the fear of the Lord and find His wisdom. That we seek His knowledge as silver and search for it as hidden treasure. He will give it to us if we are seeking and asking.

Abba, Your ways are so far above ours—Your thoughts, wisdom, knowledge, and understanding. Please increase our desire to want to seek and search after it so we can have a true understanding of Your awesomeness and walk in the knowledge of You, in Your Son Yeshua's powerful name, amen.

June 24

Romans 8:15

For ye have not received the spirit of bondage again to fear; but ye have received the Spirit of Adoption, whereby we cry, Abba, Father.

Abba Father, my Daddy, the lover of my soul, I am Your very own, and You are my Daddy, my King. This is what we can say and stand on when we surrender ourselves and ask Yeshua to forgive, cleanse, and make us right before the Father. Yeshua makes the way for us, and we become adopted into the family of Abba; our hearts become His home, and His Spirit comes and dwells in us, and we indeed cry out: Abba Father, my Daddy, my King.

I saw a video of a couple that left their five-year-old child all alone at the border. It wrecked my heart watching as he sat there, clenching his teddy bear, screaming and crying, "Don't go, come back, don't go." I bawled. I pray for that boy, that God will wrap His arms around Him and hold and keep him, and I thank the Lord with **all** my heart that we will **never** be left like that when we have Him as our Father. What an awesome gift we have being adopted by Him and becoming His very own. We won't ever have to worry or live in that horrific fear of being abandoned and left standing alone, screaming, "Don't go." **He never will**. He will never leave or forsake us. When we ask Yeshua to come into our lives and cleanse us from all sin and unrighteousness with that precious blood He shed, He will, and we become part of the family. We then receive the spirit of adoption, whereby we cry Abba Father, and we can say, "My Daddy, my King, You are the love of my soul."

Abba, thank You for sending Your Son to make a way for us to be united with You, to become part of Your family, one of Your very own. **Nothing** compares. Thank You, Yeshua, for being obedient and coming and giving Your life for us. It's in Your name, Yeshua, we pray, amen.

June 25

Psalm 18:2

The LORD is my rock, and my fortress, and my deliverer; my God, my strength, in whom I will trust; my buckler, and the horn of my salvation, and my high tower.

Oh, to give our lives to Him and know that He will be all this to us as well. What a freedom, a treasure beyond treasures. He will be that strong tower we can run into in times of trouble. He will hide us under the shelter of His wing. He will uphold us with His mighty right hand. He will sing and rejoice over us. He is the rock and firm foundation we can stand on in surety without fear. He is our deliverer and will deliver us from the enemy's ploys, bondage, and snares that so easily beset us.

He will order our every step in His perfect way and will lead and direct us where we need to go. He will give us strength for each step so we don't tire and faint. He will provide for our every need and satisfy our desires. He will protect us from the fiery darts that are aimed to take us out. He will be a fortress and hiding place to us always. He longs to be all this for us and so much more. What a blessing and treasure to be had. Who wouldn't want all this?

Abba, thank You for being all these things to us and so much more. Thank You for loving us so greatly and unconditionally. There is **none** like You. In Your Son Yeshua's name, we pray, amen.

June 26

2 Thessalonians 3:16

Now the Lord of peace Himself give you peace always by all means. The Lord be with you all.

Peace that passes understanding—I pray He equips and empowers you for each moment of every day in the journey that lies ahead of you; that perfect peace that keeps your heart and mind wrapped in Him. His sweet peace keeps you free from doubt, worry, and keeps you rested in His arms of love, knowing He holds your every moment and directs your every step. That powerful peace dispels fear and keeps you held and calm in the face of destruction and chaos. That healing peace washes over you in times of sickness, despair, and loss.

May His peace be yours for each situation and circumstance you may face, and may you know how to rest in it. There is truly nothing like His peace, for it is sweet, beautiful, and vastly out-weighs the peace the world tries to offer. Grab hold of His peace and allow it to engulf your entire being; let it wash over each fiber so you may truly know the power of it, and it will keep your heart and mind in Him always.

Lord, thank You for that sweet, powerful, healing, and per-fect peace You so long for us to have and walk in. Help us to truly immerse ourselves in it so we can walk free from the weights of the world and so the world around us can see You, the hope of glory, in us, in Yeshua's name, amen.

June 27

Galatians 6:9

And let us not be weary in well doing: for in due season we shall reap, if we faint not.

Life can get hard, trials and struggles come, storms will brew, and complicated situations are sure to arise, but if we continue to do our best and stand strong, knowing the Lord is for us, we **will** make it through and have the victory. I know firsthand how tiring it can get, but we mustn't give up; we must keep our eyes set on the goal, the end result we will reap if we don't faint. As it states in Philippians 3:14, "I press toward the mark for the prize of the high calling of God in Christ Jesus." If we press on and continue to pursue in the face of exhaustion and discouragement, we will eventually prevail; with God for us, who can stand against us? He will be our shield and strength.

Nehemiah 8:10 states, "The Joy of the LORD is your strength." If we remain joyful, encouraged, and positive, speaking His words of life along the way, we will make it through and reap a bountiful harvest.

Abba, help us to not be weary in well doing, to remain joyful and steadfast, knowing you are with us, helping us each step of the way in each moment. Help us to remember we will have the victory in You and reap in due season if we faint not, in Your Son Yeshua's beautiful and powerful name, amen.

June 28

Ecclesiastes 4:12

And if one prevail against him, two shall withstand him; and a threefold cord is not quickly broken.

As I sat writing this today, I was looking out on the pond and was watching this bird sit ever so patiently on the side, then all of a sudden, he swooped in and grabbed his fish. It was crazy, and a picture story came into my mind. The enemy sits on the sidelines of our lives, waiting and watching ever so patiently to swoop in, grab us, and swallow us whole. He knows the Word better than we do, and he knows this verse too. He knows a threefold cord is **not** quickly broken but knows if he waits patiently, the cares of life will happen: distractions and busyness that will leave us vulnerable to navigate alone at times; it's then that his prime opportunity opens, and he swoops in.

It seems marriages are one of his favorite targets. He attacks marriages, knowing if he can get them divided, get a wedge in somehow, and cause a weak link, his battle becomes much more effortless. Deceiving one is so much easier accomplished, and his victory begins. That's why it's so important to start each day in prayer together, putting God first and in the forefront of your marriage. This verse is so true, and that covenant with each other and the Father has so much power if you hold fast to it, remember it, honor it, and cherish it. If you make this the first and most important part of your agenda and schedule daily, then when the storms come, they won't seem as rough; when the night comes, it won't seem as dark, and that threefold cord will hold you, strengthen you, and you'll watch Abba flourish in and through your marriage.

Abba, please help us to bind together in our marriages and keep You forefront and first in them always so we never lose that threefold cord, in Yeshua's name, amen!

June 29

Psalm 90:12

So teach us to number our days, that we may apply our hearts unto wisdom.

James 4:14 says that our lives are but a vapor. We are bound by time, and our days are short. Psalm 103:15–16 says: "As for man, his days are as grass, as a flower of the field so he flourisheth, for the wind passeth over it, and it is gone; and the place thereof shall know it now more."

The older I get, the more I wish I knew this in my younger days; the more I desire that I would have sought for wisdom early and applied my heart to it, to cherish and number my days and use each moment wisely, to never waste time and thoughts idly but to purposefully live each moment for Him. As it states earlier in Psalm 90:10 that "it is soon cut off, and we fly away." Life is fleeting, so **be wise**, **seek His wisdom early**, and **make the most of every moment for Him**. He has purposed so much for you; walk in it always and make each minute count.

Lord, help us to know and realize the importance of each moment and breath, and help us to live and walk every bit of it purposefully for You, in Yeshua's name, we ask this, amen!

June 30

Song of Solomon 8:6–7

6) Set me as a seal upon thine heart, as a seal upon thine arm: for love is strong as death; jealousy is cruel as the grave: the coals therof are coals of fire, which hath a most vehement flame. 7) Many waters cannot quench love, neither can the floods drown it: if a man would give all the substance of his house for love, it would utterly be contemned.

I **love** this passage, I **love** the song about it, "You Won't Relent,"[27] and how beautifully it relates our hearts and desire toward Him. How awesome it is as we make a declaration to the Lord that we will set Him as a seal upon our hearts, upon our arms; may we continually set you as a seal, Lord because it is truly You who are the lover of our souls.

As I was reading this though and reading the footnotes, I saw how this is the Shulamite woman's desire that her lover, the king, set her as a seal upon his heart. It stated that the seal was a mark of official commitment; it gave a sense of security, knowing she was on the seat of her lover's affection, her lover's heart. What a beautiful portrayal of the bond between a man and a woman. God designed it to be a portrayal of His covenant and commitment to us. It should imitate that. God created the woman to desire to be the seal upon her lovers' heart, the desire to want to be all he needs, and gave the man the desire to want to give his woman that place in his heart, the security she needs, and a desire to be her protection and strength. It is truly a mirror of Yeshua and His bride.

Abba, You are so perfect in all Your ways. Help our eyes to be truly opened to Your perfect ways so we can see, understand, and walk in them always. Help our lives to always imitate Your heart, in Yeshua's beautiful name, amen!

July 1

Colossians 3:2

Set your affection on things above, not on things on the earth.

Things on this earth can look so good; lust of the flesh, riches of the world, praises of men, carnal knowledge that exalts us above others, and on and on. Oh, the enemy can paint a pretty picture stirring us to desire so easily the things that just dissolve like dust. The things of the Lord, though, are where we should set our affections. Eternal things, things above, sometimes we can't even fathom the good things He has awaiting us. Sometimes because they're not tangible at the moment, we forget about them; sometimes it's just plain hard with all the worldly distractions. Setting our thoughts, desires, and affections above takes acquiring a daily mindset that is set and fixed on the Lord, His Word, and His Law; that is so good. The more we set our eyes on Him, the easier it becomes. To truly know and believe this world has **nothing for me**, but He is **everything** I could ever desire and need is where I want to live always.

Abba, teach us and help us to fix and set our minds and affection on You, Your Word, and ways; when we rise, throughout our day, and as we lay our heads down, for there is truly nothing better to think on. In Yeshua's holy and precious name, amen!

July 2

Philippians 2:15

That ye may be blameless and harmless, the sons of God, without rebuke, in the midst of a crooked and perverse nation, among whom ye shine as lights in the world.

We live in a dark world, a world that seems to be growing further and further apart from the Father and His truth. The further it goes away from Him, the darker it gets. Darkness is the absence of light. We are called to be lights for Him, to shine bright in the midst of a dark, crooked, and perverse world. Light shines brightest in the darkness, so Him shining brightly through us presents a great opportunity for others to see Him, His truth, and their lives to be touched! A lit candle or flashlight in the middle of the day doesn't seem so bright, but in the darkness of the night, it illuminates everything in its path and clearly reveals what lies before us. That's what His light in us does for those living in darkness; it illuminates and lights the path for them to find their way to the Father. This is why it's so important that we do our best to live blameless and harmless, holy as He is holy, so our lights can shine bright without being dimmed by the sins and cares of the world, so others may come to know the same hope of glory we have in Abba.

Father, help us to walk uprightly in all we do and live blamelessly before You, so we may shine brightly in the darkness that is so quickly filling this world, in Yeshua's mighty name, amen!

July 3

Ephesians 4:1–2(ESV)

1) I therefore, a prisoner for the Lord, urge you to walk in a manner worthy of the calling to which you have been called, 2) with all humility and gentleness, with patience, bearing with one another in love.

Being humble, with all humility; what does that truly mean? The definition in the dictionary states, "having or showing modest or low estimate of one's own importance."[28] Being *gentle* is "having or showing a mild, kind or tender temperament or character," according to the dictionary.[29] *Patient* is "able to accept or tolerate delays, problems, or suffering without becoming annoyed or anxious."[30] **Wow**, that's a hard one. I am learning to wait, but can I do it without getting annoyed or anxious? This is how we are to be and act in our relationships and dealing with others.

The King James version states: "with all lowliness and meekness, with long suffering." We are to put the other first and become low so the other can be lifted up; to be quiet, slow to speak, and slow to anger, not jumping to conclusions or assuming, patient in our every move and response. Sometimes things can sound really easy until broken down, read, and understood in this manner.

Abba, help us to not just read Your words but to understand, digest, and let them become life in our lives. Help us to deal humbly, gently, and patiently with each other always, in Yeshua's powerful name, amen!

July 4

Psalm 94:12

Blessed is the man whom thou chastenest, O LORD, and teachest him out of thy law.

Hebrews 12:6 says, "for who the Lord loveth He chasteneth." He disciplines the ones He loves, His children. I remember thinking as a child that my dad and mom really didn't like me and couldn't stand seeing me have fun. It seemed every time I'd have fun and would do things with my friends, I would get in trouble, grounded, or spanked. What they knew that I didn't was those supposed fun things really weren't fun at all; they would end in a bad way, and my parents were only trying to protect me from that. They loved me and wanted to protect me from the lies of the enemy and the ways of the world.

Just like the Lord, He knows the beginning from the end. He knows the things that will hurt us and end bad. He disciplines and stops us when we start walking in the wrong direction. He chastens and corrects us because He loves us so much and wants to quickly stop us from walking down a worldly path or from the wrong turn we have made. He does it swiftly, so we don't get too far from Him and don't forget or walk away from the truth of His Word. He doesn't do it just to spoil our fun but because He loves and cares enough to keep us from harm and destruction. We need to count it a blessing when Abba disciplines us, when He stops us dead in our tracks, even when it makes us so angry and we don't understand; we must trust and believe He knows what He is doing, and He is doing it for our good. In this, we know we are His children because He only disciplines His own; what a comforting thought knowing we are His, His very own.

Thank You, Abba, for the chastening and discipline You administer to us, Your children when we need it. Help us to learn, grow from it, and know it's done out of Your deep love for us. We pray this in Your son Yeshua's beautiful name, amen.

July 5

Romans 12:10 (ESV)

Love one another with brotherly affection. Outdo one another in showing honor.

Wow, this can be a hard one, especially on those days we feel we've been wronged or forgotten about and are hurt deeply. How do we honor the other above ourselves then? How do we die to ourselves and give more when we feel there's no more left to give? This is when we must truly lean on the strength and help of Yeshua! We must allow Him to come in and fill all those places, the hurts and the emptiness, and trust Him to right the wrongs for us. Then we need to ask Him to fill us with His unconditional love so He can flow out of us in these times when we have nothing.

We can learn from Him how to always esteem the other more than ourselves in all things so we can remain genuinely devoted to one another. It is impossible on our own, but with Yeshua's help and strength, we can be the way He is and love like He does.

Father, help us to learn from Your Son's example, to be filled with that love and spirit that transcends ourselves and thinks on and honors others first, in Yeshua's holy and precious name, amen.

July 6

Leviticus 19:2

Speak unto all the congregation of the children of Israel, and say unto them, Ye shall be holy: for I the LORD your God am holy.

He must have known we could do this, to be holy, that it wasn't impossible. In and of ourselves, it would be, but knowing Him and walking with Him, we take on His righteousness, and it becomes possible to be holy as He is. We don't have to succumb to the flesh, to our desires, but we can put on Yeshua and walk as the Father has commanded. It requires not only a life change but an attitude and heart change as well. Our hearts must become sold out for Him and engulfed in His heart. Our attitudes must become one of obedience and sacrifice, and our lives must become one of total commitment to Abba and His truth.

To know as Yeshua knew this world has nothing for us. To die to ourselves and the flesh as Yeshua did and to know fully as Yeshua did that Abba is and has is all we need. Knowing His truth and way is perfect; walking in obedience to His law because we believe as Yeshua did that there is no other way but Abba's perfect way, and allow Him to fully wash over us and fill us so we can walk and be holy as He is holy. May we hear this and know today that it is possible, and we are called to it.

Abba, please help this command from You become truth to us, that we may believe we can be holy as You are holy and that we may walk in Your holiness, in Yeshua's name, amen.

July 7

Zechariah 4:6

Then he answered and spake unto me, saying, This is the word of the LORD unto Zerubbabel, Saying, Not by might, nor by power, but by my spirit, saith the LORD of hosts.

We can try with everything in us to work hard, push, and strive to do and be all we are called and created to, but we will continue to come up short, empty, and frustrated if we're doing it of our own accord. It is the Spirit of the Living God that breathes life into the situation and brings victory, and that causes us to overcome. When we realize that it's only by His Spirit, then life becomes so much easier and peaceful.

Allow His Spirit to fight your battles, order your steps, and breathe life into every situation, today and always. Wow, the difference it makes.

Abba, please fill our lives with Your Spirit and surround and fill us so we will walk and live by it and not by our own might or power, or man's, but by Your Spirit alone, in Yeshua's powerful and holy name, amen.

July 8

Proverbs 31:11–12

11)The heart of her husband doth safely trust in her, so that he shall have no need of spoil. 12)She will do him good and not evil ALL the days of her life.

This shows her forever commitment and covenant to her husband **all** the days of her life. To be this virtuous, extraordinary woman should be every woman's desire. Verse twenty-eight says, "Her children arise up and call her Blessed, her husband also, and he praiseth her." Be such a woman to capture your children and husband's heart in such a way. The ones that mean the most, that we cherish most, the ones who know us best, who see all of us; our character should speak such volumes to those closest to us that they arise and call us blessed.

My Bible footnotes state: "Such praise should encourage every woman to follow in the steps and acquire such wisdom as did this Proverbs 31 woman!"

Abba, help us to seek to always be this beautiful, virtuous woman, full of Your wisdom and leading and loving our husbands and children in Your love, in Yeshua's name, amen.

July 9

Matthew 12:36–37

36)But I say unto you, that every idle word that men shall speak, they shall give account therof in the day of Judgement. 37)For by thy words thou shalt be justified, and by the words thou shalt be condemned.

Yeshua, in verse thirty-four, called them a generation of vipers, saying, "how can ye being evil speak of good things? For out of the abundance of the heart the mouth speaketh." This means the words that we will be justified or condemned by come out of the heart. When junk comes out of our mouths, it reveals the garbage in our hearts. When idle words come out of our mouths, words that don't edify or build up, it's a sign of what condition our hearts are in, a sign that we might need to step back and truly examine our hearts; it's all about the heart condition.

On that day, when I stand before His throne, giving an account for my words, I want Abba to see through the words that I have spoken, a pure and genuine heart within, that by my words, I may be justified.

Father, shine Your floodlight into our hearts and show us where we need work, so we may speak right things, and our words won't be hurtful or idle words, but they will bring life, in Yeshua's name, amen.

July 10

1 Kings 19:11–12

(11)And He said, go forth, and stand upon the mount before the LORD. And, behold, the LORD passed by, and a great and strong wind rent the mountains, and brake in pieces the rocks before the LORD; but the LORD was not in the wind: and after the wind an earthquake; but the LORD was not in the earthquake: 12)And after the earthquake a fire; but the LORD was not in the fire: and after the fire a still small voice.

So much wind, so many voices, and thoughts that go ninety miles an hour across the highway of our minds. We get so used to all the noise and distractions of this world. Life is so loud and busy; it's easy to think that God is the same way. I mean, come on, He has over 7 billion people in this world He's watching, working, and moving in and around. He must be used to the chaos, confusion, and busyness of this world. We tend to look for the grand displays of His wonder and greatness for answers and direction, waiting for bolts of lightning to strike to know it's Him or a thundering voice coming out of the sky. I think sometimes it is the only way He'll get through all the noise and distractions and be heard. He can and will talk to us through these grand displays, but most of the time, He is waiting for us to slow down and settle down enough to hear His **still small voice**.

When the winds of life are raging and thoughts swirling and racing ninety miles an hour in your mind, try to just sit quietly somewhere and settle yourself and listen for that **still small voice** through all the noise. It will bring comfort and assurance amid a loud, chaotic world and will guide you in and through it all.

Father, help us to take time to step back from the commotion and busyness of life to spend time with You and listen for Your **still small voice** beyond the noise, that we may learn it and be led by it all the days of our lives, in Yeshua's name, amen.

July 11

Deuteronomy 6:2

That thou mightiest fear the LORD thy God, to keep all His statutes and His commandments, which I command thee, thou, and thy son, and thy son's son, all the days of thy life; and that thy days may be prolonged.

They are not idle words. Keeping His Word, statutes, and commands bring life. He is a good Father, and He is perfect in all His ways! His words are true and His ways are sure; they keep and protect us. He is God, and we are not. He knows what He is doing, and He **never** changes. He is the one and only God. Isaiah 45:18 says, "I am the LORD, and there is NONE ELSE," and it repeats again in verses twenty-one, twenty-two, and throughout the Bible. He is the Alpha and Omega, the beginning and the end, the Creator of all things, the Creator of us, and the lover of our souls, who only wants good for us and wants to protect us from evil.

Why would we think following His ways and commands would be wrong? Why would we think they would be a burden? They are so **not** when we truly fall in love with the one who first loved us; in fact, they become a delight.

Thank You, Abba, for loving us so much to give us such beautiful and perfect laws and decrees that keep and protect us from the schemes of the enemy; for setting hedges about us to safeguard us from going off the cliff and gifting us with prolonged days. You are so good and worthy to be praised!

July 12

Genesis 3:11–13

11)and He said, who told thee that thou wast naked? Hast thou eaten of the tree, wherefore I commanded thee that thou shouldest not eat? 12)And the man said, The woman whom thou gavest to be with me, she gave me of the tree, and I did eat. 13) And the LORD God said unto the woman, What is this that thou hast done? And the woman said, The serpent beguiled me, and I did eat.

Getting trapped in the blaming game is so easy to do: "But he told me," "Well, she said," "But they did." It's time to recognize it for what it is, **wrong**. It will only bring division and brokenness. We must, as children of God, take responsibility for our own actions and reactions. It doesn't matter what others do, what they may tempt us with, how they may treat us, or how the enemy may lie to us, we have God's Word, His truth at our fingertips. We know right from wrong and have His Word to guide us in all truth.

Making excuses, playing the blame game, and shifting the guilt onto something or someone else only ends in destruction. Let's run to God to help us see and take responsibility for our own actions and reactions and let us become more like Him in them.

Lord, help us to own up to our own actions and take responsibility for our own choices and decisions. Help us to make the right ones and be obedient to all You have commanded always, in Yeshua's holy name, amen.

July 13

John 12:49–50

49)For I have not spoken of myself; but the Father which sent me, He gave me a commandment, what I should say, and what I should speak. 50)And I know that His commandment is LIFE EVERLASTING: whatsoever I speak therefore, even as the Father said unto me, so I speak.

I love Yeshua's words here and His obedience to the Father. He could have come, saw how things were, changed things, and did it a different way, even just slightly, but He didn't. He was perfectly obedient to Abba. He knew that His Father's ways were perfect and needed no changing; there was no better way.

Yeshua's words, saying, "His commandment is LIFE EVERLASTING" are so powerful! He knew Abba intimately, knew His ways, thoughts, commands, and knew they were and are completely perfect, inside and out, and if followed, which Yeshua did perfectly, brought **everlasting life**! Confirming it is **all** about the Father and His will. It is a powerful and beautiful truth to realize and live by, and it's life changing.

Father, help us to see Your ways and commands have never changed, and help us to live and walk by them as Yeshua did, knowing they are protection for us and bring us life, in Yeshua's name, amen.

July 14

I Thessalonians 5:24

Faithful is He that calleth you, who also will do it.

It is so good to know that the Father, the one and only true God, calls us. He calls us by name, hears our prayers and petitions, knows what we actually need before we even ask, and is forever faithful. He will never leave or forsake us and will do and accomplish His will and purpose in our lives if we just allow Him to. What other God is like Him that is mindful of every single detail of our lives and faithful to us, His children, throughout **all** eternity, time without end? Wow, are we blessed and privileged to have such an awesome Father!

Thank You, Lord, for being faithful to Your children always and for calling us by name unto You. What a blessing it is to be a child of Yours. You are worthy of our highest praise, always.

July 15

Psalm 127:1

Except the LORD build the house, they labour in vain that build it: except the LORD keep the city, the watchman waketh but in vain.

If God's not in what we set our hands to, then whatever it is our hands are working at is in vain. He must be the very foundation of it all, the master builder; we are but the vessels. We can guard something and watch and protect it with all our might, but unless we truly have given it to Him to watch and keep, it isn't kept. For example, there have been times where I've tried with all my might to make circumstances and situations happen out of my own selfishness, and though I may have succeeded and accomplished it, they ended up void of joy and lasting memory. Then there are those times I've learned to say, "Lord You do it, if it's what You have and want," then He makes it work and happen, and it's those times that are filled with true meaning and a joy to last a lifetime.

Everything true, lasting, and substantial is in Him, through Him, and by Him; all else is in vain. It will blow with the wind, crumble in the storm, and have no lasting purpose or effect.

Lord, help us to not labor in vain but to be Your vessels that You build and work through. Help us to truly let go and allow You to be the keeper of our whole lives and everything in it, in Yeshua's beautiful, powerful, and worthy name, amen.

July 16

Revelation 21:6–7

6)And He said unto me, It is done. I am Alpha and Omega, the beginning and the end. I will give unto him that is athirst of the fountain of the water of life freely. 7)He that overcometh shall inherit all things; and I will be his God, and he shall be my son.

This is the fountain of life that will **never** run dry, the fountain that quenches one's thirst, and they will **never** thirst again. Who wouldn't want a drink from that fountain? All the false gods in the world can't offer this, only the one true God, the one and only, the Alpha and Omega, the beginning and end; only He can offer this fountain of life. What a God He is. There is **none** like Him. We don't deserve Him, but He chose us, loves us, and longs to give us a drink from that fountain.

When we make that simple choice to drink from the fountain of life, it will bring life and overcome all things, even death, and we will inherit all things with Him for all eternity. This isn't something I decided; these are not just idle words. They are His words and truth; words we can stand on and rest in. What a foundation to build our house and lives on, the truth of the spoken Word of the one and only Almighty God.

Abba, quench our thirst with a drink from this life-changing fountain so we never thirst for anything ever again, in Yeshua's name, we ask this, amen.

July 17

1 Peter 5:8

Be sober, be vigilant; because your adversary the devil, as a roaring lion, walketh about, seeking whom he may devour.

Webster Dictionary's definition of *devour* is: "Swallow whole."[31] I will never forget the first time the Lord brought this verse to life for me. I was getting ready to speak to the twelfth-grade class at Bethesda Christian School when He gave me this verse. As I looked back at my life in light of this verse, I was speechless, overwhelmed, and astounded. To look back at the imagery of Satan being that lion and me being in his mouth as he was getting ready to swallow my life in one gulp, then Yeshua reaching in his jaws ripping me out and saving my life, just took my breath away and brought me to my knees in humility and gratefulness.

I love when He gives us such profound visuals in a real-life way. I now can celebrate daily with a deeper appreciation of life, God's love, and His saving grace. We **must** stay **sober, vigilant, and wide awake** because there truly is an enemy awaiting us to take us out of the grand picture with no trace of our footprints to be left. We **must** take Abba's Word seriously here and heed it, so we don't become a statistic of the enemy.

Lord, help us to truly hear Your words here and do them; to be sober, vigilant, and watchful always, keeping our hearts and minds girded and steadfast in You, where our safety and help comes, in Yeshua's powerful name, amen.

July 18

Deuteronomy 4:9

Only take heed to thyself, and keep thy soul diligently, lest thou forget the things which thine eyes have seen, and lest they depart from thy heart all the days of thy life: but teach them thy sons, and thy sons' sons.

The Lord knew how quickly man would forget. History proves we will forget quickly if we don't stay diligent. The saying goes, "Out of sight, out of mind," and it actually holds some truth to it. We must be careful to remember, reflect, and meditate on all those things the Lord has done for us, and not just for us, but all the things He's done for His people, His children, over and over again. We live in a society that wants to only live in today, do away with history, and say some things never happened and didn't exist. The further we move away from something, the harder it is to remember details of it and its validity, even when it's documented. That's why it's so important to remember, meditate on, and teach our children and our children's children, so we don't forget, don't let all He's done in our lives, our parents' lives, and our ancestors' lives depart from our hearts.

It is the anchor that steadies us in our faith; knowing what He's done and that He'll do it again, remembering the deliverance He's done of His people with His **mighty right hand**, the battles He's won over and over again by the **power** of **His might**, and the healings He's done by the **power** of **His touch**. It all needs to be remembered and woven into the very fabric of our lives, our children's lives, and our grandchildren's.

Abba, help us to remember, heed, and diligently keep our souls in remembering all You've done today, yesterday, and all the years previous, and help us to teach it to the future generations so it doesn't ever depart from our hearts, in Yeshua's precious name, amen.

July 19

Jeremiah 17:7–8

7)Blessed is the man that trusteth in the LORD, and whose hope the LORD is. 8)For he shall be as a tree planted by the waters, and that spreadeth out her roots by the river, and shall not see when heat cometh, but her leaf shall be green; and shall not be careful in the year of drought, neither shall cease from yielding fruit.

This is literally the verse I want to govern my life by. Oh, how I want to be that tree. I want my roots to be so deep into the Father's heart and way that I'm immovable. When the storms come, I stand; when the heat comes, I flourish; and when the drought comes, I am well-watered in His river of life. I want to trust in Him alone. I want my hope to be found in Him alone. I want to grow and be a tall tree, yielding beautiful fruit for my Savior and Redeemer.

I want to have full, green branches that bring cool shade to those He is bringing out of the scorching heat for a moment's rest, tall enough to house the mother eagle and her nest of babies— growing taller day by day, roots deeper day by day, and leaves greener day by day for Him alone and His glory.

Abba, help us to grow and be this tree Your Word speaks of. Help our roots grow deep and solid in You and make our fruit plentiful for You and Your kingdom, in Yeshua's beautiful name, amen.

July 20

Ecclesiastes 3:1

To everything there is a season, and a time to every purpose under the heaven:

There is a chosen and appointed time for all things. God holds all things in His hand and has ultimate control over **every** circumstance and situation; absolutely nothing happens without His say. His will and ways are **perfect** along with His appointed times. Life is so much easier and less stressful if we surrender to His will. Hard and painful times will come, no matter what, as well as joyful and beautiful times; it's guaranteed, but it's also guaranteed that if we accept and trust His way, surrendering to His control as He directs our steps and lives, allowing His sovereignty to reign, we will live with great peace and contentment in the midst of it all.

He is such a good, good Father, full of compassion, perfect in all His ways, and always faithful. We do ourselves a great favor when we let go, fall into the hands that hold all things, and trust His sovereignty in each season and step of our lives. There will be a time of birth and death, mourning and laughing, rending and sowing, and war and peace. We can fight against it all and feel the anguish and misery as we try to control our circumstances and life events, or we can **know** that **nothing** happens that doesn't go through Him first, set our will in line with His **perfect** will, **let go, let God**, and live in His peace that passeth understanding and His joy unspeakable. Ecclesiastes 3:14 states: "I know that, whatsoever God doeth, it shall be forever; nothing can be put to it, nor any thing taken from it; and God doeth it, that men should fear before Him." God is sovereign and possesses supreme and ultimate control in all things.

Help us, Father, to stand in reverenced awe before You, knowing You truly do have ultimate control. Help us surrender to Your authority and control, knowing there is no better way than Yours and that in surrendering, we find rest, in Yeshua's name, amen.

July 21

Isaiah 6:9

And He said, Go, and tell this people, Hear ye indeed, but understand not; and see ye indeed, but perceive not.

God was telling Isaiah to tell His people that though they thought they were hearing His Word, they were really not because if they were, it would have changed them, and they would have turned from their own ways. Though they might have seen with their eyes, they were not perceiving it in their hearts and living and walking by what He said. They were a hard-headed, stiff-necked people that didn't take His words seriously and to heart. It is truly not any different from how we are today.

To truly hear and understand His Word brings change; to truly see through His eyes helps us perceive the perfection of His will.

Abba, help us to not just hear Your Word but to truly understand it; to not just see but to truly perceive Your truth in our hearts. Help it come to life in us so it changes everything we do and say, and it changes everything about us. In Yeshua's powerful name, amen.

July 22

1 Timothy 2:9 (ESV)

Likewise also that women should adorn themselves in respectable apparel, with modesty and self-control, not with braided hair and gold or pearls or costly attire.

We live in a world where modesty has been forgotten about within a great majority of our population. So many today think we must dress a certain way to get attention or advancement, whether it be in our jobs, social status, or even our close circles of friends. We live in a society of competition, always trying to be first or better. I see so many willing to compromise themselves or sell themselves short just to accomplish this. Others just follow to fit in or be accepted. Humility and modesty are deteriorating rapidly all around us. It is so important to preserve these quickly-fading attributes that separate God's children from the world.

I remember going through this transition from the worldly sparkle Barbie me (and I don't mean worldly in the sense that I was out sinning and walking in darkness), but more as I didn't have my heart and priorities right. I cared more about sparkling and standing out, more about the attention and looks I would get than allowing the reflection of Abba in my life to sparkle and shine and draw all attention to Him. 1 Peter 3:3 says, "Do not let your adorning be external-the braiding of hair and the putting on of gold jewelry, or the clothing you wear." Not that we can't wear gold or do our hair, but in doing so, we should remain modest and not let our worth be wrapped up in it or seek attention with it. Proverbs 11:22 says, "like a gold ring in a pig's snout is a beautiful woman without discretion." It surely makes it sound very unappealing.

Help us, Abba, to be Your children in every area of our lives. Even in how we dress and present ourselves, we are a representation of You. Help us to live modestly always so You can shine through us. In Yeshua's name, amen.

July 23

Luke 11:28

But He said, Yea rather, blessed are they that hear the word of God, and keep it.

So, the other day, we were talking about not just hearing but understanding. Today in this verse, Yeshua takes it an additional step, which, from the beginning, should have been known, as God was saying in Isaiah, that by hearing, we should understand, and if understood, we would do, and it would change us. Blessed are they that hear the Word of God and **keep it**.

The definition of the Greek word *phulasso/keep* is watch, guard, obey, do, observe, and preserve.[32] So not just hear and understand, but by truly hearing and really understanding, you will do and walk out His Word. You will live, obey, protect, and keep it. Wow, it kind of changes everything!

Lord, help us to hear, understand, and do, to keep and put into practice daily in our lives Your Word. In Yeshua's name, amen.

July 24

Psalm 33:11

The counsel of the LORD standeth for ever, the thoughts of His heart to all generations.

His counsel, thoughts, will, and way stand **forever**, to and throughout **all** generations; not just for a time long ago because of their obedience or rebelling, not just for today because of our obedience or rebellion, but for the future and their obedience and rebellion also. Nothing is new under the sun, and history just repeats itself, and God never changes. That just makes it so sweet and simple.

His counsel, will, and thoughts were established once and stand forever, throughout all eternity; not much more clarification is needed.

Thank You, Lord, for making it simple, cut, and dry for us, and please help us **not** to complicate and change it. You are **perfect** in **all** your ways. In Your Son Yeshua's perfect and beautiful name, amen.

July 25

Isaiah 29:13

Wherefor the Lord said, Forasmuch as this people draw near me with their mouth, and with their lips do honour me, but have removed their heart far from me, and their fear toward me is taught by the precept of men.

The Lord is not happy with just lip service. He wants our hearts. From the beginning, it's always been about a heart condition. He always only ever wanted our hearts, offered to Him in genuine and true love and desire for Him; genuine and true fear, reverence and awe of Him.

Not what man says or teaches it should be, but how Abba wanted and desired it from the beginning. It is genuine and deep love that causes us to believe and trust Him always in all things, every word, and command because we know He is good and perfect in all His ways. Just as Yeshua did, and He is our example.

Help us, Abba, to wrap our hearts in Yours always, in all things, each minute of every day, just as our Savior Yeshua taught us and showed us by example to do. In Yeshua's holy and precious name, amen.

July 26

John 10:27

My sheep hear my voice, and I know them, and they follow me.

If we are His sheep, then we hear His voice; we spend enough time with Him that we know His voice well, and when He speaks, we hear Him and follow. The Father knows us inside and out. He sees our hearts, motives, and desires to be with Him and know Him more. He knows we are His sheep. I like to put things in a literal context so I can truly grasp what it is saying, so I think about my dad. My dad could speak in a room full of people, and nobody else would recognize and acknowledge his voice like I, his child, would. I would hear it, know above all the other voices, and be like, "That's my dad," and I would follow it. Of course, there were those rebellious years, but even in those, I still heard his voice.

Yeshua was telling the Jews who came around Him that they didn't hear Him or believe Him because they were not one of His. He saw their hearts and knew they couldn't accept who He said He was. He knew they wouldn't follow Him because they were not His.

It is vital that we spend time with Yeshua, getting to know who He is, the only begotten Son, the perfect sacrifice, the perfect example that we should learn from. It is vital for us to learn, hear, and know His voice and follow it, for it leads us to eternal life. Verse twenty-eight says, "where we shall never perish or be plucked from His hand."

Help us, Yeshua, hear Your voice and follow You as You walk out perfectly the example of how we should walk in our lives before Abba. In Your powerful name, Yeshua, we ask this, amen.

July 27

Proverbs 1:5

A wise man will hear, and will increase learning; and a man of understanding shall attain unto wise counsels.

The Hebrew definition of *hear* is: listen, consider, perceive, obey, understand.[33] Jeremiah 5:21 talks about having ears but not hearing. A wise man will **hear** and **increase** learning; it will go down and take root, and he will obey and do. Proverbs 1:7 says, "The fear of the Lord is the beginning of KNOWLEDGE: but fools despise wisdom and instruction." The Hebrew definition of *fear* in this verse is: morally reverence, reverent obedience[34]; another word to reverently obey the Lord is the beginning of knowledge. The fool hears but doesn't attain to, doesn't do.

For so long in my life and still many times today, it is hard for me to truly hear instruction. Instead, I would get offended by it or become hurt by it because I would regard it as negative toward my person or character. It is so important to be teachable, to yearn for and follow instruction, to be humble enough to hear and increase learning. I now can see and understand a little more that instruction was to help and better me, that when I would choose to not be offended by it but heed it, my situation and life would actually become simpler.

Being on the defense continually will cause our ears not to hear. Approaching our situations and life with a teachable attitude will help us grow in wisdom and understanding as we learn to stand in a reverent awe of the Almighty and His ways that are **sure** and **true**.

Father, help us to attain wise counsel, to hear and increase learning, and to lay down our pride and be teachable. In Your Son Yeshua's name, we ask this, amen.

July 28

Nehemiah 8:10

Then he said unto them, Go your way, eat the fat, and drink the sweet, and send portions unto them for whom nothing is prepared: for this day is holy unto our Lord: neither be ye sorry; for the Joy of the LORD is your Strength.

To give a little history of what is happening here in this verse, Ezra the priest had just got done reading the book of the law of the Lord to all the people. It was the first day of Tabernacles. Nehemiah, Ezra, and the Levites stood before the people as they wept while hearing the words of the Law. They were proclaiming to them to "WEEP NOT, nor be SORRY, for this is a Holy day unto the LORD your God, a day of rejoicing, for the Joy of the LORD is your Strength."

This is a time set aside by the Father to remember and celebrate all He has done for them. Read His law and see how beautiful and perfect it is and how it is their lives and protection. Be joyful in this, for it is the **joy** of the Lord that is their strength and ours as well. Having His Word and these times that He has set aside and appointed for us, His children, should fill us with a **joy** that holds and sustains us in and through all things; it is our strength. When we celebrate Him, His Word, and His ways like this, it literally transforms and changes our lives. Walking in this joy daily, the **joy** of the Lord is vital to being **victorious**!

Father, help us to know Your true and real **joy** deeper than we ever have, that it truly will be our strength daily in all we do and face, in Yeshua's name, amen.

July 29

Ezekiel 36:26–27

26) A new heart also will I give you, and a new spirit will I put within you: and I will take away the stony heart out of your flesh, and I will give you an heart of flesh. 27) And I will put my spirit within you, and cause you to walk in my statutes, and ye shall keep my judgments, and do them.

Walking about in this world we live in today with sin so prominent all around can cause our hearts to become numb to the truth of the Lord's Word. Little compromises here and there with this world slowly causes our hearts to harden. Sin conceived births rocky, stony places in our hearts that lead to death.

The Lord says He will take our stony hearts, if we allow Him, and replace it with a heart of flesh. He will put a new spirit in us that will cause us to want to do, follow, and obey His statutes and judgments. I believe a heart like Yeshua is only about the Father's will and heart. Once again, it's **always** and **only** been about a **heart condition**.

Abba, please give us new hearts; take our hearts that have been numbed and hardened by the world around us, sin, and the enemy, and replace it with new hearts, hearts of flesh that want only Your heart and will. Breathe Your Spirit, Your Holy Spirit in us so the desire of our hearts will be to walk in Your way all the days of our lives, in Yeshua's holy name, amen.

July 30

Romans 12:2

And be not conformed to this world: but be ye transformed by the renewing of your mind, that ye may prove what is that good, and acceptable, and perfect, will of God.

It's so easy to conform and mold to the world around us, the people around us, or the workplace we spend a good majority of our time in. All the things that try to drag us away little by little from His truth or convince us to compromise just slightly, then step by step, we begin to conform. That's why it's so important to spend quality time with the Father in prayer, reading and meditating on His Word and just being in His presence so He can transform our hearts and minds.

In doing this, we begin to learn who He is and come to know His acceptable and perfect will. We begin to know beyond a shadow of a doubt, so when we go out into this crazy world around people from every walk of life and into our workplaces, we can stand firm in His truth and shine.

Abba, transform our hearts and minds by renewing them in You, Your Word, and Your truth, that we may know and walk in Your acceptable and perfect will and not conform to all the winds that blow around us, in Yeshua's powerful name, amen.

July 31

Matthew 11:28

Come unto me, all ye that labour and are heavy laden, and I will give you rest.

How the stresses of everyday life, work, study, children, responsibilities, and deadlines can weigh on us and steadily drag us down. I don't know about you, but I know there have been times for me where the weight has become so heavy. I feel like I'm drowning and gasping for air. I'm guessing I maybe should have come to Him before it got so bad, but in the beginning, it didn't feel so heavy and felt tolerable to navigate through and handle. Then it just hits, each little thing like a thousand-pound weight, multiplied and multiplied.

I am learning there is one sure way to keep this from happening, **come to Him early**. We should be giving all our cares to Him like His Word says, "Cast all your cares on me," then things will never become too heavy to bear. When we come to Him and give it all to Him, the unbearable becomes bearable. In fact, when we come to Him from minute one, it never becomes unbearable or too heavy because He fights our battles. He calms the storms and sustains and holds us in and through the tough times that come. He does give us rest in the middle of the chaos; we just must learn to come to Him.

Help us, Abba, to know You are here to carry and bear the weights of this life for us, and we don't have to, in Yeshua's precious and powerful name, amen.

August 1

Deuteronomy 30:16

In that I command thee this day to love the LORD thy God, to walk in His ways, and to keep His commandments and His statutes and His judgments, that thou mayest live and multiply: and the LORD thy God shall bless thee in the land whither thou goest to possess it.

I love this verse, the God of the universe, the one and only true God, Creator of heaven and earth, and of you and me tells us plain and simple what to do to multiply, prosper, and live a blessed life. In fact, He doesn't just tell us, He commands us. It wasn't an if you agree, if it's easy enough, a maybe, or even an if you need to change it a little to fit your life, desire, or schedule better. **No**, there are **no absolutes**, just a simple command: **love Me**, **follow Me**, and **obey**.

Knowing He is God of all things, knowing He created us and loves us beyond what we could comprehend, knowing His ways are perfect, beautiful, and blessed, why wouldn't we want to believe, follow, and obey Him? Why wouldn't we want to keep His commands? All of them. It seems like a love beyond all others to me, a win-win situation. It is protection from evil, a holding and keeping in our every step and blessings beyond what we deserve and can comprehend, something so simple we choose to make so hard. There's an acronym I learned in recovery: KISS-Keep It Simple, Stupid. If need be, we must remind ourselves daily to keep it simple because it is. Just love Him, follow Him, and do what He says.

Abba, help us to love, hear, follow, and keep Your words always, for they are our life and blessings, in Yeshua's name, amen.

August 2

Isaiah 1:19

If ye be willing and obedient, ye shall eat the good of the land.

Back in Isaiah 1:10–11, it says; "hear the word of the LORD, ye rulers of Sodom, give ear unto the LAW of our God, ye people of Gomorrah. To what purpose is the multitude of your sacrifices unto me, saith the LORD," and it goes on to say their sacrifices He doesn't delight in. He calls them vain oblations. Incenses are an abomination unto Him. Their Sabbaths, new moons, and appointed feasts, He hates them, and they are trouble to Him, the many prayers He will not hear. See, though they gave their sacrifices still and kept the Sabbaths and feast days, their hearts had not changed; they were full of impurity, rebellion, defiance, and evil. They thought that following His commands would make them holy without a heart change. It didn't mean God hated the Sabbaths that He created, His appointed feast days, or even sacrifices, but what He hated was the context of how they were being used. His delight is in His children keeping and following His Word with willing hearts, genuine and true, wanting to be obedient to Him who knows best and is ultimate holiness and righteousness. I often say keeping the Law won't save us, but it will keep and protect us if our hearts are pure and genuine. Verse eighteen of this chapter says, "Come let us reason together, saith the LORD; though your sins be as scarlet, they shall be white as snow; though they be red like crimson, they shall be as wool." He will wash our sins away and give us a new heart; are we willing? Will we be obedient when He does?

Abba, please help us to have a genuine and true heart change, hearts that are willing to hear and follow You, hearts full of love for You, knowing and having a genuine want for You and all You are, in Yeshua's name, amen.

August 3

Philippians 4:13

I can do all things through Christ which strengtheneth me.

It is vital for us to **know** that it is not in and of ourselves ever that we succeed and accomplish the impossible, but it is **Christ** in us that strengthens and enables us to do and accomplish His will in our lives. We don't need to fear anything He sets before us, but we can confidently approach it, knowing we can do **all** things through Yeshua. He is our strength, rock, our very breath, and will surely equip us for any task He calls us to.

The next time you may feel the enemy, the world or others telling you that you can't, confidently and unwavering, stand and say, **I can do all things through Christ who strengthens me**; proclaim it loudly, knowing and believing He's got you. In and of ourselves it is impossible, but with Yeshua, **all** things are possible. His strength is made perfect in our weakness.

Abba, help us to know through You alone we can and will do all that You've called us to, and help us to not be afraid or doubt but to believe and stand on Your Word always, in Yeshua's mighty and powerful name, amen.

August 4

Habakkuk 3:18

Yet I will rejoice in the LORD, I will joy in the God of my Salvation.

When I read the book of Habakkuk and truly processed and understood all the feelings, thoughts, and doubts he was having and struggling with, but then found resolution in it all with realizing who God truly was, all I could think was, **wow**. It began to help me with some of my own conflicts, questions, and struggles I had been facing. Here, Habakkuk is having to look at the reality that God is allowing the Babylonians to come and threaten his land and people, that his people were declining spiritually, and his faith, in the midst of it all, was faltering.

I believe we all go through this in our lives; we wonder where God is, why He allows certain things, and is He really intimately involved in each and every aspect of this world and our lives? Sometimes we forget that He is a sovereign God who has a perfect plan and knows exactly what He is doing and is perfectly just in all He does. His ways or thoughts are far above ours. Habakkuk eventually changed his thoughts and questions to a trust and faith in his God who would sustain him in the midst of the things He allowed, and he declared, "I WILL REJOICE IN THE LORD, THE GOD OF MY SALVATION." He went from an overwhelming amount of questions, thoughts, and doubts to a sure-footed **faith** in the God who would hold him, no matter what.

Abba, help us to be like Habakkuk, that no matter what situations in life we must face, we can do it in the assurance of knowing You will sustain and keep us and with the attitude of praise to **rejoice** in the **God of our salvation**, in Yeshua's precious name, amen.

August 5

Romans 5:8

But God commendeth His love toward us, in that, while we were yet sinners, Christ died for us.

I never really knew the full meaning of this verse. I grew up in church knowing Yeshua died for me and my sins, but always thought He died for this cute, good little girl. It wasn't until He met me the day He delivered me from my addiction that it truly resonated in me the complete and deep meaning of this verse. As I sat there after a weekend binge from my drug addiction, a total wreck, my hands all cut up and burnt from a crack pipe, stinking from not showering for days, broken from my life crumbling in pieces all around me, losing everything, including my children, my hearts—absolutely nothing was left and surely nothing good in me. This is when the Lord met me and revealed to me that it was at this moment, seeing this beat-up, broken mess, awful, sin-laden girl that He went to the cross for me. **What**? **Say what**? I lost it, knowing He **loved** this **unlovable** person enough to die for me. It was at that moment, with that revelation, that His **love** changed my life.

Today, I have hope because of Him meeting me where I was at! Today, I have life because of Him loving me just as I was. I walk today and every day in the revelation of this love that He has for me, and it changes everything, and when I start forgetting to walk this way, it becomes evident in my attitude, and I must quickly grasp hold of this revelation once again. He **loves** us in the middle of our messes and garbage. He **loves** us and will come and find us, pick up our broken pieces, and gently put us back together with an unconditional, unending love that will take our breath away.

Thank You, Abba, for coming and finding us when we lose ourselves, our way, and our direction. Thank You for loving us so greatly that You sent Your **only begotten Son**, Yeshua, to lay His life down for us so that we may have life and come to know You. Thank You, Yeshua, for being obedient to the Father and being that **perfect** sacrifice for us.

August 6

Exodus 15:2

The LORD is my strength and song, and He is become my salvation: He is my God, and I will prepare Him an habitation; my father's God, and I will exalt him.

This is the song Moses and the children of Israel sang when they arrived safely on the other side of the Red Sea and the Egyptian Army was lost as the water crashed back down on the dry riverbed. What a sight it must have been, what a feeling of exultation, happiness, joyfulness, and gratefulness. The adrenaline must have been at a crazy level as they rushed through those last couple of steps, knowing Pharaoh's army was closing in behind them. I just can't even imagine. I do know I would be jumping, dancing, shouting, and singing praises to Him as they were. The only problem was that just a few miles down the road, they forgot all about what had happened and what the Lord did, and all that exhortation of praise turned to worry, doubt, and complaining. This became a common trait for the Israelites, and for us as well.

We must brand, imprint, etch, and engrave these moments in our hearts and minds so they're never forgotten; that way, when the hard times come, and they will, we can still sing these **beautiful** songs of praise because we know and remember that Abba has done it before, and **He will do it again**. So even in the midst of the worst battle, storm, or situation, we can dance, sing, jump, and shout over the awesomeness of our God, knowing He will bring us to the other side victoriously.

Abba, thank You for Your unending faithfulness, amazing goodness, and powerful right hand that delivers us from our enemies. We worship, praise, and adore you always, with **all** we are and have, in Yeshua's perfect and beautiful name, amen.

August 7

1 John 3:4

Whosoever committeth sin transgresseth also the law: for sin is the transgression of the law.

Our world today tends to believe and teach that the law of the Lord is bad, burdensome, and impossible to keep. This verse tells us quite the opposite; it's saying if we transgress against it, we sin. I think we are being led to look at it through the wrong eyes or lens. The law of the Lord is perfect, and He gave it to His children, **us**, to protect, keep, and set apart and free us, free from the true bondage Satan has planned to entrap us in with all his lies and deceit. Abba loves us so much to set these guardrails in place to keep us from the danger and death that awaits us on the other side, the fatal end He sees, and we don't. The deliberate and intentional breaking of these safeguards subjects our lives to a world of sin, bondage, and death.

It is pretty slick of the enemy to flip the scenario and say that God's way is bondage, that you're not truly free, and to deceive one into believing that his way, the way that leads to death, is true freedom. That is just so crazy to me, but he is good at what he does and trips the best of us up with it. Praise the Lord, He has given us His written Word to have so we can know the truth. Sin is the breaking of God's law, the law He set in place to keep us set apart and separate from the world. We are His children, a holy people and these laws are life and keep us safe. We are blessed when we obey them and when we trust and believe He knows best and established them for our good. He is a good, good Father who loves us beyond comprehension and is **perfect** in **all** His ways.

Thank You, Abba, for loving us so much to want to protect and keep us from Satan and all his lies and tactics. Help us to know and believe **all** you set in place is perfect, and it is a blessing to be **obedient** to you in it **all**, in Yeshua's name, amen.

August 8

Proverbs 3:1–2

1) My son, forget not my law; but let thine heart keep my commandments: 2) for length of days, and long life, and peace, shall they add to thee.

I know I want length of days, long life, and sweet peace to see my children's, children's children. Yes, how I long for extra days, and to have His peace that passeth understanding through it all. It seems unreal and impossible, but His Word is true and sure, so it's **not** if I listen and do! Verses five and six say, "Trust in the LORD with ALL thine heart, and lean NOT unto thine own understanding, in ALL thy ways acknowledge Him, and He shall direct thy paths." The Hebrew definition of *direct* is to make straight, smooth, right.[35] We must **trust**, **lean not**, and acknowledge Him in **all** things. We must learn to die to self and know His way is far better. When He chastens and corrects us, we must **not** become weary but know it is good; it is out of His love for us He is doing it, and it shows we are His children, verses eleven and twelve says.

We must desire to find wisdom and get understanding. His Word says they're better than silver and gold and more precious than rubies, that **nothing** we can desire compares to them. Wisdom to know and understanding to do; it's a Tree of Life, it says, to them that lay hold. It says to **not** let them depart from our eyes and keep sound wisdom and discretion; they are life and grace to us: when kept, thy foot shall not stumble and we shall walk safely, we shall not fear and our sleep shall be sweet, we shall not be afraid of sudden fear, for the Lord shall be our **confidence**! How I long to live and walk daily in this place; just reading and meditating on it brings such peace. Imagine what living and walking in it would bring.

Abba, help us to desire and seek wisdom, to get understanding and walk, follow, and acknowledge You in **all** our ways, always, in Yeshua's powerful name, amen.

August 9

Matthew 23:12

And whosoever shall exalt himself shall be abased; and he that shall humble himself shall be exalted.

Yeshua made it very clear that we should never exalt ourselves, worry about another being exalted over us, or be concerned with having the chief seat, rank, status, or popularity. All those who exalt themselves and find their identity in these things He says will be abased. The Hebrew word for *abased* is *Tapeinoo*—and its definition is: "to be given a lower rank, humiliate, to be brought low, depress, make lower in value."[36] Yeshua said the Pharisees were guilty of exalting themselves, that they care more about status and what they looked like than about justice, mercy, and matters of the heart. Being the greatest should have made them a servant to all.

It's important to learn from and use this example in our own lives and actions. We never need to worry or fight to exalt ourselves, for if we always remain humble in all things, He **will** exalt us. We need to remember that in being exalted, we must become servants with the attitude of, "What can I do for you" and "Let me help you find the one who can do for you what He did for me." A servant should get excited and happy about helping others succeed. Sometimes I wonder when I've been humiliated or embarrassed if it may have been God's way of abasing me to bring me back into a proper light of who I am in Him because I may have been exalting myself beyond where I belonged. I think it's an easy thing for our flesh to fall into, and we must be alert, watchful, and careful to remain **humble** in **all things always**.

Abba, help us to stay humble always, and when You exalt us as Your Word says You will, help us to remain humble with a pure heart before You, in Your precious Son Yeshua's name ,we ask this, amen.

August 10

Jeremiah 29:11

For I know the thoughts that I think toward you, saith the LORD, thoughts of peace, and not of evil, to give you an expected end.

I love how Abba delivers His children a word of hope amid their being taken into captivity by His hand and allowing. Even in His execution of judgment, He still loved His children and gave them hope for a future. In verse seven, He tells them to seek the peace of the city that He caused them to be carried captive to and to pray unto Him for it. Then He says these profound words "For in the Peace thereof shall ye have Peace," basically saying, "Hey, it's up to you, I've allowed this in My perfect judgment to happen, but I am giving you a choice to choose peace amid it and trust Me to deliver you in due time," conveying throughout that He has thoughts of peace and not evil toward them and to give them an expected end.

What God executes such perfect judgment and discipline with such genuine and true love that carries and holds us through it all. What an awesome, beautiful and perfect Abba we have.

Thank You, Abba, that even when we don't deserve it, You are still true to Your nature, a loving Father who holds and keeps us, giving us an expected hope in the middle of our discipline and correction. There is just **none** like you that has such **perfect ways**, **perfect justice**, and **perfect love**.

August 11

Genesis 2:24

Therefore shall a man leave his father and mother, and shall cleave unto his wife: and they shall be one flesh.

Earlier Genesis 2:18, it says the Lord said that it was not good that a man should be alone, that He would make a help meet for him, and He took a rib from Adam and made what Adam called *woman*. He said, "this is now bone of my bones and flesh of my flesh." Abba knew it was not good for a man to be alone, that he needed companionship, he needed a help mate. Ecclesiastes 4:9 says: "Two are better than one; because they have a good reward for their labor, for if one falls the other will lift him up, if two lie together, then they have heat to stay warm."

Marriage was part of God's plan for man, for a man and woman to fall in love, marry, and fill the earth with more of God's children. When finding that one God has for us, we need to rejoice, be grateful, and cherish it with every part of our being. God's heart cared so deeply about every need we would have and perfectly made ways of meeting and filling each one of them. His thoughts and provisions for us are constant and without end, setting the example of how a husband and wife should love and care for each other.

Help us to cherish and love each other as You do us, Abba, to always put the other before ourselves, and love each other unconditionally and relentlessly with all we have, **always**, in Yeshua's name, amen.

August 12

John 1:17

For the law was given by Moses, but grace and truth came by Jesus Christ-Yeshua Hamashiach. (His proper Hebrew name)

So, Moses delivered the Law to us, God's instructions, for how we should live. Yeshua delivered the truth that His Father's law and ways are right and perfect and showed us by walking it out perfectly. Then He said, "**Follow me**" and "**Do what I do**." He delivered grace by laying His own life down and being that perfect blood sacrifice for our sins to wash and cleanse us from **all** unrighteousness so we may become part of His family. Talk about the perfect plan, the perfect example, the Son coming and walking out His Father's perfect will, then dying and shedding His perfect blood to wash us clean so we can become family and walk out the Father's perfect will as He did.

God set in stone His perfect law, Moses delivered it, Yeshua came in the flesh and walked it out to show us what it looked like, and then shed His blood to wash away all our sins and give us the opportunity to walk and live like Him. How much clearer can it get?

Thank You, Abba, for sending Your perfect law for us, for sending Your only begotten Son for us. Thank You, Yeshua, for being obedient to Abba and walking out His will perfectly for us to learn from and then laying Your life down for us so we can now live.

August 13

Philemon 1:2

And to our beloved Apphia, and Archippus our fellowsoldier, and to the church in thy house.

I love this, a church in his house, how beautiful. Home churches are not something new. In fact, they are extremely old. It's so funny thinking about this because just tonight at the dinner table, we were playing this table topics game that we play sometimes when eating. The question was, "When are old things better than new things?" This would have been a great one to bring up and talk about. I believe here the old is better because having church in a home made it more personable and intimate compared to the church's today filled with hundreds of people that just get lost in the shuffle.

Philemon had church in his home, and people came and gathered on the Sabbath and read the Word. Read their instruction manual on how to live, remembering and teaching their children of all the ways God continued to always show up and deliver His people, how He never left or forsook them, and how He led them continually. Reading this tonight just gave me such encouragement seeing as this past Saturday, it's exactly what we did in our house—what we have been doing for a couple of years now, and sometimes I must remind myself that God brought me here for a reason, and this is **good**.

Thank You, Abba, for taking me back to some old so I could learn something new. You are above and beyond **amazing** and loved with a whole heart.

August 14

Isaiah 54:17

No weapon that is formed against thee shall prosper; and every tongue that shall rise against thee in judgment thou shalt condemn. This is the heritage of the servants of the LORD, and their righteousness is of me, saith the LORD.

This was the word spoken over Dad and I when we graduated from Minister Candidate School. I know God saw my heart and mind and knew how afraid and worried I was about what people may say about me as I began whatever it was He had awaiting me. My past addiction the Lord delivered me from had plagued and scarred my life with many terrible memories, situations, and circumstances. There was **no** pretty tapestry of my life; only ugly, dark, horrific memories of a life that was worse than most people's nightmares. How would anyone ever listen to me, take me seriously, or care about anything I had to say?

I was believing the lie that they would all only ever see me as the useless, lying, good-for-nothing addict I used to be. Then the Father spoke this verse over me. He knew exactly where I was and what I needed to hear and know. This verse has given me the courage to share all the ugliness of my past with others and the security and surety that He's got my back if anyone has anything to say. Any tongue that rises against you in judgment shall be condemned. It's **all** for **His glory**! If we are His servants, doing what He's called us to, and our righteousness is now found in Him alone, then He will handle the weapons and tongues that may try to rise up against us. This **is** our heritage. He's got it, and we need **not** worry. **Go, do,** and **be all** He's called you to, knowing you never have to worry or fret.

Thank You, Lord, for giving us this heritage, this security and surety in You that You will always have our back and fight our battles. You are surely more than we deserve. In Yeshua's holy name, amen.

August 15

Psalm 111:10

The fear of the LORD is the beginning of wisdom: a good under-standing have all they that do His commandments: His praise endureth forever.

Hmm, so I can try to understand His commands, what they mean, who they were for, if they are still to be followed today, if they are burdensome or good, or I can just **do them** and have a **good understanding**, as this verse says. Why must we complicate everything and try to dissect every aspect of everything instead of just taking Him at His Word and **obeying** it?

The fear of the LORD, the reverent awe and respect of Him is the beginning of wisdom. Then wisdom directs us to obedience to Him and His commands, which leads to a good understanding of the loving Father's fullness of goodness and mercy that we have. **His praise endures forever, amen!**

Help us, Abba, to have that reverent fear before You that we don't question but just **do** Your commands, knowing You are good and perfect in every way, and so are Your commands, in Your Son Yeshua's perfect name, amen.

August 16

James 1:22

But be ye doers of the word, and not hearers only, deceiving your own selves.

When we hear the Word, I mean truly hear it, it should change us so we begin to walk it out. If we never begin to walk in the Word and do what it says, then we are just deceiving ourselves and truly haven't heard it at all.

The Word brings life and blessings when not just heard but obeyed. It's like using a map to get to a certain location but not following what it says; you come up lost in the wrong place. The Word is our map to navigate us through this place that is really not our home to a safe arrival at our true home for eternity with the Father. If we never truly hear it, follow it, and do it, we end up deceived and lost for eternity.

Abba, help us to take Your Word seriously and not just be hearers of it but truly become doers of it, all of it, and all the truths it holds, so eternity with You becomes our reality, in Yeshua's name, amen.

August 17

Leviticus 10:8–9

8) And the LORD spake unto Aaron, saying, 9) Do not drink wine nor strong drink, thou, nor thy sons with thee, when ye go into the tabernacle of the congregation, lest ye die: it shall be a statute for ever throughout your generations.

Just six verses prior in Leviticus 10:2, the Lord devoured Aaron's sons Nadab and Abihu for offering strange fire before the Lord in the tabernacle. What is the strange fire they offered in verse one that got them killed? There's been many debates over the years, but as I read this and continue on, just six short verses later, the Lord is commanding Aaron that **no** wine or strong drink shall be drunk before entering the tabernacle or they will **die**! I can only be led to think that they must have had something to drink before going in to light the fire, and it was strange fire, so they died at the hand of the Lord.

Proceeding on to verse ten, the Lord says, "That they may put difference between Holy and unholy, and between unclean and clean." As I prayerfully thought and meditated on these verses, there was a question posed in my spirit, which I believe was the Lord, asking: Where does He live today? Where does His Spirit live and dwell today? 1 Corinthians 6:19–20 states: "Know ye not that your body is a Temple of the Holy Spirit which is in you, which ye have from God, and ye are not your own: for ye were bought with a price: glorify God therefore in your body." 1 Corinthians 3:16 states: "Know ye not that ye are a Temple of God, and the Spirit of God dwelleth in you," and verse seventeen goes on to say, "the Temple of God is Holy and such are ye." It reminded me of verse ten in Leviticus, where God says: "that ye may put a difference between Holy and unholy." So if we are the Temple today, He dwells in us, and we are to be holy as He is and put a difference between holy and unholy, does what He told Aaron for him and his sons and all the generations apply to us as well? I believe it's definitely something to thoughtfully meditate on and pray about.

Abba, help us to hear and understand how You would have us walk and live as Your temple that Your presence dwells in so we may be set apart and holy as You are, in Yeshua's holy name, amen.

August 18

Mark 9:49–50

49) For every one shall be salted with fire, and every sacrifice shall be salted with salt. 50) Salt is good: but if the salt have lost his saltness, wherewith will ye season it? Have salt in yourselves, and have peace one with another.

Matthew 5:13 says: "Ye are the salt of the Earth: but if the salt has lost his savour, wherewith shall it be salted? It is thenceforth good for nothing, but to be cast out, and to be trodden under foot of men." As I researched this verse and what it truly means to be the salt and have that salt in ourselves, I had to take a deeper look into the qualities of salt. I was astonished to find out salt has many more great uses than just a flavor enhancer and preserving agent. I learned that it is a texture enhancer as well. For example, it takes the correct amount of salt when making yeast bread to come out with the proper texture for the bread. It is a nutrient source essential for survival; it helps contract muscles and conducts nerve impulses, and it sustains the proper balance of minerals and water in the body, all in moderation, of course. It is used as a binding agent by causing the gelatinization of proteins, which holds products together. It raises the boiling point of water, which causes water to boil quicker. It's a color enhancer, preventing meats from turning gray or muddy. It brightens the golden color of bread crust by increasing the caramelization. It melts freezing ice and snow. It has been known to kill some types of bacteria, help heal wounds faster, and help heal a sore throat.

Wow, I was overwhelmed seeing all the properties and qualities of salt and comparing it to how we as God's children should be. I believe one would benefit greatly from researching and studying the qualities and uses of salt and then learning how God meant for those uses and qualities to be applied in our lives as His children. He says we are to be the salt and light. Taking time to dig and study this gave me a better understanding of what it truly means. Take time to study each one and put it in perspective of human life instead of food. Like a little salt in us can melt a **cold**, **icy heart**, the salt in us can heal a wounded heart and so on. We are the salt of the earth. Let's truly figure out what that means and **be it**!

Abba, help us to dive into Your Word deeper always so we can know and understand the words You are speaking to us and all You're calling us to be. It truly changes everything, Lord, when we do, in Yeshua's beautiful name, amen.

August 19

Numbers 18:25-26

25) And the LORD spake unto Moses, saying, 26) Thus speak unto the Levites, and say unto them, When ye take of the children of Israel the tithes which I have given you from them for your inheritance, then ye shall offer up an heave offering of it for the LORD, even a tenth part of the tithe.

This verse confirmed to me what I already believed to be true, that giving back to God the first fruits of our labor, only a tenth of all He's given us is extremely important and comes with a promise. In this verse, God told the Levites, the priests, that they were to give a tithe just like everyone else He required it from. Out of all the tithes that came into the Temple from the children of Israel, which was the Levites inheritance and livelihood, they were to give the first fruit, the 10 percent to the Lord.

God doesn't need our first fruits, that 10 percent; everything in existence belongs to Him anyway. He wants our obedience and hearts in it. When we learn the importance of obedience in this area, we will watch our lives prosper and bloom beyond our wildest expectations. We can't outgive the Lord; it all belongs to Him, so why not just give back the little bit He requires. Malachi 3:10 says it best: "Bring ye all the tithes into the storehouse, that there may be meat in mine house, and prove me now herewith, sayeth the LORD of Hosts, if I will not open you the windows of heaven, and pour you out a blessing, that there shall not be room enough to receive it." **Yes**, I want that. There is no losing when you obey Him. Ask Him where He would have you give those first fruits and then do it. Watch the windows of heaven open.

Abba, teach us this biblical truth deep in our hearts so we don't miss out on all You have for us, in Yeshua's name, amen.

August 20

Proverbs 4:23

Keep thy heart with all diligence; for out of it are the issues of life.

There will be times when I'm in a conversation, and all of a sudden, I spew something out of my mouth and I'm like, "Where did that come from?" Or when I'm angry and upset with someone I love and junk comes out of me, and I think, "How am I capable of this? What is really in me? How is this possibly coming out of me if I love the Lord?" Jeremiah 17:9 says: "The heart is deceitful above all things and desperately wicked, who can know it?" Then it says in 1 Kings 8:39: "For thou, even thou only, knowest the hearts of ALL the children of men." The Lord searches the hearts of man and knows them. He knows all the junk and garbage in our hearts, even when it is not clear to us. I believe that's why Solomon gave warning to keep our hearts with **all** diligence; He knew the heart was and would be the problem.

In Matthew 12:34, Yeshua told the Pharisees that "out of the abundance of the heart the mouth speaks." How important it is to guard our hearts, to have a heart like Abba. David cried out to the LORD in Psalm 51:10: "Create in me a clean heart, O God; and renew a right spirit within me." The heart is where all the issues of life begin; it is a place where we need Abba to shine His flood-light, clean it, and make it pure, then we must guard it with all diligence daily, minute by minute, with each step we take. Pray this prayer with me today.

Abba, create in me a clean and pure heart. Help me to guard it and not let any junk grow or take root, so my words and life can be a reflection of You always, in your Son Yeshua's powerful name, I pray this, amen.

August 21

Titus 1:2

In hope of eternal life, which God, that cannot lie, promised before the world began.

This is our hope of glory, our goal which we should be aiming for, everlasting life, eternity with Abba and Yeshua. What a paradise it will be: no more tears, no more pain, brighter than the brightest day ever, seen as His glory illuminates all eternity. Wow, our infinite minds can't come close to conceiving the fullness, greatness, and beauty awaiting those who set their affections, hearts, and minds on the Lord, His truths and way that uphold His laws and walk in them.

Romans 6:23 says the wages of sin is death; but the gift of God is eternal life through Yeshua Hamashiach, our Lord. This is a promise to those who love and chose the Lord. He cannot lie. It is impossible for Him to; it is against His very nature! So, we can know that this is a rock-solid truth we can stand on, hope in, and look forward to.

Abba, help us to choose You every minute of every day as we look forward in anticipation to a glorious eternity with You, in Yeshua's name, amen.

August 22

Hebrew 4:9–10

9) There remaineth therefore a rest to the people of God. 10) For he that is entered into His rest, he also hath ceased from his own works, as God did from His.

The Sabbath is a vital day to keep and remember. Jeremiah 17:21–22 states: "Thus saith the LORD, take heed to yourselves and bear NO BURDEN on the Sabbath day, nor bring it by the gates of Jerusalem; neither carry forth a burden out of your houses on the Sabbath day, neither do ye any work, but HALLOW ye the Sabbath day, as I commanded your Fathers."

It wasn't open for debate; His day was to be **hallowed**, and it was for our good. In Mark 2:27, Yeshua in His own words, said: "The Sabbath was made for man, and not man for the Sabbath." It was a good thing, a Blessing for us. Hebrews 4:11 goes on to say: "Let us labour therefore to enter into that rest, lest any man fall after the same example of unbelief." These are simple commands that we complicate when they bring such amazing blessings and joy.

Abba, engrave Your commands on our hearts and minds so we can know the full blessing of walking in them, in Yeshua's powerful name, amen.

August 23

Ruth 1:16

And Ruth said, Intreat me not to leave thee, or to return from following after thee: for whither thou goest, I will go; and where thou lodgest, I will lodge: thy people shall be my people, and thy God my God.

Through the tragic loss of her husband, her sons and all her earthly belongings, Naomi believed that the Lord had stretched forth His hand against her. She felt as if He had dealt very bitterly with her and turned away from her. She wanted her daughters-in-law to go back to their home, where they could still have hope for a future. Orpah, her one daughter-in-law, kissed her and went home, but Ruth, even through her own loss of her husband, father-in-law, and brother-in-law, saw something more in Naomi and her God. It was something worth staying for.

Through all the loss and hardship, she saw glimmers of a true God and His faithfulness. How Naomi lived her life must have spoken volumes to Ruth about her character, and not just the character of Naomi, but of Naomi's God as well, to cause Ruth to want to make Naomi's people her people and Naomi's God her God. Because of her choice to follow Naomi and the only true God, her life was blessed beyond measure as she became part of the lineage of our Savior Yeshua. What a tragic and devastating situation that God used and purposed for greatness and joy. He **always** has a **perfect** plan.

Lord, help us to trust You in and through the pain and tragedies of our lives, knowing Your perfect plan will use it all for our good and Your glory, in Yeshua's holy name, amen.

August 24

Lamentations 3:22–23

22) It is of the LORD'S mercies that we are not consumed, because His compassions fail not. 23) They are new every morning: Great is thy Faithfulness.

We serve an **awesome**, **powerful**, and **faithful God** who executes judgment and discipline perfectly but loves and has mercy faithfully as well. I was reading in Jeremiah 24 today, and it was talking about how the Lord allowed His people to be carried away by Babylon into captivity for their own good, to protect the true remnant and reject King Zedekiah and his princes and followers. He executed justice, judgment, and discipline perfectly on the evil Zedekiah and his people, all the while, loving and having mercy on His true remnant, even though they fell and failed, and preserving them.

It is of the **Lord's great mercy** we are **not consumed**. I began to think about how many times in my own daily walk with Abba how I fall and fail; sometimes it might just be a little slip, and sometimes it's a crashing fall, but **praise Yah.** His compassion **fails NOT** and **His mercies are new every morning**. **Great is His faithfulness**.

Thank You, Lord, for Your mercies are new every morning, for not consuming us when, at times, it would be perfectly understandable if You did, but instead, having such great compassion on us. Truly, Thy faithfulness is great, in Yeshua's name, amen.

August 25

Jude 1:24–25

24) Now unto him that is able to keep you from falling, and to present you faultless before the presence of His Glory with exceeding joy, 25) To the only wise God our Saviour, be Glory and Majesty, Dominion and Power, both now and ever. Amen.

If we set and fix our eyes on Yeshua, fully putting our hope and trust in Him, continually looking unto Him, the Author and Finisher of our Faith, He will keep us from falling. He will present us faultless before the Father, joyfully. It actually says with exceeding joy. *Exceeding* means **very great**, **extreme** or **go beyond**.[37] He will keep us from falling and will present us with **exceeding joy!** Now that's something that should make us **exceedingly grateful** and **joyful**, causing us to easily proclaim. To the only wise God, our Savior, be glory, majesty, dominion, and power, now and forever, amen!

Abba, thank You for Your Son, our Savior, who came to earth to shed His precious blood for us, to wash us clean and present us before You faultless, to guard, protect us, and keep us from falling. Thank You, Yeshua, for your obedience and faithfulness, for it's only through You and all You did that we can come to the Father and have eternity in His presence.

All glory, majesty, dominion, and power be yours, both now and forever, amen!

August 26

Psalm 91:1

He that dwelleth in the secret place of the most High shall abide under the shadow of the Almighty.

Living in today's world comes with a lot of chaos and craziness. It's hard to slow down and find a place of refuge, place of rest, shelter to just run into for a moment and disconnect from the world. Abba has that place, a secret place in Him we can run into and not just for a moment, but we can remain there always; we can live in that secret place in Him. The word *dwell* in Hebrew translates to *Yaw-shab*, and its definition is: "To have one's abode, inhabit, tarry, stay, **remain**."[38]

There's no other place that compares. Nothing the world has to offer comes close to being in that **secret place** of Abba's, to abiding under the **shadow** of the **Almighty**; it's here we find rest, protection, renewal, and strength. I bid you to read Psalm 91 in its entirety today. It will bless and encourage you.

Father, help us to make our abode in that secret place of Yours, to find our shelter under the shadow of Your wing, and to take up camp there that we will remain forever and never leave, in Yeshua's holy name, amen.

August 27

Matthew 4:10

Then saith Jesus unto him, Get thee hence, Satan: for it is written, Thou shalt worship the Lord thy God, and Him only shalt thou serve.

I just love how every time Satan put something forth in front of Yeshua to tempt Him, Yeshua always answered with; "**It is written**!" He was the Son of God and knew what His Father spoke, but also, He was brought up in the Word as well; He was raised knowing Torah. His parents were Jewish and raised their child knowing God's Word. They studied and taught it to them as the Torah teaches them to do. Luke 2:41 talks about how Yeshua's parents went to Jerusalem every year for the Feast of Passover. They knew Torah and followed it, knew God's feast days, and kept them.

Mary said in Luke 1:38; "Behold the handmaid of the Lord; be it unto me according to thy Word." She was a handmaid of Abba—handmaid is a servant. She served Abba, which means she knew His Word, followed it, and taught it to her child. This gives a powerful example of how important it is for us to know the Word and teach it to our children. I find it so funny that later in this same passage in verse six, Satan quotes scripture to Yeshua and says, "It is written, He shall give His Angels charge concerning thee." So even Satan knows the importance of knowing God's Word, and Satan knows it to the point that he can quote it. That only confirms to me that we might want to make it a priority to really begin to know His Word, to start reading, studying, and meditating on it. We need to allow it to fill us so we can not only stand on it but deflect the attempts of Satan when he tries to use it against us, as he clearly will, for he used it against the Son of God.

Father, help us to yearn for and desire to know Your Word, to begin to pick it up daily and fill our hearts and minds with it so we can learn it, know it, obey it, and stand on it always, in Yeshua's holy name, amen.

August 28

Judges 8:34

And the children of Israel remembered not the LORD their God, who had delivered them out of the hands of all their enemies on every side.

This is once again how the children of Israel would quickly forget all the Lord had done for them. In Judges 6:12, the Angel of the Lord appeared to Gideon and said unto him, "The LORD is with thee, thou mighty man of valour." Gideon was wondering, if this was true, then where were all the miracles which their fathers had told them, saying, "Did not the LORD bring us up from Egypt, but why now is he forsaking us and delivering us into the hands of the Midianites'' (Judg. 6:13). It is here the Lord chooses Gideon to fight and save Israel from the hands of the Midianites.

I encourage you to read these chapters in Judges about Gideon and all he did in defeating the enemy with only 300 men against thousands, so all could see and know it's **not** through man **but only** through God. It is a powerful read and great passage to hold close to in remembering the awesome and miraculous works of our God. Too quickly, we can forget them as the Israelites did if we don't continue to read them, dwell on them, meditate on all He has done, and His goodness to His children. Let's flood our hearts and minds with His Word, remembering constantly all He has done over and over again for His children, so we **never** forget it and be led astray and delivered into the hands of the oppressor who seeks to destroy us.

Abba, thank you for Your Word to remind us always of Your faithfulness over and over again and help us to **never** forget who You are and all You've done, for You are our **only hope**, in Yeshua's mighty name, amen.

August 29

Colossians 1:10–11

10) That ye might walk worthy of the Lord unto all pleasing, being fruitful in every good work, and increasing in the knowledge of God; 11) Strengthened with all might, according to His glorious power, unto all patience and longsuffering with joyfulness.

Our daily walk should be all pleasing to the Father; all the work of our hands should be good and bear fruit. Our hands shouldn't be idle or in mischief of any sort. We should constantly be seeking and searching out His Word, filling ourselves with His truths and ways, and meditating day and night on His Word as it says in Joshua 1:8: "This book of the law shall NOT depart out of thy mouth, but thou shalt meditate therein day and night, that thou mayest observe to do according to ALL that is written there in, for then shalt thou make thy way prosperous, and then thou shalt have good success."

I so love that verse. He should be the very essence of our lives, and we should constantly increase in His knowledge, continually growing deeper in our walk with Him. We walk strengthened in Him, by the knowledge of His Word and trust in who He is. We put on Him in all things that we may be and remain **joyful** in times of trouble, walking through the struggles and offenses, temptations and tests, with all patience and longsuffering knowing it's on the **Rock which we stand**, truly believing He works all things for good. Romans 8:28 tells us that He works all things together for good to them that **love God** and are called according to **His purpose**. It's when this truth takes hold that we can remain **joyful** in and through **all things**, eyes on Him, fully engaged, and in love with our Abba.

Help Your Word, Daddy, to truly go down deep and take root in our hearts. Help us to love it more than life so it literally becomes life, and we can walk, knowing You and having our full confidence in You, shining Your light and joy always, in Yeshua's beautiful name, amen.

August 30

Exodus 3:14

And God said unto Moses, I AM THAT I AM: and He said, Thus shalt thou say unto the children of Israel, I AM hath sent me unto you.

Wow, the name alone should have been an eye opener, should have spoken loud enough to **who He was**; it should have been beyond enough to make them say, "Hey, this is someone we can believe in and trust." It should be enough for us today, but how many times does He move on our behalf and split the seas, and we take the next step and begin to fear, doubt, and cry again?

He says, "I AM THAT I AM," not, "I was," not, "I will be," but "I AM." Yesterday, tomorrow, and forever, He is the I AM for every situation; we can **always** stand on that and not fret.

Thank You, Lord, for all that You are, for being the **great** I AM today and forever in our lives, so we never have to question or doubt, in Yeshua's name, amen.

August 31

1 Peter 1:15

But as He which hath called you is Holy, so be ye Holy in all manner of conversation.

Holy in Hebrew is ἅγlos/*hagios*, meaning: "sacred, physically pure, morally blameless, consecrated."[39] *Conversation* in Hebrew is ἀναοτροφή, meaning: "Manner of life, conduct, behavior."[40] Peter goes on in verse sixteen to say: "Because it is written, Be ye Holy, for I am Holy." Peter knew it was written in Leviticus 11:44, where the Lord told them to be holy as He is holy. The Father must have known it was possible for us to attain holiness if He tells us to be holy. He knew we could stay physically pure, morally blameless and consecrated to Him if we tried. He didn't say it would be easy to live in a fallen world, but it would be possible to do because He called us to it and would be with us in walking it out.

If we truly love Abba, then we will want to obey and please Him, and we will dedicate and consecrate ourselves unto Him and work hard to be holy as He is. It will take work, dedication, and a genuine desire to want to be obedient. It might mean we will have to say no to certain things, let go of some stuff we want, and be separated from things we may long to be part of, but it will be so worth it, even though it may be difficult and painful at times. Holiness is possible!

Help us, Abba, to be pure, blameless, consecrated and set apart for You, to be holy as You are in **all** our conversations, conducts, and life, in Yeshua's holy name, amen.

September 1

2 Corinthians 10:5

Casting down imaginations, and every high thing that exalteth itself against the knowledge of God, and bringing into captivity every thought to the obedience of Christ.

Daily, many thoughts will come across the highway of our minds. We live in a world that bombards our minds with information—good, bad, old, and new. We can't escape it; God made our minds like an expressway for thoughts to travel and get things done. It's up to us, though, to pay close attention to the kind of thoughts we allow to travel on the highways and byways of our minds.

The Bible tells us we should think on good things, and our thoughts should line up and be in obedience to His Word. We should think on things above, like Him, His will, and way. Think on positive things His Word says about us, like Psalm 139:14, "You are Fearfully & Wonderfully made," and Luke 12:7 says: "The very hairs of your head are numbered, Fear Not." Philippians 4:8 tells us to think on true things, honest, just, pure, lovely and of good report. These are the thoughts we should have on the highways of our minds. The enemy wants to bombard our minds with lies, thoughts that are wrong and negative, and thoughts that don't line up with God's Word; thoughts that will drag us down or only bring temporary joy, but as the mother bird that fiercely chases the predator away that's trying to get to her nest, that's how we should be chasing away the thoughts that don't belong. Taking those thoughts into captivity, discarding them before they ever have a chance to run through the highways of our minds and set up camp.

Abba, help us to make sure every thought is lined up to Your Word. Help us to cast out all the bad and false thoughts and lies and not give them any place for any amount of time, but to only allow Your thoughts of good and truth to be established in our hearts and minds, both now and always, in Yeshua's powerful and mighty name, amen.

September 2

Malachi 3:6

For I am the LORD, I change NOT; therefore ye sons of Jacob are not consumed.

He is the same yesterday, today, and forever, Hebrews 13:8 states. He will **never** change. He spoke the Word; it went forth and established the world. His truth and purposes remain forever unchanging, unwavering, consistent and permanent **truth**; Unaltered by even Yeshua, but actually walked out in **perfect obedience** as an example for us.

He will **never change**, His Word will **never change**, and His will will **never change**. He is perfect in all His ways and needs no changing. We might be better if we believe Him, take Him at His Word, and stop trying to change it or believing those who have. His Word and truth will stand unchanged forever!

Thank You, Father, for being true to who You are and Your Word, for never changing and always faithful, remaining the same in a constantly changing world. It's a blessing to know there is one truth that never will change, in Yeshua's name, who gave it all to show and save us, amen.

September 3

Isaiah 46:9

Remember the former things of old: for I am God, and there is none else; I am God, and there is NONE like me.

We read yesterday how He never changes, and here He is telling them, and us, to remember the former things, the things of old, for they are truth and life. If we choose not to follow them, then it will end as before in the same way, destruction, and death.

He doesn't change. It is good to remember who He is and all He has said, His love, mercy, justice, and judgments. He is the only one true God, and when all the false gods and idols utterly perish forever, He, His Word, and counsel will continue to stand. There is **none** like Him and **nothing** comes close to comparing; **always remember**.

Help us, Lord, to know and remember Your Word is truth and is the only thing that will stand forever; there is **no one like You**, in Yeshua's name, amen.

September 4

Genesis 18:14

Is anything too hard for the LORD? At the time appointed I will return unto thee, according to the time of life, and Sarah shall have a son.

I love when God makes the impossible possible. Sarah was well past the childbearing age, so the very thought of her conceiving was preposterous, but it's times like this that God loves to shine and show just who He is and what He is capable of. He is a mind-blowing God, and **nothing** is too hard for Him. I can't even tell you the amount of times He has taken my breath away, turning the impossible into reality. Just like with my miracle daughter, Bethany, when all the doctors said she would never make it, God said it won't be how they say, but how I say, and here she is today, twenty-four years old and thriving. Don't ever underestimate or second guess what He is capable of because when you think He can't, He'll rock your world!

Is there anything too hard for the Lord? Will you doubt? Will you laugh? Will you dismiss it as crazy? Or will you take Him at His Word and believe there is **nothing impossible** for our God; nothing too big, nothing too hard, absolutely nothing impossible for the one who created **all** and holds **all** things. He is a mountain-moving, sea-parting, sick and lame healing, raising from the dead, miracle-working God that makes the **impossible possible**.

Thank You for being the God of the impossible, Abba. Help us to believe, trust, and stand firm in the truth of this always, **never** wavering, in Yeshua's Mighty name, amen.

September 5

Psalm 103:17–18

17) But the mercy of the LORD is from everlasting to everlasting upon them that fear Him, and His righteousness unto children's children; 18) To such as keep His covenant, and to those that remember His commandments to do them.

This is the blessing for them that keep His covenant and do His commands that stand in awe and reverence of Him and His righteousness and do their best to be obedient. His mercy will be from everlasting to everlasting to our children and our grandchildren. They and us will experience the awesome reality of His unchanging love when we live and walk in His commands and are sincere in this covenant relationship with Him.

His mercy will remain unchanging and will continue **forever**, something we are not even worthy of, He will shower us, our children, and our children's children. It's beyond worth it to me to follow all He is and says. His mercy and grace alone cause me to stand in awe and wonder, for He is such a loving and perfect Father.

Lord, Your commands are beautiful and perfect, and though we fall short at times, it doesn't change how perfect they are. Your covenant is a blessing we don't deserve to be a part of. Help us to always stand in reverence and awe before You, Your glory, and righteousness, for there is **none** like You who loves so deeply, waits so patiently, and gives so freely everything that is so **good, right, and true**. May Your praise continually be on our lips and Your Word always hidden in our hearts, in Yeshua's beautiful name, amen.

September 6

Ecclesiastes 3:11

He hath made everything beautiful in His time: also He hath set the world in their heart, so that no man can find out the work that God maketh from the beginning to the end.

We will never be God or know what He knows, those secret things that are for Him alone. I remember one time struggling deeply, trying to figure something out that wasn't meant for me to know. I was seriously a wreck sobbing in true fear before Him, trying to just hear an answer when I heard, "If you knew all things, you'd be God, and I wouldn't."

Though I didn't get the answer I was looking for, I got one profound enough to give me peace in not knowing. Sometimes I find myself going back to that question, and I have to remind myself He's God, and I'm not, and it's OK that I don't know. What we are to know is that He has made **everything beautiful** in **His** time, and we must find rest in knowing that and live each moment to its fullest in the beauty of that, not worrying about what we're not even meant to know.

Abba, help us to find true contentment in every step of our journey, experiencing Your beauty in and through it all, things known and things unknown, in every season, with the beauty each one holds, in Yeshua's name, amen.

September 7

Philippians 4:11

Not that I speak in respect to want: for I have learned, in what-soever state I am, therewith to be content.

I'm not sure I have fully learned this yet, but I do know I want this to be where I live; content wherever I am, knowing that having and walking with my heavenly Father is **all** that is needed for complete fulfillment.

I lived most of my life in the state of, "I want what I want when I want it, and I'm going to have it." I thought those wants would bring happiness and feelings of fulfillment, only to find out the small amount of joy it brought **never** lasted. In fact, many times, getting what I wanted only ended up in more problems and in a worse state than before. If I only knew the words of this verse much earlier in life and truly took them to heart, learning to be content in whatever state I was, I could have saved myself from a lot of grief and hurt.

Abba, help the words of this verse take root in our hearts so we can truly be content in whatever state we are in because we have You, in Yeshua's holy name, amen.

September 8

Jeremiah 17:5

Thus saith the LORD; cursed be the man that trusteth in man, and maketh flesh his arm, and whose heart departeth from the LORD.

We are imperfect beings, and though we try and have the best of intentions, we, at some point, somehow, will let someone down. We will fail them or even hurt them. I remember a point in my life when the Lord had just delivered me from my addiction. He sent somebody to take me under his or her wing and help me. I began putting my trust in that person, running to him or her instead of the Lord, and he or she began to occupy that seat on the throne of my heart. The Lord started showing me that this couldn't be, and I needed to give Him that rightful place in my heart and life, that my hope and trust needed to be in Him alone.

All I can say is when God brings something to your attention and tells you it needs to be fixed, it's best to heed and listen. If we, as I did, become rebellious and hardheaded and choose not to listen, then things can end in an extremely painful way. "Cursed be the man that trusteth in man," ouch! The lesson was hard, but I learned it well.

Father, help us to always put our hope and trust in You alone, knowing in doing so, You will help us, keep us, and not leave or forsake us ever, and we will be blessed, in Yeshua's name, amen.

September 9

Psalm 113:3

From the rising of the sun unto the going down of the same the LORD'S name is to be praised.

All day, every day, He is more than worthy of our praise and worship. We should be praising Him when the sun rises, when it sets, and all the minutes in between, not just in our devotion time, studies, awesome concerts, or Sabbath or worship nights; not just when things are good, when we're happy, or just when we are feeling it, **but always, all day**, and **in all things**. That is what it says!

So many times, I've thought, "How is this possible, Lord? It seems actually impossible in this life we live in and flesh we walk in, but it can't be because your Word wouldn't tell us to do it if it wasn't possible." It may be hard, it may take dying to the flesh, so out of **obedience,** we can, but it is possible. It will take work and fixing our minds minute by minute on Him, and even when we don't feel it, make the conscious choice out of obedience and do it. Psalm 118:24 says: "This is the day that the LORD hath made; we WILL rejoice and be glad in it!" It takes daily waking up and choosing to praise Him and being glad and rejoicing in another day to worship and serve Him with and in **all** we do.

Abba, we love You so much and long to worship You. Help us to learn to do it minute by minute, from the time the sun comes up until the time it sets, and in **all** things, always, in Yeshua's name, amen.

September 10

Romans 8:1

There is therefore now no condemnation to them which are in Christ Jesus, who walk not after the flesh, but after the Spirit.

If we are walking according to the Spirit of the Lord, then we may suffer through correction and chastening when we, as His children, mess up like children often do. Hebrews 12:6 says the Lord chastens those He loves, and Proverbs 3:12 states who the Lord loveth He corrects, but one thing we will not experience from Him is condemnation.

Condemnation is not of the Lord, for there is now **no** condemnation to them in Christ Jesus who walk after the Spirit. If you're feeling condemned in any way, then you need to stand firmly and boldly, declaring this verse with your mouth and tell Satan you **will not** be held bondage through condemnation. Yeshua, who **loves** us, **corrects** us but the enemy, who **dislikes** us, **condemns** us. It's important to remember that.

Abba, thank You, Father, for loving us enough to not condemn us when we mess up or make a wrong turn, but instead, You discipline and correct us with a genuine, unconditional love that turns our feet and hearts back to You and keeps us held in You. In Yeshua's name, amen!

September 11

John 6:35

And Jesus said unto them, I am the bread of life: he that cometh to me shall never hunger; and he that believeth on me shall never thirst.

Yeshua was telling the multitude around Him that He is the true Bread of Life, not to labor for the meat that perishes but for the meat, which endures to everlasting life. The Father sent manna from heaven to feed and sustain His children in the wilderness, then He sent the True Bread, His Son Yeshua, who will feed us with the Bread of Life, and we will never hunger again. He will give us a drink, and we will never thirst again, for He is the fountain of everlasting life that never runs dry.

We must believe that He is who He says He is, the Son of the Living God, and He came down from heaven, from the Father, to be the bread that gives life to the world. In verse thirty-eight, He says, "I came down from Heaven NOT to do my own will, but the will of HIM WHO SENT ME." It's the Father's will and way that leads to eternal Life through the Bread of Life, His Son, Yeshua.

Father, help us to know and believe Yeshua is that Bread of Life that came down from You to teach us Your **perfect will** and feed us with Your **truth**, where we will never hunger or thirst again, in Yeshua's mighty name, amen.

September 12

Proverbs 28:9

He that turneth away his ear from hearing the law, even his Prayer shall be abomination.

You don't hear this verse much today. Instead, it's more common to hear that the law is burdensome, too hard, and that's why it was done away with. That sure is a **stark contrast** to what God is saying here in Proverbs.

He says the one who turns his ear away from hearing the Law, his prayer will be an **abomination** to Him; ouch, that's a **harsh** word. *Abomination*, in its full definition, means: "disgust, detest, loath, hate, disgrace."[41] Our prayers will be a disgust to the Lord. He will detest and hate them; they will be a disgrace to Him if we refuse to hear His law. I know I desire my prayers to rise to a Father who **delights** in hearing and answering them, which causes me to **delight** in hearing and following His law. How about you?

Abba, help our ears to not turn away from hearing Your law so our prayers **never** become an abomination to You, in Yeshua's beautiful name, amen.

September 13

Psalm 119:9–16

9) BETH. Wherewithal shall a young man cleanse his way? By taking heed thereto according to thy word. 10) With my whole heart have I sought thee: O let me not wander from thy commandments. 11) Thy word have I hid in mine heart, that I might not sin against thee. 12) Blessed art thou, O LORD: teach me thy statutes. 13) With my lips have I declared all the judgments of thy mouth. 14) I have rejoiced in the way of thy testimonies, as much as in all riches. 15) I will meditate in thy precepts, and have respect unto thy ways. 16) I will delight myself in thy statutes: I will not forget thy word.

OH, what beautiful and powerful and lasting and true words to walk and live our lives by. His Word stands **forever**. It's proven the test of time, and we are blessed for holding tight to it and walking by it. Psalm 119:1–2 says, "Blessed are those who walk in the Law of the LORD and Blessed are they that keep His Testimonies, and that seek Him with their WHOLE HEART." *Blessed* means "special favor, mercy or benefit, endowed with divine favor and protection, privileged."[42] I want that; it's a win-win situation.

Lord, help us to know Your Word more and more daily, to truly make it the source of life we live and walk by, to meditate on it, hide it in our hearts, and delight in following it always, in Yeshua's precious name, amen.

September 14

1 John 3:18

My little children, let us not love in word, neither in tongue; but in deed and in truth.

Anyone can say pretty much anything, but to put those words into actions shows the genuine and true intent of the heart. What would life look like if Yeshua said all He did and then never went to the cross? Life would be pretty hopeless and bleak.

We must back up our words with actions. In fact, maybe we should be people of **few words** and **great deeds**. There is an old saying that says: "Preach the gospel; if necessary, use words." Words are a dime a dozen, but loving, living, and giving in truth is a precious and rare treasure that can change a heart, life, and history.

Abba, help us to be people of few words but great and genuine actions that make a real difference in this desperate world, in Yeshua's powerful name, amen.

September 15

Proverbs 6:16–19

16) These six things doth the LORD hate: yea, seven are an abomination unto Him: 17) A proud look, a lying tongue, and hands that shed innocent blood, 18) An heart that deviseth wicked imaginations, feet that be swift in running to mischief, 19) A false witness that speaketh lies, and he that soweth discord among brethren.

Wow, once again, that word *abomination*—this is deep. In reading these, there are some that I was like, "Hmm, well, I don't think I devise evil thoughts. I don't think I would shed innocent blood, not even run to mischief. In fact, I flee from it." Some of these, though, might be done more easily and without thought, not realizing they are an abomination to Him. Like a proud look, to exalt yourself, your thoughts, or ways above another's, always thinking in your own mind you're better or right. We are to be humble in our thoughts and actions.

Telling little white lies, thinking it might be less harmful or offensive, instead of being completely honest as His Word says we should be in **all** our dealings and affairs. Like speaking falsely of someone else, how often do we say things about someone we're not really sure of, or how often do we say things when we're mad that really aren't completely correct and have a sided curve to them? I know there have been times I didn't even realize it was what I had been doing. Accusing one of something without evidence or proof is stating falsehoods. What about sowing discord? Wow, this one is tough; talking about maybe a hurt, a deep hurt that causes others to form an opinion of another or deliberate gossip. It might do us well to dig into these and examine our lives and hearts and then guard them to keep clear and far from these things that God hates.

Help us, Abba, to search ourselves honestly so that we don't walk or act in any of these things that You **hate**, in Yeshua's name, amen.

September 16

Ephesians 4:23–24

23) And be renewed in the spirit of your mind; 24) And that ye put on the new man, which after God is created in righteousness and true holiness.

How do we become renewed in the spirit of our minds as Paul is talking about here? It's not a difficult answer to figure out; it's actually quite simple. It's by putting the right stuff in our minds, filling our minds with the Word of God and allowing His Word to wash over us and change us.

Put off the old man, the old way of thinking, the sinful nature, and lusts of the flesh that so easily trip us up, and put on Christ. Learn and acquire His attributes, taking on His character and walking in His truth, putting on the new man He died to make us. Take on His righteousness and holiness, with our eyes fully fixed on Him and our hearts rooted in His Word, allowing it to wash and renew our minds daily.

Father, teach us to daily fill our minds with Your Word that we may always walk renewed before You in holiness and righteousness, in Yeshua's holy and righteous name, amen.

September 17

Isaiah 5:20–21

20) Woe unto them that call evil good, and good evil; that put darkness for light, and light for darkness; that put bitter for sweet, and sweet for bitter! 21) Woe unto them that are wise in their own eyes, and prudent in their own sight!

It seems to be man's natural trait to think we are smarter than Jehovah. That we actually have the right to decide what's good and bad, to name what's sin and what's not, to change what He said by manipulating it to fit our wants and lifestyles. In trying to act so wise, we become major fools. The creation creating ways opposed to the **Creator**—imagine that.

Oh Jehovah, forgive us for our wrongs, for our trying to change the things that You have established from the beginning of time, for walking in a false belief that we are greater than our Creator and have the right, for following our own wisdom, which has only made us fools. Help us to get back to your **unchanging Word**, the Word spoken and established by You, the only Truth, to live and walk by Your wisdom, which is the only thing that makes us wise and brings life, in Yeshua's powerful and mighty name, we ask all this, amen.

September 18

Hebrews 4:16

Let us therefore come boldly unto the throne of grace, that we may obtain mercy, and find grace to help in time of need.

Daily, I need to remember and put this scripture to use. Daily, I need to come boldly unto His Throne of Grace because I fall short daily; whether it's in actions or reactions. My own actions in being too busy to notice the one placed right in front of me that needs a hug, smile, or meal, or I'm late and justify going ten miles over the speed limit to get where I need to be. How about when I purchase something I know I can't afford but justify it by saying I need it or think I deserve it; better yet, I want to bless someone else with it when there are so many other ways I could bless someone. All the things I know better but do anyway because of the cravings of the flesh; from eating to vacationing to just plain wants that aren't prayed about or truly justified.

Then there are the reactions, and that list is far too long to list; negative reacting in a great majority of situations: offenses, hurts, jokes and so on. Needless to say, I am so beyond **grateful** for His Throne of Grace that I can come before and find mercy for all my junk. Just the fact that He extends so much grace to the messes I make and gives me so much Mercy I don't deserve humbles me and takes my breath away.

Abba, help us all to see daily what a **blessing** it is having that Throne of Grace to boldly come before and help us realize just how much we mean to You and how much favor You shed on us, even when we are a mess and don't deserve any of it. Thank You so much for loving us so **greatly**, in Yeshua's name, amen.

September 19

Deuteronomy 6:7–9

7) And thou shalt teach them diligently unto thy children, and shalt talk of them when thou sittest in thine house, and when thou walkest by the way, and when thou liest down, and when thou risest up. 8) And thou shalt bind them for a sign upon thine hand, and they shall be as frontlets between thine eyes. 9) And thou shalt write them upon the posts of thy house, and on thy gates.

There's a saying that goes: "out of sight out of mind," and it holds great truth. If we don't consistently think on things, remember them, teach them, or write them down, we will have a difficult time remembering and walking by them. When we don't meditate, dwell, and know them, it's easy for us to forget. The Lord knew if not taught daily, if not talked about throughout the day, at bedtime, and at rising, if not meditated on, thought about, talked about, His Words and commands would fall by the wayside and eventually be forgotten, like how so many are trying to rewrite history and say some of it never happened.

It's important that we heed these verses, that we truly place them on our door posts, write them on paper, and place them around our homes to see and talk about them with our families so they are constantly on the tip of our tongues; teach them to the future generations so they are **never forgotten**, and allow them to be written on our hearts so we walk by them daily. Forgetting is easy; remembering takes time and work. This is vital for the future of God's children, and it's important that we walk by and teach the Father's commands, so His ways are **never** forgotten.

Lord, may Your words govern our lives, help us to be diligent with all You tell us to do, let us never stop talking about, never stop teaching, and never forget any of Your words and commands to us, in Yeshua's name, amen.

September 20

Psalm 103:11–12

11) For as the heaven is high above the earth, so great is his mercy toward them that fear Him. 12) As far as the east is from the west, so far hath He removed our transgressions from us.

I'll never forget the Lord speaking these words to me over twenty-some years ago now. I wasn't much accustomed at that time to hearing His voice, as I was drowning and dying in my addiction. In fact, when I heard Him speak them to me, I wasn't even aware that they were in the Bible until I read it one day and was like, "That is what You spoke to me, Lord." His Word is powerful, true, brings life, and **never** returns void. It's supreme, and you can stand on it because He and His Word are always faithful! Micah 7:19 says He will cast our sins into the depths of the sea.

God doesn't give us what we deserve because He is merciful, and He does for us what we can't do for ourselves. He does not treat us the way we deserve to be treated; He loves us through the junk. I was hopeless and powerless, and He stepped in and threw all the garbage and sin from the sunrise to as far as the sunset; mere words cannot explain just how awesome, miraculous, powerful, beautiful, faithful, and merciful He is!

Abba Father, You are such a good, good Father, and You meet us where we are with open arms waiting to rescue us from the grip of the enemy. Thank You so much for Your endless, unconditional love and for Your faithfulness and mercy always, in Yeshua's name, amen.

September 21

Revelation 21:4–5

4) And God shall wipe away all tears from their eyes; and there shall be no more death, neither sorrow, nor crying, neither shall there be any more pain: for the former things are passed away. 5) And he that sat upon the throne said, Behold, I make all things new. And he said unto me, Write: for these words are true and faithful.

What a glorious day it will be. No more tears, pain, death—it's almost inconceivable in this world we live in. The last year and a half for me have been a difficult one, to say the least, and that's sugar-coating it. I think I shed more tears, felt more pain, and experienced more loss than in fifty-four years of my life! God is good, though, and He does hold and comfort us through this life. I am grateful beyond words for His steadying hand, peace beyond understanding, saving grace, and His mercies that are new each morning to help me through another day.

Reading this verse gives me **great** joy and anticipation for that day when He makes **all** things new. It gives me comfort in the middle of all this, knowing there is a day coming where all my tears will be wiped away. I will feel no more sorrow, pain, or the sting of death; for God is true and faithful, and the former things will be passed, and **all will be new**. I am excited and look forward to that day.

Father, thank You for Your promise of a new day when **all** the hurts, pains, and worries of this world will be gone, and we will spend eternity in the beauty and peace of Your presence, and though glimpses of it here and now are so comforting, it doesn't compare to what You have awaiting Your children. **You are so good**. Thank You, in Yeshua's powerful name, amen.

September 22

Galatians 5:25

If we live in the Spirit, let us also walk in the Spirit.

In Galatians 5:16, Paul says if we walk in the Spirit, we shall not fulfill the lust of the flesh. When we walk in the Spirit, we crucify the flesh. When we walk in the Spirit, we walk, looking like Yeshua, bearing the fruits of the Spirit as He did. Struggles and temptations will come, but His Spirit in us will steady and hold our feet, keep our minds on Him and things above, and help us to walk according to His law and perfect will so we won't be suffering the disciplines from it.

His ways are good and perfect, and when we walk by His Spirit, we walk in those ways; we produce good fruit and godly character and are protected from the lusts of the flesh and the ways of the world.

Lord, help us to crucify the flesh daily and walk in the Spirit. Let that Spirit wash over us and help us to walk as Yeshua did; obediently, in love, being Patient, and full of joy as we head toward that prize of eternity with You, in Yeshua's mighty name, amen.

September 23

Numbers 22:28

And the LORD opened the mouth of the ass, and she said unto Balaam, What have I done unto thee, that thou hast smitten me these three times?

Alright, first off, if a donkey opened his mouth and began speaking to me, I'd be wondering who put what in my coffee on the way down to the ground in utter hysteria. Seriously, though, these are truly things God must resort to sometimes because we are so hardheaded. I wonder how many times the different roadblocks throughout my life could have been an angel of the Lord in front of me as an adversary opposing my direction and my hardheadedness. I remember back in the day, someone told me that the angels God sends to watch and protect us actually fight with each other when my feet hit the floor and say, "No way. It's your turn today. I get a break." Hmm, cute, but I am not sure it's accurate, but imagine how the angel of the Lord felt when it came to Balaam.

Balaam was in direct opposition with what God said and in his hardheadedness, almost got smote by the angel of the Lord. He needed to thank his donkey for saving his life instead of smiting her. How many times have we been guilty of this in our own life circumstances and situations? What a powerful event that should speak volumes to us all. Crazy how the donkey saw the angel of the Lord, but Balaam was completely blinded from seeing it. How often are we completely blinded, yelling, and smiting the wrong things because of it? We would do well when we come up against oppositions as such in our lives to stop and inquire of Abba if it is Him and His redirection instead of just forcing our way forward.

Abba, help us to notice the roadblocks as signs from You. Help us to stop and seek You for direction or redirection, in Yeshua's name, amen.

September 24

Matthew 6:33

But seek ye first the kingdom of God, and His righteousness; and all these things shall be added unto you.

I love how in verses twenty-eight and twenty-nine, Yeshua talks about the lilies and says: "Consider the Lilies of the field, how they grow; they toil not, neither do they spin: and yet I say unto you, that even Solomon in all his glory was not arrayed like one of these." Wow, I just love this image, the lily of the field arrayed in all its glory, splendor, and beauty, and how God perfectly grows and keeps it, how it stretches forth in all its beauty toward heaven as to give praise to the Creator, and it doesn't worry about a thing; it is just magnificent. Yeshua uses this to tell us not to think or worry about what we will eat or drink or be clothed with. He said they are more arrayed than King Solomon. Thinking about the lilies and pondering Yeshua's words, I think He knows what He's talking about, and we shouldn't worry about a thing.

I have some Asiatic lilies in my front yard, the bright fire orange ones, and the beauty of them just takes my breath away, as with all of His beautiful handiwork; from the flowers to the trees to all of the nature He created. It's just breathtaking. He takes such loving and constant care of it all. How are we to even think that He wouldn't do the same to His children? He says in verse thirty-two that "after all these things the Gentiles do seek," what they will eat, drink and wear, but not so for us, for our heavenly Father is fully aware of all we need, and if we seek the kingdom of God and His righteousness first, all these things we are in need of will be taken care of with no thought or worry on our part. Is it worth seeking Him first for this? I think so!

Abba, help us to always seek You first so we can be assured that we will be taken care of just as the beautiful lily is with no worries, in Yeshua's beautiful and perfect name, amen.

September 25

Jeremiah 31:33

But this shall be the covenant that I will make with the house of Israel; After those days, saith the LORD, I will put my law in their inward parts, and write it in their hearts; and will be their God, and they shall be my people.

The new covenant, where His law will no longer be written on stone tablets, being taught by man, but now they will be written on the very hearts of man by the Spirit of the Living God. He says He will cleanse and forgive us from our iniquity and remember our sin no more. Yeshua came and shed His perfect, pure blood to wash and cleanse us so we can stand faultless before the Father; our sins gone and remembered no more. Then Abba sent the Holy Spirit, the Comforter, our helper, to come and write the Father's laws on our hearts to be known and not forgotten so we could walk upright before Him. The **renewed** covenant in its complete fulfillment, Yeshua's blood applied to our lives and Abba's perfect law, written on our hearts to walk and live by.

Thank You, Abba, for a perfect plan from the beginning and executing it so beautifully and perfectly, and thank You, Yeshua, for your great sacrifice and obedience to the Father in laying Your life down for us, in Your precious Son Yeshua's perfect name, amen.

September 26

John 19:36

For these things were done, that the scripture should be fulfilled,
A bone of Him shall not be broken.

In Exodus 12:46 and Numbers 9:12, it speaks of the Passover lamb, and they were not to break a bone of it. Yeshua is our Passover Lamb, the Perfect Lamb, without spot or wrinkle, and for prophecy to be fulfilled, He had to have no broken bones as well. How perfectly God orchestrates everything; details so intricate and completely fulfilled with precise perfection a thousand and some odd years later. That's our God, yes!

As the Sabbath was approaching, Jewish law stated that no bodies could be left hanging on crosses on the Sabbath. The Jews approached Pilate and asked for their legs to be broken, as it would quicken death. The soldiers then broke the legs of the men on each side of Yeshua, but when they got to Yeshua, they saw that He was already gone and did not proceed to break His legs; instead, they pierced His side, which is also another confirmation of Scripture. Wow, I Love how the Word **always** confirms itself.

Yeshua, thank You for being obedient and sacrificing Yourself, the perfect Lamb, for us; how I fall on my knees in grateful adoration and praise. Thank You, Abba, for loving us so much to send Your only begotten Son and having such a perfect plan to save us, so we could have eternity with you. All glory, honor, and praise to You, our Most High God. With every breath, I will sing of Your greatness forever, in Yeshua's name, amen.

September 27

Ezra 6:19

And the children of the captivity kept the Passover upon the fourteenth day of the first month.

Jeremiah prophesied that after they were taken into captivity for a time by the Babylonians, they would be set free and restored to their homeland. This happened during the reign of King Cyrus when he overthrew Babylon. He issued an edict for the Jews to return to their land and rebuild the house of their God. Finally, after many years and much trouble, being commanded to stop building, then being allowed to build again by the decree of King Darius, the Temple was completed at last. They dedicated the Temple and kept the Passover. They knew God's Word, His commands, His chosen holy days, and immediately restored them all.

Verse twenty-one says: "And the Children of Israel, which were come again out of captivity, and all such as had separated themselves unto them from the filthiness of the heathen of the land, to seek the LORD God of Israel did eat, and kept the Feast of Unleavened Bread seven days with Joy." In Ezra 3:1, 4–5, it talks about how they gathered themselves together in the seventh month, kept the Feast of Tabernacles, and kept **all** the feasts of the LORD. They knew the importance once again of being separated and set apart for the LORD, following His commands, and keeping His appointed times. They would remember, be grateful, and follow for a time until rebellion and sin set in again. We have a choice; we can become rebellious, forget His ways, and do our own thing or we can refuse to be rebellious and follow Abba and His ways and be blessed. His ways never change, and His Word and truth stand forever. Let's remember and celebrate His appointed times with great joy, praising, and thanking Him for His perfect will in it **all**.

Thank You, Abba, for restoring Your people back to You always and putting Your ways in our hearts so we remember and do them, in Yeshua's name, amen.

September 28

Leviticus 16:29–31

29) And this shall be a statute for ever unto you: that in the seventh month, on the tenth day of the month, ye shall afflict your souls, and do no work at all, whether it be one of your own country, or a stranger that sojourneth among you: 30) For on that day shall the priest make an atonement for you, to cleanse you, that ye may be clean from all your sins before the LORD. 31) It shall be a sabbath of rest unto you, and ye shall afflict your souls, by a statute for ever.

The Day of Atonement is a high, holy day, one of God's appointed times, known as the Sabbath of Sabbaths. It is the time that we humbly come before the Father, examine our hearts and lives, confess our sins, and receive atonement for them. It is the **only** commanded fast day throughout all of Scripture. It is a solemn day as we fast, take time to look deep inside our hearts, lay at Abba's feet all the junk that still may beset us, ask the Lord for His mercy, and reflect and remember all Yeshua went through to be that ultimate sacrifice for our atonement. It is time to thank Abba for His immeasurable love for us, knowing we can't even come close to comprehending how He felt as He watched, from heaven, His only begotten Son suffer the worst death ever for us, so we can have right standing with Daddy. Being obedient to and keeping this day, as He commanded, in light of all this shouldn't even be a question in our minds.

Yeshua, thank You for shedding Your precious blood to atone for our sins so we may be reconciled with our Father, our Creator. You are worthy of all praise forever!

September 29

Acts 1:7

And he said unto them, it is not for you to know the times or the seasons, which the Father hath put in His own power.

Some things just aren't for us to know. **We** are not God. He is. He knows all, and we don't. That's just the way it is, whether we like it or not. We can try, work our whole lives trying to figure things out, study and dig, research, and study some more just to get to the end, still not knowing and finally realizing it wasn't meant for us to know. Not that we shouldn't spend our lives studying and going deeper into His Word and Him; we absolutely should. In doing that, we must know, though, that there are some questions that may not get answered; some secret things that are for Him alone, and we may never know.

Instead of using all our time trying to figure things out, trying to beg for the answers that aren't ours to know, maybe we would be better using that time to truly just grow closer to His heart and **all** that He is. We will **never** figure out the things we're just not meant to know, but we can **always** learn more about our Abba and grow closer to His heart, desire for us, truth, and perfect ways if we only put our sights and efforts there.

Thank You, Father for creating us to be finite beings, totally dependent on an infinite God who controls and handles our destiny and orders our steps on the journey there; taking all worry out of having to solve all things, knowing You, who created and holds the whole universe and all of us, have it all, in Yeshua's beautiful name, amen.

September 30

Lamentations 1:18

The LORD is righteous; for I have rebelled against His commandment: hear, I pray you, all people, and behold my sorrow: my vir-
gins and my young men are gone into captivity.

So often we have to come to the end of ourselves to see the
error of our ways. God's people seem to experience this quite
often; the flesh tends to fight against God's ways. The one thing
that is sure is that judgment and discipline will come. God's
people believed nothing could ever happen to them because they
were His chosen; they believed they were always protected and
couldn't be destroyed, that their enemies would never prevail
over them. The bottom line is that sin is sin, and God hates sin
and warns us consistently that the wages of it are death.

He is a God of judgment and justice and will not tolerate sin,
and though He is a patient God in hopes that we will turn from it,
if continued in it, sin will not go unpunished. Judgment and punishment here came at a high cost; they lost **everything**; their city,
homes, the Temple, their freedom, and some their lives. Wow, He
is a just God, and He says what He means and means what He
says. We should be careful to take Him at His Word.

Lord, help us to hear Your Word and believe it always; to know
it is solid and never play around with the things You tell us not to,
to not even give the slightest opening to sin or disobedience in
our lives, in Yeshua's name, amen.

October 1

Proverbs 11:16

A gracious woman retaineth honour: and strong men retain riches.

The definition of *gracious* is: "courteous, kind, pleasant, compassionate, favor, merciful, precious, elegance, charm"[43]; to possess such things bring a woman *honor*, which is defined as: "dignity, splendor, glory."[44] A strong man is a man who is awe-inspiring, awesome, mighty and powerful. In Proverbs 12:4 it says a virtuous woman is a crown to her husband; but she that maketh ashamed is as rottenness in his bones. Again, the definition of *virtuous* is "having or showing high moral standards, strength, wealth."[45] A woman must strive to be gracious and virtuous in all her dealings and ways; not only is it beneficial to her personally, but it is to her husband as well. She will be a crown to him. He will walk about feeling highly favored of God to have such a beautiful, gracious, virtuous woman by his side. Other men will greatly admire him. He will feel encouraged in the man he is and the things he sets forth to do because he has a precious and pleasant wife that believes in him and lifts him up.

I long to be this woman. I long for my heart to be set on these treasures of character, to retain honor and be a crown for the man God has blessed me with. May I never be rottenness to his bones by shaming him, degrading him, or dragging him down. I read in the footnotes of my women's study Bible that a woman like that is compared to enduring an infestation of maggots in the bones. It's a horrible irritant and fatal disease. Ouch, how horrifying. I know I've been guilty of not being a good wife and so many times fail greatly and must come before Abba and ask for forgiveness and help to learn to be the wife He has purposed and called me to be. Also, for a man, he must strive to be a strong man, display dignity, might, integrity, and to be awe-inspiring in all of his dealings, that he may retain wealth and riches—not only materially, but also the wealth of the heart, that a virtuous wife can trust and confide in him, knowing he will keep her safe and provided for. May our aim always be to become the men and women these verses speak of.

Abba, help us to be men and women of godly character, and please forgive us for when we haven't been or we're falling short. Teach us to be more like You in **all** our ways, in Yeshua's name, amen.

October 2

Song of Solomon 2:15

Take us the foxes, the little foxes, that spoil the vines: for our vines have tender grapes.

I remember growing up and always hearing my mother say, "It's the little foxes that spoil the vine." I never completely understood what she was saying or even that it was biblical. I've learned throughout my growing up and studies in the Word that though it can be used in an array of situations and would stand true, here in Song of Solomon, it is used in the context of marriage. The little things can come in to try to divide and separate two hearts. We can have big, life-shattering things that rock our world at times, but we tend to run and cling to Abba to weather those storms of life, knowing He will sustain and hold us. Now those little situations, disagreements, differences, problems, and foxes, we tend to try to navigate ourselves. We assume it's not a big deal.

Just a few examples could be: continuing to do something your spouse has asked you a number of times not to do, being too busy to listen to him, feeling what he's saying might not be the most important thing at the time, talking to an opposite sex when your spouse is uncomfortable about it, or hanging out one night with some friends when you notice it makes your spouse a little sad. These are just a few things that could take root in an unhealthy way and destroy the whole vine, the whole relationship, without even seeing or knowing until it's too late. There are so many more things that can be the little foxes that come in and destroy our vineyard, love, and relationship. In this passage, it was saying let us take them. When I was researching ancient Hebrew, it gave the definition: "to perceive, the ability to see beyond what is seen in the physical." Also, "to come upon, fasten, take hold, possess them, to see the deeper side of them and uproot them before they destroy the whole vine,"[46] dissolve the harmony of a beautiful marriage.

Abba, please help us to be aware of the little foxes, the little things. Help us to perceive them and take hold of them before they take hold of us, before they destroy all You've done and brought together, in Yeshua' name, amen.

October 3

Psalm 121:1–2

1) I will lift up mine eyes unto the hills, from whence cometh my help. 2) My help cometh from the LORD, which made heaven and earth.

All of my help cometh from the Lord. He is my defender, deliverer, strength, shield, healer, and the Rock upon which I stand. He is my portion, fortress, and strong tower I run into in times of trouble and my shelter in the storm. He is my keeper, the one who orders my steps, He is my stay and the lover of my soul. He is always my very present help. I **will** lift up mine eyes unto the hills, knowing it is He alone that is all I need, every second, day, and situation and circumstance.

The rest of Psalm 12 goes on to say "He will not suffer thy foot to be moved, he will not slumber, He is thy keeper, the LORD is thy shade upon thy right hand, the sun shall not smite thee by day, nor the moon by night, the LORD shall preserve thee from ALL evil, He shall preserve thy soul, the LORD shall preserve thy going out and thy coming in from THIS TIME FORTH, AND EVEN FOR EVERMORE! AMEN & HALLELUJAH!"

Thank You, Abba, that we can always look to You for all things, for You are always here in and with us, before us, behind us, all around us, and You will never leave us, in Yeshua's name, amen.

October 4

Philippians 4:8

Finally, brethren, whatsoever things are true, whatsoever things are honest, whatsoever things are just, whatsoever things are pure, whatsoever things are lovely, whatsoever things are of good report; if there be any virtue, and if there be any praise, think on these things.

There's so much negativity in the world around us; heartache, strife, fear, and darkness. We live in a world that seems to be so separated from Abba and His ways. It's hard not to get discouraged when looking around or listening to the news or others, and it becomes easy to dwell on these things.

I like how Paul instructs us here on the things to think on. I believe His time was not much different than ours, and they struggled with the same issues of focusing and thinking on the not-so-praiseworthy things that wouldn't edify but tear down. If we want to have victory in our lives and walk in joy and peace, let's be careful to remember Paul's words and think on the things that are true, honest, just, pure, lovely and of good report. Let these things be the central focus of our thoughts.

Abba, help us to keep our minds healthy and free from the garbage of this world by thinking on these things that are good, praiseworthy, and cause us to be a people of virtue, set apart for You, in Yeshua's name, amen.

October 5

James 3:16

For where envying and strife is, there is confusion and every evil work.

Webster's definition of *envy* states: "Desire to have a quality, possession or other desirable attribute belonging to someone else." The Hebrew definition states: "Jealousy."[47] Envying is simply wanting what another has or striving to be the same. It may show up in the desire of a social status, leadership position, godly gifts, talents, material possessions, personal praise, admiration, family relationships—be it sibling, children, or spouse—rewards others get, spiritual power, others children or husbands receiving more acknowledgements than ours, and the list goes on and on. Proverbs 14:30 says: "a sound heart is the life of the flesh: but envy the rottenness of the bones." Ouch! James says envy exists with every evil work. Romans 1:28–32 includes it in a reprobate mindset, being turned over to things which are not convenient; Galatians 5:19–21 has it in the list of the "works of the flesh"; 1 Peter 2:1–2 includes it in the lists of things to lay aside so we may grow on the sincere milk of the Word.

When we seek to have what others have, we minimize, if not dissolve our own potential, and we fail to become the valuable person He created us to be. We become a copy, a phony, a counterfeit, **not** genuine. We never want to be, do, or have what others are, have, or do. We are to be content with what God has for us, His plan, and His purpose, trusting that He knows best and will always provide for all we need. We must find contentment in Christ alone and what He calls us to. When we are, do, and have what Abba has purposed for our lives, then we are genuine and no other person can be us. We are one of a kind, rare, special, and valuable.

Abba, help us to always put aside these things that will so easily beset us. Help us to be happy and content in Your will and plan for our lives, in Your Son Yeshua's beautiful name, amen.

October 6

Jeremiah 23:23–24

23) Am I a God at hand, saith the LORD, and not a God afar off?
24) Can any hide himself in secret places that I shall not see him?
Saith the LORD. Do not I fill heaven and earth? Saith the LORD.

God is omnipresent. He is everywhere simultaneously. He's not bound by space, time, or a place. He sees all things, and nothing is hidden from Him. Our tiny minds can't grasp this because we are bound to space and time. It is mind-blowing when looking at the size of our world and the amount of people in it, wondering how it is utterly possible that He is everywhere, always, and how He knows all things, even our thoughts before we think them, but He is and He does. He is intimately involved in every detail of all His creation.

There is nowhere we can go to escape from Him; no secret place apart from His presence. We can't hide from His sight; it's impossible. If we think there is even a chance we can do something and get away with it, we should quickly think again. Numbers 32:23 says: "be sure your sin will find you out." I remember my mom telling me this as a child. I would think, "Hmm, she's not here; she will never know," then lo and behold, somehow, she did. The Lord always revealed it to her. He saw it all. It's true, beyond a shadow of a doubt, that there is nothing He doesn't see and no escaping His presence, but if we are living uprightly before Him, this is the best blessing **ever**. Abba's eyes are always on us and He always has our backs. **Nothing** is better than that.

Lord, thank You for being ever-present everywhere, always in our lives. Help us to remember it in all our actions and reactions, in Yeshua's name, amen.

October 7

Esther 4:14

For if thou altogether holdest thy peace at this time, then shall there enlargement and deliverance arise to the Jews from another place; but thou and thy father's house shall be destroyed: and who knoweth whether thou art come to the kingdom for such a time as this?

Esther was facing the possibility of losing her life if she went before the king unsummoned. Mordecai spoke some powerful truth to her that caused her to consider his proposal. What if she was created for **such a time as this**? To save her people! I can't even imagine the thoughts that must have swirled around in her head, the doubt, the fear.

If Esther would have let that fear and doubt dictate her decision and chose not to trust and believe that God perfectly orchestrated and ordered her steps to this exact place in time for such a time as this, we wouldn't be reading about her today. It's because she chose to step out in faith that Abba could use her to save and deliver His people. What a powerful lesson and example for us to think about and remember in our own daily walk with Him. You are here in this place, and this time, not by chance, but **for such a time as this. Make it count**!

Lord, help us to answer whatever call it is that You have created us for and placed us here and now for such a time as this to do, in Your Son Yeshua's mighty name, we ask this, amen.

October 8

Ezekiel 3:10

Moreover He said unto me, Son of man, all my words that I shall speak unto thee receive in thine heart, and hear with thine ears.

God wants His Word to be engrafted in us and become a part of our daily lives. He wants us to receive them in our hearts, so they become what we live and breathe, so they begin to change and cause us to do them. We must know it, not just in our heads, but in our hearts if we're going to share it with the world. We must truly be listening to what He is saying—hearing with our ears and receiving with our hearts so we can be the difference for Him.

There are so many lost and dying apart from Him that need Him, and we are His vessels to bring His truth and life to them. Let's truly be vessels of honor for Him, His hands, and feet, and share His powerful and life-changing truth with those who so badly need this hope of glory we are so fortunate to have in Him.

Abba, help us to honestly and deeply receive Your words in our hearts so that they transform the very way we think, speak, and act; that we truly become Your vessels used by You to reach a dying world, in Yeshua's mighty name, amen.

October 9

1 Timothy 4:12

Let no man despise thy youth; but be thou an example of the believers, in word, in conversation, in charity, in spirit, in faith, in purity.

You're never too young to start living and walking uprightly. You're never too young for God to speak to and use. Shine for Him in your conversation, words, and deeds. Stand for Him in that steadfast faith, no matter how young or seasoned you are. That faith will speak volumes to the world around you.

Don't let any man stifle the fire inside you but instead let the flame of His love burn brightly for those around you to see. Stand purified and rooted for an example as His Word says. Never disregard what Abba is doing in you, for He will use you in **big** ways if you stand steadfast in Him.

Abba, help us to know and be sure of who we are in You and to always be an example before men in that, no matter what, in Yeshua's name, amen.

October 10

Deuteronomy 6:5

And thou shalt love the LORD thy God with all thine heart, and with all thy soul, and with all thy might.

We are to love the Lord with everything, holding nothing back. He is worthy, and nothing else compares, so why wouldn't we love Him with **all** we have and are?

He deserves **no** seconds, only the first of all we are and the best of all we have. When we love like that, I think we will be amazed at how He showers our lives and drenches us with all He is.

There is nothing to lose and everything to gain. Love Him with no limits, reservations, and your whole hearts, all the time, in every season. Give Him your **all** and watch what He does.

Abba, teach us to love You with every fiber of our being and show us the manifestation of what that genuine true love is when we love You without measure and hold back nothing, in Yeshua's beautiful name, amen.

October 11

Jude 1:22–23

22) And of some have compassion, making a difference: 23) And others save with fear, pulling them out of the fire; hating even the garment spotted by the flesh.

There will be those we need to be humble, gentle, and kind with. We will have to deal with them in love and compassion as we walk alongside them, sharing Abbas's word of life and truth with them. Then there will be those we literally need to grab by the nape of the neck, dragging them out of the fire.

There may be different approaches but the same heart and mindset of hating the very sin that contaminates them and sentences them to eternal death if not dealt with and turned from. We have a tendency in our world today to treat sin as normal, typical, or common when we should despise even the slightest appearance of it. We need to look at sin for what it really is: filthy, hopeless, and empty; a death sentence from the devil himself. We need to let that vision move us to being clothed in righteousness and helping others to do the same.

Abba, strengthen and equip us to help others find You and Your saving grace and power that will set them free from the chains of sin and will lead them to finding eternal salvation in You, in Yeshua's powerful name, amen.

October 12

Isaiah 6:3–4

3) And one cried unto another, and said, Holy, Holy, Holy, is the LORD of hosts: the whole earth is full of His Glory. 4) And the posts of the door moved at the voice of him that cried, and the house was filled with smoke.

We serve the Holy Lord. He is sacred, set apart, the one and only, and the **true** God. Nothing compares to Him; His glory and fame go on from generation to generation throughout all eternity. He is worthy to be praised, for there is none like Him. His holiness brings me to my knees. I bow before Him in awe and wonder, in deep reverence of His power and authority. I am speechless. His beauty and glory is like a consuming fire that sets my heart ablaze.

Though we try with mere words to describe His majesty and holiness, it's impossible, for it is beyond words. Mountains tremble at His voice, and the earth quakes at the sound of it. His name alone was so holy people wouldn't even utter it. I fall on my face in His presence, for who can stand before Him? Every knee shall bow to the Living God, for He alone is God and worthy. Though we live in a world that doesn't seem to reverence how holy He is anymore, we must. We must be different and set apart for Him. We must be the example, remembering that it is He who speaks, and stars are born, knowing mountains will always move at His command. Holy, holy, holy is He. The whole earth is full of His glory, and one day, every knee shall bow and every tongue shall confess this truth.

Abba, help us to be children who see, who genuinely, truly, and deeply realize who You are and how holy You are. Help us to reverence You as the angels that behold Your face daily do; crying and singing before Your throne, always. Holy, holy, holy, is the Lord God Almighty, in Yeshua's magnificent name, amen!

October 13

Acts 2:17

And it shall come to pass in the last days, saith God, I will pour out of my Spirit upon all flesh: and your sons and your daughters shall prophesy, and your young men shall see visions, and your old men shall dream dreams.

I don't know about anybody else, but I **know** I want His Spirit to be poured out upon me; to live and breathe in me. I'm tired of operating in the flesh, succumbing to its wants and desires, seeing through fleshly eyes, thinking and walking in the decaying of it, and always feeling powerless and weak because of it.

I want to be empowered and governed by the Spirit of the living, Almighty God. I want to walk in His Spirit, see through His eyes, dream His dreams, think His thoughts, speak His Word, and walk in the power of His truth that leads to everlasting life.

Abba, pour out Your Spirit and drench us, cause us to see visions, dream dreams, and prophecy Your words, in Yeshua's mighty name, we ask this, amen.

October 14

Psalm 139

I encourage you today to take a moment out of the business of life and just read this Psalm in its entirety. Dive into it and allow Abba to engulf you in His Presence and Love.

The title to this psalm is: "Praise to the All-Knowing God." It's a powerful psalm by King David of God's ever-abiding presence in our lives. Verse two talks about how He knows our sitting and rising. Verse four states there's not a word on our tongues that He doesn't know before we speak it. Verse five says He is behind and before us, and His hand is upon us. Verse six says that such knowledge is too wonderful for us, so high we can't attain unto it. Then he continues to talk about where can one go from His Spirit? Or where can one flee from His presence? Absolutely nowhere is David's conclusion, for even in his mother's womb, Abba covered him. Verse fourteen says, "I will Praise thee, for I am fearfully and Wonderfully made: MARVELOUS are thy works." Verse seventeen goes on to say: "How precious also are thy thoughts unto me, O God! How great is the sum of them." Verse eighteen continues with: "If I should count them, they are more in number than the sand, when I awake, I am STILL WITH THEE." Then his plea in verse twenty-three is: "Search me, O God, and know my heart: try me, and know my thoughts." Verse twenty-four: "see if there be any wicked way in me and lead me in thy way everlasting."

Wow, such a beautiful, powerful, and soothing psalm, knowing that God is ever-present in **every** detail and aspect of our lives, and He knows us intimately. **Nothing** is hidden from Him.

Thank You, Abba, for loving us beyond our comprehension and being so mindful always of Your children. Thank You for the assurance of knowing Your presence is with us wherever we go, always, in Yeshua's name, amen.

October 15

Hebrew 4:12

For the word of God is quick, and powerful, and sharper than any twoedged sword, piercing even to the dividing asunder of soul and spirit, and of the joints and morrow, and is a discerner of the thoughts and intents of the heart.

God's Word is truth, the one and only truth; it doesn't change, and it will stand **forever**. It is absolute, powerful, and life-changing. Those who read it, hear it, and walk by it will be **blessed**. God's Word is alive and brings life to those who heed and believe it. Anything apart from His life-breathed Word is death. Nothing can get around it or disqualify it; it stands alone in its power and authority and has stood the test of time.

God's Word is good; it is wisdom and righteousness and reveals our true hearts. Yeshua used it to defeat Satan, and we can too. Satan **can't** stand against it; he will be defeated by it every time. He knows it better than we do, though, so we must make it our job to learn it and fill our hearts and minds with it. It is our most powerful weapon and should be in our mouths always, ready on the tips of our tongues.

Abba, Your Word is powerful and sharper than any two-edged sword. Help us to know it and fill our lives with it so we can walk continually by it and know the truth of all it holds always, in Yeshua's name, amen.

October 16

Ezekiel 8:16

And he brought me into the inner court of the LORD's house, and behold, at the door of the temple of the LORD, between the porch and the altar, were about five and twenty men, with their backs toward the temple of the LORD, and their faces toward the east; and they worshipped the sun toward the east.

In the verses prior to this, the LORD was taking Ezekiel through the Temple in a vision and showing him the great abominations that were being done in His house behind closed doors. The elders worshiped abdominal things, every form of creeping things, and all other idols, and the women were weeping and crying to Tammuz, the fertility land god, in the entrance of the sanctuary. Then He goes on to tell Ezekiel to come and look at an even greater abomination and takes him to the door of the Temple at the porch and shows him the twenty-five men, most likely priests since he was in the inner court and they had their backs toward the LORD'S House and the LORD as they stood facing the east worshiping the sun. Wow, all this was done against the Father in pure rebellion to His Word and commands in His own house.

So it now becomes about more than just the iniquities and the sins of His chosen, but it's now the blatant rebellion of their hearts doing it all right there in His temple. Oh, can history, for once, not repeat itself in this instance, even though it seems to already be? God calls rebellion the sin of witchcraft in 1 Samuel 15:23. It completely disregards Abba's merciful warning to us and His patience in executing discipline and just pushes buttons (as my husband would say) of His hurt and fury into a greater depth. It is no wonder why His punishment was so great.

Abba, search our hearts; rip out and remove whatever rebellious spirit may be there against You. Help us to live and walk upright in Your perfect commands all the days of our lives, in Yeshua's name, amen.

October 17

2 Timothy 2:15

Study to shew thyself approved unto God, a workman that needeth not to be ashamed, rightly dividing the word of truth.

It is up to us to search out God and His Word. We can't go off the coat strings of our parents, pastors, leaders, counselors, or teachers forever. I remember a few years back when I first started seriously studying the word on my own. Wow, the things I learned. I always relied on someone else to teach me instead of picking it up, studying it, and learning it for myself. I went off my parent's, friends', and pastors' relationships, and I just called it mine. Their beliefs were my beliefs and their opinions were my opinions until the day I started my own relationship with Abba when I started searching Him out for me, personally.

I learned who the Father was in a whole new way. I learned His heart and truths, how to be still and listen to Him, and I'm still learning. I'm doing my best to find out who this most beautiful and perfect Father is and trying to learn all His perfect ways. I know we won't know everything—we can't—some things are only His, but to search out and learn Him in the essence and truth of all He is has been the **best** thing that's ever happened in my life. When the end comes, there will be but one I stand before and give an account to. I better get to know Him, His heart, and His words now, so on that day, He knows me.

Abba, help us each individually dive into You and Your Word and study to show ourselves approved. Help us to know You, Your truths, and Your heart, that we may go deeper into all You are, Lord; deeper than we ever have before, in Yeshua's name, amen.

October 18

1 Chronicles 29:11

Thine, O LORD, is the greatness, and the power, and the glory, and the victory, and the majesty: for all that is in the heaven and in the earth is thine; thine is the kingdom, O LORD, and thou art exalted as head above all.

David here is blessing the LORD before all the congregation; he uses such beautiful and eloquent words describing the supreme perfection of our Lord. He knows how perfect, right, and true the LORD is and calls us to know it as well. It explains why in 1 Samuel 13:14 and Acts 13:22, the Lord called David "a man after His own heart." David loved the Lord, knew how to worship Him, and genuinely wanted to.

I want to be known as a person after God's own heart. I long to worship Him with everything in me, know Him more, and always go deeper into the wonder of **all** He is. May that be our hearts' desire, run after Him, fall in love with Him, know His heart, and be a people after His heart.

Lord, help us to be children after Your own heart, to genuinely lavish all our love, worship and praise on You, to truly know how good and perfect You and Your ways are, and to want nothing more than to be one with You, Your heart becoming our very own, Your ways becoming our deepest desires, just as it was David's and Yeshua's, in Your Son's precious and perfect name we ask this, amen.

October 19

1 John 3:6

Whosoever abideth in Him sinneth not: whosoever sinneth hath not seen Him, neither known Him.

1 John 3:9 also states: "whosoever is born of God doth NOT commit sin, for His seed remaineth in Him, and He CANNOT sin, because he is born of God." So, is this saying we can live a life without sin once we come to know and abide with the Lord? I believe it's pretty clear. If we abide in the Lord, we will want to live and do right as He has called us to do, and He, by His Spirit, will equip and enable us to do just that. Now it's not to say as we are learning Him and His ways, we won't have a stumble here or there, more like unintentional sin, when we mess up because we haven't learned yet and don't fully know, which is completely different than knowing and blatantly doing it anyway, intentional sin.

We now have a choice and can say **no** to sin because the blood of Yeshua has cleansed us from it and rendered sin powerless in our lives unless we choose to submit to it again. If we truly abide in Him, we walk by and are led by the Spirit, and sin will **not** have a place in us.

Father, help us to abide in You and be born new in You through the precious blood Yeshua shed for our redemption, that we may live righteous before You, free from the bondage of sin, that it will be powerless over us from here on out as we are led and walk by Your Spirit, in Yeshua's powerful name, amen.

October 20

Ruth 2:12

The LORD recompense they work, and a full reward be given thee of the LORD God of Israel, under whose wings thou art come to trust.

The LORD was making amends to Ruth. He was compensating her for all her loss, Boaz told her. Ruth knew in her heart that Naomi's God was a true and real God through walking alongside her, watching her, seeing her character, how she carried herself, and how she was selfless, even in the midst of great loss and thought of her daughters-in-law above herself.

Ruth chose to stay and walk with Naomi and her God instead of turning back to her own people and their false gods. God rewarded her for that and showed her that trusting in Him came with great blessing. God went on to bless Ruth's faithfulness by giving her a place in the line of Yeshua; this became part of her legacy. Wow, how awesome is that? Could it get any better?

Abba, help us walk in Your ways, knowing they are right, true, and good, even when we don't feel, see, or think they are, and help us to trust and rest in You as You build and preserve our place in Your greatest story ever told, in Yeshua's beautiful name, amen.

October 21

Titus 2:3–5

3) The aged women likewise, that they be in behavior as becometh holiness, not false accusers, not given to much wine, teachers of good things; 4) That they may teach the young women to be sober, to love their husbands, to love their children, 5) To be discreet, chaste, keepers at home, good, obedient to their own husbands, that the word of God be not blasphemed.

God calls us to be good examples, not just in word, but in actions before the younger generation, to teach them according to His Word how one should live, conduct themselves, and act as children of the Most High God; showing and teaching them through examples to be sober, do the right thing, be honest, love their husbands the way God says we should, be discreet, modest, humble, pure, having a heart toward God alone first, then their husbands alone, and not giving parts of it in other places, whether it be a job, friend, or anything else. Then to their children, love and teach them in love to live righteously, be obedient, and teach them by example to be good keepers of their homes, families, and the treasures God has entrusted them with. It sounds easy but takes a heart devoted and wrapped in God's love and Word to walk it out. I think so much of this in our current generation has been forgotten and pushed under a rug. Women are too busy focusing on their own lives, chasing after their own dreams, that there isn't much being taught to the younger generation about these values anymore. Make it a priority to live and walk in God's way. Teach our younger generation by example the importance of these **values** so they don't get lost and forgotten for good.

Abba, help us to be the kind of woman Your Word speaks of, the woman of God You called us to be. Help us to teach the younger girls by example how to live and walk in Your holiness, in Yeshua's name, amen.

October 22

Ephesians 4:26

Be ye angry, and sin not: let not the sun go down upon your wrath.

DON'T GO TO BED ANGRY

It's not a sin to be angry or upset; it's an emotion God created us with and can be useful if used correctly. It's all about how we react to it and the responses we allow it to dictate in us. Will it be a healthy response and bring about a good change? Will we deal with it prayerfully first and then be led from there, or will we let it fester, grow, and have its way in our hearts? If not taken under control immediately and dealt with, anger can turn into a deep-seeded hatred that can end up dictating a world of ugliness and destruction in our hearts and lives.

Deal with anger quickly and wisely and always with prayer before it has the chance to turn into a destructive force. At all costs, **never go to bed angry**. If it's a person who's caused you to become angry or hurt, talk it out before your head hits the pillow for the night, making sure not to give the enemy space and time to grow it. If it's a situation, bring it before the Throne, lay it at the feet of the Father, and leave it there. Sometimes we're angry at ourselves and must find grace to forgive ourselves and give ourselves another chance. Whatever it may be, don't go to bed with it left undone; deal with it so your head can lay down in peace and have sweet sleep.

Lord, help us to always recognize anger before it grows into sin, to deal with it prayerfully and lay it down so it never has the chance to establish a root in our hearts and lives, in Yeshua's name, amen.

October 23

Exodus 23:22

But if thou shalt indeed obey His voice and do all that I speak; then I will be an enemy unto thine enemies, and an adversary unto thine adversaries.

The Lord had given all His instructions and commandments and then He said He was sending an angel to go before His people to keep them and bring them safely into the place He had prepared for them, that they were to beware of Him and obey. Obedience, that's what God wants of us; a heart that just wants to hear and do what He says. In doing so, He will have our backs, be our defender, and fight our battles. He will take care of our enemies and be a wall of defense around us against our adversary. Those against us will really be standing against Him; those devising evil and fighting against us will really be picking a fight with the Most High God, not us.

If we will just listen to His words and **obey** all He says, we will make it into the Promised Land safely. Pondering this, I wonder why so often we don't, knowing His ways are perfect, and this is the promise we receive if we do and follow what He says; why wouldn't we? It's truly a win-win situation for us.

Abba, help us to see the beauty and blessing in being obedient to You and help our hearts to desire to always follow You. There truly is no better way. In Yeshua's name, we ask this, amen.

October 24

1 Samuel 15:22

And Samuel said, Hath the LORD as great delight in burnt offerings and sacrifices, as in obeying the voice of the LORD? Behold, to obey is better than sacrifice, and to hearken than the fat of rams.

The Lord captured my attention this morning with the **amazing** picture He painted in the sky; the hues of pinks, purples, blues, and tints of orange took my breath away as I sat just taking in the beauty of His handiwork. I began to think that if He paints such beautiful and perfect pictures in the sky, then His ways and everything about Him must be just as beautiful and perfect. If He is so beautiful and perfect in His pictures and ways, why wouldn't we want to follow them and be obedient to Him? If obedience is simply what He requires, and His ways are perfect and beautiful, why would we want anything less?

Obedience is greater than sacrifice! Obedience leads to God's heart, which is beautiful and perfect; there is nothing better. Obedience is a choice and surely doesn't seem like that hard of one. Knowing how wonderful He is, that He gives good gifts to His children, paints such beautiful pictures, and has such perfect ways, why would we even question obeying Him? I know it's what I want. How about you?

Abba, help us to see the beauty in obedience to You. Help us to choose to walk in it, in Yeshua's name, amen.

October 25

Mark 12:38–40

38) And He said unto them in His doctrine, Beware of the scribes, which love to go in long clothing, and love salutations in the marketplaces, 39) And the chief seats in the synagogues, and the uppermost rooms at feasts: 40) Which devour widows' houses, and for a pretence make long prayers: these shall receive greater damnation.

So, while reading this and the warning it gives, it brought to light that not only should we beware of them, but we should also beware we don't become like them, that we don't let our hearts become clouded with the wrong things. Popularity and status are a funny and tricky thing and will come in and set up residence in our hearts if we are not carefully guarding them.

Feeling special, fitting in, and being liked by others always makes one feel important and good. Having knowledge and talents can be an awesome thing and truly help and bless others, but it can also be the proving ground of a prideful heart if we are not careful. God must be the one who always receives all the glory in every area of our lives, in all our accomplishments and all we do. We must always remain humble and give God His rightful praise and due in it all, always. We must never let it go to our heads and hearts and let it set up place in a wrongful way. We must beware of the scribes and becoming like them.

Father, help us to always guard our hearts in all things, never letting them detach from You and Your Word by allowing wrongful issues to take root, in Yeshua's name, amen.

October 26

Proverbs 13:20

He that walketh with wise men shall be wise: but a companion of fools shall be destroyed.

My mother always told me you will become the company you keep, so make sure you keep the right people around you. When I was younger, she didn't like the choice of some of my friends and would point-blank tell me they would be my downfall. I didn't listen or believe her until I hit rock bottom. She was right. She had discernment that I didn't at that time, and her words lined up with the Word of God. I Corinthians 15:33 says: "Be NOT deceived: evil communications corrupt good manners," and 2 Corinthians 6:14 says: "Be ye not unequally yoked together with unbelievers: for what fellowship hath righteousness with unrighteousness? And what communion hath light with darkness?" Then in Proverbs 14:7, it says: "Leave the presence of a fool, for there you do not meet words of knowledge."

I've always said that you can have a bushel of bad apples and put a good one, even one hundred good ones in there, and it will not make the bad ones good, but you can have a bushel of good apples and put only one bad one in there, and it will make every good apple bad. That powerful analogy, along with all of God's precious words, has caused me to carefully consider the company I keep today.

Abba, please fill us with Your discernment to know those You send into our lives and those we're not to keep company with. Help us to always be wise and walk wisely in the company we keep so we are not destroyed, in Yeshua's holy name, amen.

October 27

Hebrew 6:19

Which hope we have as an anchor of the soul, both sure and sted-fast, and which entereth into that within the veil;

Yeshua Messiah is our hope of glory, who entereth into the veil, into the Holy of Holies before Abba and stands in our place, the Perfect Lamb, slain for us, making atonement to the Father on our behalf for our sins. Wow, this truly is the anchor of hope for our souls, for our eternal salvation. He is our hope, anchor, salvation, and redemption. He stood in our place, took our sin upon Himself, paid the price, canceled our debt, and reconciled us through His righteousness to Abba.

We can now boldly say we have this hope as an anchor of our soul, sure and steadfast. Yeshua became our hope of glory and is worthy of our praise, **all our praise**. I know my debt was huge, one I could **never** pay, and I will forever stand in praise and thanksgiving for Yeshua having paid it for me, and I will forever hold to Him, my anchor and hope.

May this prayer be for all: Thank You, Yeshua, for taking my sin upon Yourself and standing in my place so I can be washed in Your perfect blood and stand righteously now before the Father. I love You with all my heart and being, in Your mighty and pow-erful name, Yeshua, amen.

October 28

Psalm 25:10

All the paths of the LORD are mercy and truth unto such as keep His covenant and His testimonies.

The Lord's paths are full of mercy and truth. His ways are right and good. If we faithfully walk in His covenant and hear and follow His testimonies and commands, we will experience His mercy, new every morning. His goodness exceeds our wildest dreams. His blessings are beyond what our minds can comprehend. There's **truly nothing better** than this world can offer; nothing else has ever or will ever compare.

Abba, thank You for allowing us to come into covenant with You, for giving us Your commands and testimonies that are so good, perfect, and true. Help us to hold fast to Your covenant always, in Yeshua's name, amen.

October 29

Matthew 21:16

And said unto him, Hearest thou what these say? And Jesus saith unto them, Yea; have ye never read, Out of the mouth of babes and sucklings thou hast perfected praise?

Wow, hear this: not out of the aged, the matured, the learned, but out of the mouths of babes and sucklings comes **perfected praise**; those who come not from a place of knowledge or schooling, not skilled or educated, but those who come with a simple, genuine, grateful heart, in praise and thanksgiving, from a place of humility and simplicity.

The definition of *babe* in Strong's Concordance is "infant, simple minded, untaught, unskilled, innocent."[48] The definition of *suckling* is "unweaned child, still on milk."[49] It's out of this innocence and genuine heart that perfected praise comes. So, praise Him in that place of beginnings; sing loud, sing with your whole heart, and let the world hear your perfected praise.

Abba, help us to not get stuck in the aged and the old when it comes to praising You but to come as babes in the innocence and simplicity of our hearts before our minds come in and complicate it all. Help us to be that child crying out, "Hosanna, hosanna, hosanna in the highest." In Yeshua's precious name, we ask this, amen.

October 30

1 Peter 5:5–6

5) Likewise, ye younger, submit yourselves unto the elder. Yea, all of you be subject one to another, and be clothed with humility: for God resisteth the proud, and giveth grace to the humble. 6) Humble yourselves therefore under the mighty hand of God, that He may exalt you in due time.

To have a humble spirit is a genuine treasure. Yeshua, being the Son of God, who had all things, gave it all up to come and give His life for us. He humbled Himself and put the welfare of everyone else first. His life was an example to us all of genuine humility. Proverbs 16:18–19 says: "18) Pride goeth before destruction and haughty spirit before a fall. 19) Better it is to be of a humble spirit with the lowly, than to divide the spoil with the proud." Back in Proverbs 16:5, it states that every one that is proud in heart is an abomination to the Lord. A proud look is the first thing listed in Proverbs 6:16–17 as one of the things God hates, and 2 Samuel 22:28 says: "His eyes are upon the haughty, that thou mayest bring them down." Wow!

In today's world, pride seems to be one of mankind's biggest downfalls. Everyone has to be right, from our government to the corporate world to personal relationships; everyone's too proud to give in, see a different way, be wrong, and walk away. We must begin to truly walk and live like Yeshua in all things. Pride kills, and humility lifts up. Therefore, humble yourselves under the mighty hand of God, "that He may exalt you in due time!" It means we may have to walk away sometimes; we may have to say we're wrong when we know we're right and let our way go as we watch another way get chosen, even though we know our way would have been better. We'll have to learn to lay things down, humble ourselves, let go, and **let God**. As I stated earlier, a humble spirit is a genuine treasure.

Help us, Lord, to humble ourselves under Your hand, trusting and believing You will always exalt us in due time, in Yeshua's name, amen.

October 31

1 Kings 6:11–13

11)And the word of the LORD came to Solomon, saying, 12) Concerning this house which thou art in building, if thou wilt walk in my statutes, and execute my judgments, and keep all my commandments to walk in them; then will I perform my word with thee, which I spake unto David thy father: 13) And I will dwell among the children of Israel, and will not forsake my people Israel.

It's simple; walk in His ways, obey His Word, keep His commands, and judge rightly. Doing these things will please the Father, and He will dwell among us and be faithful to not forsake us. Everything about Him is perfect, right, and good, so why would we ever want to not listen or follow Him, especially when in doing so, comes great blessing as well?

Thank You, Lord, for Your perfect Word and promise to walk with us, call us Yours, and never forsake us if we walk in it. Help us to always walk in it, in Yeshua's powerful name, amen.

November 1

John 5:30

I can of mine own self do nothing: as I hear, I judge: and my judgment is just; because I seek not mine own will, but the will of the Father which hath sent me.

I love Yeshua's words here. He declares how of His own self, He can do nothing; everything is because of, through, and by the Father. It's completely 100 percent the Father's will, and Yeshua seeks and follows it. How much more beautiful can it get? Fully, with complete obedience, the Son follows the Father's will perfectly.

Yeshua is our example, so we should do our very best to follow Him and do as He did. Just as He followed the Father and did what the Father said, we should follow Him and do the same, doing our best to be obedient children. There truly is one way only, and that is the Father's way; Yeshua knew it. It's always been about the will of the Father since the beginning, His perfect will for mankind.

Abba, help us to have a heart like Your Son did, one that wants nothing else than to follow and do Your will. In Your Son Yeshua's powerful name, we ask this, amen.

November 2

Ephesians 5:15–16

15) See then that ye walk circumspectly, not as fools, but as wise,
16) Redeeming the time, because the days are evil.

I don't know if, in my lifetime, this verse has ever held such weight and been truer than it is now. As I observe the world around me, the further it's going away from the truth, from what's right and pure, and the closer it's getting to allowing evil and darkness to hold great precedence, is truly alarming. The days are evil, and we must redeem every moment possible, being wise and not foolish, walking uprightly, cautiously making each step, each word, and each moment count.

I know His Word says there's nothing new under the sun, and history just repeats itself; well, history could repeat itself at any moment in our Yeshua Messiah returning once again. Only this time, He's to take us to our eternal home with Him and the Father. I believe it's vital now more than ever to be wise and redeem the time, each second before the time is up.

Father, help this verse resonate not just in our hearts and minds but in our lives as we walk it out and get ready for our eternal life with You, in Yeshua's name, amen.

November 3

Psalm 141:3

Set a watch, O LORD, before my mouth; keep the door of my lips.

Yes, Lord, sometimes I can say some pretty stupid things. That old saying of "think before you speak" was not spoken lightly. Our words can edify, lift up, and bring life, or destroy, tear down, and bring death. James 3:5–8 talks about how the tongue is a small part of the body but makes great boasts; it is a fire and world of evil among the parts of the body that it defiles the whole body. No man can tame it, and it's full of deadly poison.

Ouch, what a heap of trouble such a little member of our body can get us into. Oh Lord, but for You, You can set a watch before our mouths and keep the door of our lips. As King David sought and asked of You, so do we!

May our prayer be: Abba, please guard our mouths, tongues, and help our words to be Your words, always, in Yeshua's name, amen.

November 4

Hebrew 4:15

For we have not an high priest which cannot be touched with the feeling of our infirmities; but was in all points tempted like as we are, yet without sin.

Yeshua, our High Priest felt, wrestled, and dealt with all the same temptations and things we do. He fully knew what it was like to be in this world but not of this world. He knew the struggles and hardships. He felt the pain this life comes with, yet He stayed the course, kept His eyes on the Father, and overcame this world.

Through Him, we can do the same; the Father's perfect will and way before us, His Word of truth to guide us, His Holy Spirit to enlighten us, and His Son Yeshua, our Savior, who lived and walked it out perfectly, to show us. If we set our eyes on this and keep the course, we can, with Abba, Yeshua, and the Holy Spirit, walk this life out as overcomers too.

Abba, help us to keep the course, keeping our eyes fixed, walking in the steps You ordered for us, in Your Son Yeshua's perfect name, amen.

November 5

Joshua 24:15

And if it seem evil unto you to serve the LORD, choose you this day whom ye will serve; whether the gods which your fathers served that were on the other side of the flood, or the gods of the Amorites, in whose land ye dwell: but as for me and my house, we will serve the LORD.

I remember growing up and seeing these words on a daily basis hanging on our wall. I then made that same choice for my own home, and I have had a plaque since I can't even remember this verse that hangs on our wall in our house. Though we may not do it perfectly, fall short at times, or stumble and fall, it will always be a standing rule in our home that as for me and my house, **we will serve the LORD**.

We will work with all our might, hearts and all we are to serve, follow, and obey the one and only true God, the Almighty King. He truly is the **only** God, with no equal; absolutely nothing compares, and every other false god with its false promises will be absent of life, empty and void, powerless to change anything, with no hope for today, tomorrow, or life eternal. "Choose you this day whom ye will serve"—my choice is made, and as for me and my house, we will serve the Lord, the Creator of **all** things, the lover of my soul, the only true God!

Abba, help this to be the choice of all Your children and help us to stand proudly and securely in it, in Your Son Yeshua's mighty name, Amen.

November 6

Matthew 20:28

Even as the Son of man came not to be ministered unto, but to minister, and to give His life a ransom for many.

Yeshua didn't come to be served; it was just the opposite. He came to serve. He led the way for us by example, showing us how we should walk and live. Earlier in verses twenty-six and twenty-seven, Yeshua was talking with His disciples and explaining to them that he who wants to be great and chief must minister and be a servant.

We're not to sit in high places, thinking more of ourselves than we ought, making others serve us, but we are to serve others. We are to be the hands and feet of the Father as Yeshua was. As I stated earlier, He is our example and tells us to follow Him.

Abba, help us to see and follow Your Son, the greatest example You sent for us, knowing He walked out Your perfect will perfectly, so we could learn from Him and do our best to do the same. Help us to truly take notice of how He was fully obedient, fully humble, and truly a servant to all by laying His life down to ransom and reconcile us to You, in His perfect and powerful name, amen.

November 7

Ezekiel 11:19–20

19) And I will give them one heart, and I will put a new spirit within you; and I will take the stony heart out of their flesh, and will give them an heart of flesh: 20) That they may walk in my statutes, and keep mine ordinances, and do them: and they shall be my people, and I will be their God.

The Spirit of the Living God lives and breathes in us, taking our hard hearts and replacing it with a heart of flesh; hearts that desire to walk in His statutes and ways, that want Him alone. A Father, so patient, with such unconditional love, steps in, removes the very fibers of the sinful nature of our hard, ugly hearts, and gives us His heart, a heart of flesh, genuine and true that longs for truth and righteousness.

Lord, may Your words spoken here be done in our lives now as we read this. Please take the stony hearts out of us, hearts that have been hardened and made ugly by sin and the world, and give us hearts of flesh, hearts like Yours. Put a new Spirit within us, Abba, so we may continually want to walk in Your statutes and ordinances and do them always. That we may be Your people, You will be our God, and we may find joy and peace in doing so. In Yeshua's name, we ask this, amen.

November 8

Acts 1:11

Which also said, Ye men of Galilee, why stand ye gazing up into heaven? this same Jesus, which is taken up from you into heaven, shall so come in like manner as ye have seen Him go into heaven.

Praise the Lord, He's coming back! His Word is true, and Yeshua will be returning. They stood there, I'm sure, sad, broken, shocked, and astonished over seeing Him go. A Son to one, brother to some, friend to many, and a Savior to all was leaving them, being taken up to heaven to be with the Father. Two men in white standing by told them, "Hey, why are you standing here watching and gazing into the sky? He will be coming back just as you've seen Him go."

I'm sure they must have had to comfort one another, telling each other not to worry, not to be afraid, urging each other to push on, that there's a lot of work to do, knowing He's going to come back like the men said, so they must get busy. I would think they were encouraging one another as well in the midst of probably one of the craziest things they've ever witnessed. Maybe they were telling one another, "Hey, let's be joyful in having this hope and tell the world so they can have the same hope." I can only imagine the conversation that happened at that moment amongst them. It's the same today, though; we must continue with joy and tell others about this hope we have, expectantly awaiting His glorious return, believing, and knowing beyond a shadow of a doubt He is coming back to take us home to the place He has prepared for us. Hallelujah, it's not time to be sad, scared, or worried, but it is time to **rejoice** in His promised words, serve Him, and be His hands and feet while we await our Messiah's return.

Father, thank You for this promise of Your Son's return for us. Help us to remain joyful and positive in the waiting, in Yeshua's name, amen, amen, and amen!

November 9

Judges 7:9

And it came to pass the same night, that the LORD said unto him, Arise, get thee down unto the host; for I have delivered it into thine hand.

The story of Gideon amazes me and gives me hope every time I read it. Knowing it's **never** by man's hand, our strength, power, or wisdom, but **only by the Lord**. One shepherd boy could slay and kill a giant that hundreds of men couldn't because of the LORD. It's only because of Him and through Him that **all** things are done.

Man should never get the glory or boast in themselves for what is **only** because of God. Let's never forget the power He holds, and let's always remember to stand in reverence of Him, the King of kings, knowing **all** things are always and only by Him. I would much rather have the Army of **one** on my side, Jehovah, the great I Am, than the army of ten thousand or even a hundred thousand. He will **always** have the **victory**.

Abba, help us to know and fully trust in You, in all things, believing and never doubting You will win our wars, never relying on ourselves or the strength of men, but always fully relying on You **alone**, in Yeshua's name, amen.

November 10

Proverbs 30:5

Every word of God is pure: he is a shield unto them that put their trust in Him.

Wow, we read yesterday about Gideon and how the Lord cut his army way back so everyone would know that victory came not through anyone or anything else but God alone. How those men believed and trusted in His Word, that He would be there, fighting this battle for them, giving them the victory through Him. That's the result of trusting the Father.

When we trust You, Lord, You will **always** show up. Your Word is good, true, pure, and will stand **forever**. You, Abba, will be a shield to those who trust in You.

The definition of *shield* is "a protection against blows or missiles, a cover that protects, a wall of protection."[50] He will defend, protect, and keep those who put their trust in Him. Who would want to put their trust in anyone or anything else?

Thank You, Abba, for coming to our rescue, being our defender, our shield, and always protecting us when we put our trust in You. Nothing compares. In Yeshua's mighty name, amen.

November 11

Philippians 4:6–7

6) Be careful for nothing; but in everything by prayer and supplication with thanksgiving let your requests be made known unto God. 7) And the peace of God, which passeth all understanding, shall keep your hearts and mind through Christ Jesus.

In the darkest night, in the bottom of the pit, in the face of terror, in sickness and disease, in brokenness and heartache, He **will** keep our hearts and minds in perfect peace. We don't have to worry or fret; we have a **hope** and can bring our prayers and requests to the Throne, and we can come with Thanksgiving, knowing Abba hears and is mindful.

We don't have to be anxious about anything; we can rest and have perfect peace in the middle of the hardest circumstances because His Word is true, and He will hold and keep us. He is faithful! By prayer and supplication, with thanksgiving, let your request be made known unto God, and experience His perfect peace, which passeth **all** understanding.

Abba, thank You for Your beautiful and perfect peace that only You can give; it truly transcends all understanding. Thank You that we can bring our requests to You. Help us to always bring all things to You through prayer and supplication, earnest and humbly, with thanksgiving and a grateful and thankful heart because we know You are who You say You are, and You are good, in Yeshua's beautiful name, amen.

November 12

Genesis 50:20

But as for you, ye thought evil against me; but God meant it unto good, to bring to pass as it is this day, to save much people alive.

What the enemy means for evil, God will use for good. The enemy worked in the hearts and minds of Joseph's brothers, causing them to do what they did to him, selling him into slavery and almost killing him. But God knew the future and allowed it, knowing He was going to turn it around and use it for good. He was going to use it to save a nation, His nation.

If we will keep our eyes fixed on the Father and trust Him in all things, then we will rise above the cares of this world. We will walk through this life without fearing what the enemy may try to do to us. We are His children and have His promises to hold to and stand on. We can rest in knowing He will use all things for good and His glory. He goes before us, behind us, beside us, and is all around us, He will never leave us or forsake us. Praise Yah. We can trust Him with every single situation in our lives.

Abba Father, thank You for using what the enemy meant for evil, for good. You are a good, good Father, in Yeshua's good and perfect name, amen.

November 13

John 13:14–15

14) If I then, your Lord and Master, have washed your feet; ye also ought to wash one another's feet. 15) For I have given you an example, that ye should do as I have done to you.

What a beautiful picture of true love and humility. Yeshua, the Son of the Most High God, came to serve others and not be served. He became the greatest servant of all to show and teach us how to do the same. I praise and thank Him that He has taught me the power and blessing that comes through this one act of genuine love and humility. The peace that just fills the room during such a moment is life-changing and literally softens the hearts of all.

He did this because He knew how important it was for us to see and learn, and then to do the same. It truly changes things; it creates an atmosphere of humility and bonds hearts together. If there is hurt, animosity, or jealousy, it heals it and washes it away. I encourage you to follow Yeshua's footsteps in this and watch it transform hearts and lives right in front of you.

Thank You, Yeshua, for being the best example and walking everything out so perfectly for us that we may have the opportunity to be blessed in a way we couldn't perceive by following You. Thank You, Abba, for letting Your only begotten Son go, sending Him for us so we may learn from Him and receive salvation through Him, and it is in His perfect name, we pray this, amen.

November 14

1 John 3:22

And whatsoever we ask, we receive of Him, because we keep His commandments, and do those things that are pleasing in His sight.

The Lord longs for us to follow and obey Him. He knows the beginning from the end and what's best for us and what will harm us. He is the parent who is protecting His precious child by setting up boundaries to safeguard us.

By obeying and following Him, we remain safe, hidden under His covering, and stand confident, knowing He orders our steps and has our front, back, side, above us, and under us. We can walk, knowing we are pleasing Him. We can walk, experiencing His goodness and blessings and knowing we are always held. All that He has said and set in place is for our good and protection, so why would we ever want to **not** keep His ways.

Abba, help us to see that Your ways are good, and help us to know deeply how much You truly love us and want to always protect and keep us, in Yeshua's name, amen.

November 15

Daniel 4:3

How great are His signs! and how mighty are His wonders! His kingdom is an everlasting kingdom, and His dominion is from generation to generation.

These are the words from King Nebuchadnezzar to all the people after seeing God deliver Shadrach, Meshach, and Abednego from the fiery furnace. He was coming to the realization that their God was the one high God, and He is mighty, powerful, and worthy of praise.

To finally come to that place of believing and knowing beyond a shadow of a doubt that Abba is the one and only true God and none other is above or beside Him is a beautiful place to be. It's a place of complete awe and reverence, a place that causes us to drop to our knees in humble adoration. Seriously, **no** other place I'd rather be.

Abba, help us to know deep within our being how great and mighty You are, to know that there is truly **nothing better** than You. In Your Son Yeshua's name, we ask this, amen.

November 16

Galatians 1:10

For do I now persuade men, or God? Or do I seek to please men? For if I yet pleased men, I should not be the servant of Christ.

I lived the majority of my growing-up years trying to please others, doing all I could to be liked by all and fit in wherever I was. I became so many different people that I didn't know who the Joy God created me even was. I got seriously lost in the midst of it and almost completely lost my life, but for God's grace.

When He delivered me many years later from that life of bondage and destruction, the first thing He taught me was if I still sought to please people, I would **never** please Him. He had to become my only goal, hope, purpose, objective, my one and only, and the **center** of my heart, seated on the throne of my life. Making Him everything and pleasing Him alone would cause me to love as He loved, walk as He walked, and touch lives as He touched lives. I wouldn't have to worry about being liked or fitting in because I was loved by the only one that mattered, the God who created me, and He alone validates all I am.

Lord, help us to look to You alone for everything, to seek to please You alone, so we truly can become all You created us to be, in Yeshua's holy name, amen.

November 17

1 Corinthians 15:58

Therefore, my beloved brethren, be ye stedfast, unmoveable, always abounding in the work of the Lord, forasmuch as ye know that your labour is not in vain in the Lord.

The definition of *steadfast* is "Dutifully firm and unwavering."[51] *Unmovable* means "CANNOT be moved, NOT physically possible to be moved."[52] We are told by Paul here to remain dutifully firm and unwavering, to stand, making it impossible to be moved by man, the enemy, or circumstances; like that tree, unmovable and unshakeable. Always abound, overflow, flourish, and prevail in our work for the Lord.

In the face of all things, being unmovable, steadfast, firm, and unwavering, knowing that even though we can't see what it's doing, and it may seem to all be in vain, it's **not**. God sees and is using it, and we don't need to see to believe.

Lord, help us keep our eyes fixed on You, remaining steadfast in all You've called us to, knowing that even if we don't see, it's not in vain, and You are using us for Your plan. You will fulfill Your purposes if we remain unmovable in You, in Yeshua's powerful name, amen!

November 18

Luke 16:13

No servant can serve two masters: for either he will hate the one, and love the other; or else he will hold to the one, and despise the other. Ye cannot serve God and mammon.

There is only room for one on the throne in our lives. We can have, love, and be blessed with people, positions, homes, and things, but God is a jealous God and will not share His throne with anything or anyone else. We cannot have a divided heart. We must make a choice of who or what we seek and run after because that will become the master we serve and take its place on the throne of our hearts. Yeshua, here, is talking of money and wealth, but it is true for anything and everything else as well.

We must be careful to keep our affections on the Lord and our running and seeking after Him alone. He must remain the Master on the throne of our hearts, and we remain a servant to Him and nothing else. He alone deserves that rightful place, for He is our Creator and the lover of our souls.

Abba, help us to run after You alone. May You be our Master, and we always will be your servants, in Yeshua's name, amen.

November 19

Isaiah 12:2–3

2) Behold, God is my salvation; I will trust, and not be afraid: for the LORD JEHOVAH is my strength and my song; He also is become my salvation. 3) Therefore with joy shall ye draw water out of the wells of salvation.

As I sat today in the emptiness of wishing back days gone by and wrestling with the fear of tomorrow and all the change coming with it, I felt as if I was drowning in a sea of loneliness, and the enemy was having a hay day in the playground of my mind. I was thinking about having to let go of yesterday and trying to figure out how to embrace all the new changes of tomorrow, struggling with the peace of being still and trying to find joy in the journey; the joy of where I'm at here and now. All of it had me overwhelmed and sinking deeply to a place I didn't want to be, discouraged and afraid, then all of a sudden, there were these **powerful** words of this verse that just kept jumping off the page at me. I will trust and not be afraid; the Lord Jehovah is my strength and song. I will draw water from the wells with joy.

I began to think on these words and let them sink deep inside, and they began to stir me. I realized He is my song, and I need to sing. I don't need to be afraid; He is my strength; I will draw water with joy. The joy of the Lord is my Strength, and I can trust Him, for He will hold me. He is my salvation; today is my gift. His joy is my strength, so I will sing at the top of my lungs and trust with all my strength, and I will not be afraid today.

Abba, let this be all of our song always. In the empty and lonely moments, let us remember and never forget these words, in Yeshua's holy name, amen.

November 20

Ephesians 2:10

For we are His workmanship, created in Christ Jesus unto good works, which God hath before ordained that we should walk in them.

We have been saved by God's grace through the blood of Yeshua and are now set apart and instructed to walk as He walked. We are His workmanship and were created and specially designed by God to do good works. We are His masterpiece and should reflect that in all we do and say.

Just as renowned painters' masterpieces hang for all to see and be awed and inspired by, that's how our lives should look and be. Our lives should cause others to stop, take notice, and be touched by the Master's workmanship in us. We are His masterpiece on display for the world to see; let's take their breath away as we allow the Lord's beauty and love to radiate and shine through us to the world around us.

Lord, help us to truly walk in those good works You have ordained us to walk in that we may shine You always in all we do, in Yeshua, our Messiah's name, amen.

November 21

Psalm 119:10

With my whole heart have I sought thee: O let me not wander from thy commandments.

Oh that these words don't just resonate off our lips but that they may be our deepest heart's desire. That we truly see His commands as good and never want to wander from them. This whole chapter is one of my favorites.

I love how throughout the whole chapter, it just speaks of how good the LORD'S ways, His judgments, commands, laws, and statutes are. How righteous and perfect He is in **all** things, and how He's faithful to **all** generations. How fitting that this is the longest chapter in the Bible. It is worthy of the pages it fills with its admonishing of how perfect our God is and how good His commands to us are.

Abba Father, thank You for loving us so much to give us such good and awesome instructions and commands; You are such a good Father and perfect in all Your ways, in Yeshua's name, amen.

November 22

1 Timothy 5:22

Lay hands suddenly on no man, neither be partaker of other men's sins: keep thyself pure.

We must always be careful to suddenly lay hands on just anyone; we should be led by the Spirit and covered when we do. We must be cautious of what we open ourselves up to and careful we don't become partakers in the sins of others.

As we grow deeper in Him and begin to walk as His priests and elders, we must make sure we are keeping ourselves pure in all things to the best of our ability. We must be watchful to not allow the enemy any place, opening, or get a foothold in our lives. We are set apart for Him and must remain under His covering in all our dealings and steps.

Help us, Abba, to be pure before You by always remaining under Your covering, to be wise in all we do and not do anything hastily without seeking Your guidance in it, in Yeshua's holy name, amen.

November 23

2 John 1:6

And this is love, that we walk after His commandments. This is the commandment, That, as ye have heard from the beginning, ye should walk in it.

It's no new thing. John even states in the prior verse, "Not as though I wrote a new commandment unto thee, but that which we had from the beginning." This is love, to walk in His commandments, loving God, and loving one another. His commandments are good; they haven't changed, and when we obediently walk in them, it shows our love, creates more love, and shows the world His love toward us and how good He is.

Yeshua came loving the Father so much that He followed perfectly all the Father said, and then told us to follow Him and do the same. This is the definition of **love**, following Yeshua and doing the will of the Father, then our light will shine, and His love will **radiate** through us to the world.

Father, help us to show love by obediently and willingly walking in Your commands as Yeshua did so others may see how good and perfect You and Your commands are, in Yeshua's wonderful name, amen.

November 24

Jeremiah 33:11

The voice of joy, and the voice of gladness, the voice of the bride-groom, and the voice of the bride, the voice of them that shall say, Praise the LORD of hosts: for the LORD is good; for His mercy endureth for ever: and of them that shall bring the sacrifice of Praise into the house of the LORD. For I will cause to return the captivity of the land, as at the first, saith the LORD.

Sing to the Lord a new song. Exalt His name on high. He is great and mighty, perfect in **all** His ways. Rejoice and be glad. His grace has saved us. His mercy delivers us, and by His love, He is restoring us. He is faithful throughout all generations. His Word is true, and He **never** changes. He is worthy.

Let everyone that has breath shout praises to the Lord!

Oh Abba, You are so good, and we worship You and sing praises to You with **all** we have and are. You truly are worthy of it all. In Yeshua's name, we pray, amen.

November 25

1 Thessalonians 5:16–18

16) Rejoice evermore. 17) Pray without ceasing. 18) In every-thing give thanks: for this is the will of God in Christ Jesus concerning you.

God's will for us is to always be grateful and give thanks in all things; not just in the good times, when things are going as planned, when blessings are reigning and happiness is abounding, but in the difficult times too. When hopes and dreams are being crushed, you're breaking from the pain, when answers don't come, or sickness isn't healed, don't despair or lose sight. He still controls the winds and the waves, so rejoice, be glad, and give thanks unto the Lord, knowing He is good. Continue praying and seeking Him, believing He holds your every moment and works **all** things together for good.

Lord, help us to live and walk by these instructions You set before us in Your Word, for they are Your will for us, in Yeshua Messiah's name, amen.

November 26

Hosea 4:6

My people are destroyed for lack of knowledge: because thou hast rejected knowledge, I will also reject thee, that thou shalt be no priest to me: seeing thou hast forgotten the law of thy God, I will also forget thy children.

It is our individual responsibility to educate ourselves. We need to pick up the Word and allow it to feed us and transform us by the knowledge it holds. It should be our daily bread, what we feast on continually. I think sometimes it's easy to use the lack of knowledge to excuse us from things, or curt tail discipline because the "we didn't know" gets played, but nothing dismisses the fact that we all have the capability of picking up the book, His Word, and learning it for ourselves.

When you're in college and you have to take an exam, nobody can take it and pass it for you; you must put the work into studying and learning so you have the knowledge needed to pass the test. So, it is the same in this journey of life. We must put the work into getting to know the Lord, His Word, and truth. We must study to show ourselves approved so we don't perish for lack of knowledge.

Abba, Your Word has everything in it we need to live. Help us to daily feed on it and fill ourselves with it so we have life and are not destroyed for lack of knowledge, in Yeshua's powerful name, amen.

November 27

1 John 2:7

Brethren, I write no new commandment unto you, but an old commandment which ye had from the beginning. The old commandment is the word which ye have heard from the beginning.

The Word, from the beginning, unchanging, perfect, powerful, and life-changing, given to us to live and walk by. IT is **not** too difficult and definitely **not** burdensome, but beautiful and sweet, bringing wisdom and blessing.

How wonderful and awesome it is that we are so blessed to have such righteous decrees and laws that He established for our good and protection. There's never been a greater love than the Father's love toward us and the Word He's given to be a lamp to our feet and a light to our path, to be our life.

Father, help us to take Your Word, read and eat it and hide it in our hearts, so we never forget it and always walk by it, for it truly is our life, in Yeshua's mighty name, amen.

November 28

Joshua 1:7–9

7) Only be thou strong and very courageous, that thou mayest observe to do according to all the law, which Moses my servant commanded thee: turn not from it to the right hand or to the left, that thou mayest prosper whithersoever thou goest. 8) This book of the law shall not depart out of thy mouth; but thou shalt meditate therein day and night, that thou mayest observe to do according to all that is written therein: for then thou shalt make thy way prosperous, and then thou shalt have good success. 9) Have not I commanded thee? Be strong and of a good courage; be not afraid, neither be thou dismayed: for the LORD thy God is with thee whithersoever thou goest.

It's been said that there are 365 fear nots in the Bible, one for every day, and it's a good thing because fear will keep one from moving; it binds and paralyzes, making one useless. In the last couple of years, fear has really tried to set up camp in my life, trying to grab hold of the very fibers of my being, causing me to be afraid to take steps, make decisions, and afraid to move. The Lord is helping me have victory in this through daily meditating on His Word and verses like these, letting them become the very fiber of my life instead. Fixing my eyes on Him alone, no turning but fixed and unmovable, walking according to and doing all His Word says, and I don't have to worry at all because I can find rest in knowing I'm doing what I can, and He will do the rest. If you're struggling at all with fear in any area of your life, pick up the Bible and let His words wash over you, filling you with His peace and truth, encouraging you to stand unmovable, courageous, and strong, for He is and will always be with you when you put your trust in Him.

Abba, help us to have victory over fear so that we may stand and walk strong and courageous, doing all Your Word says, knowing You are always with us and we have nothing to fear, in Yeshua's name, amen.

November 29

2 Corinthians 10:4

For the weapons of our warfare are not carnal, but mighty through God to the pulling down of strong holds.

The Lord provides us with some pretty powerful weapons to combat strongholds with. The first is His Word; His Word is true and can be stood upon and trusted in times of battle. God's spoken Word has power; when He speaks, things happen. Yeshua fought the enemy with "It is written"! The Word of God is powerful, sharper than any two-edged sword. Worship is another mighty weapon. God inhabits the praise of His people. When we Worship Him, not only does He show up, but He blankets us in a peace that passeth understanding and equips us with a strength that far surpasses any human strength.

We have Yeshua and His name; His word says that at the name of Yeshua, every knee shall bow, that what we ask in His name, He will do, and those who believe in Yeshua shall be saved. We have His Holy Spirit He sent to dwell in us and enable and equip us for any battle or stronghold. One of the greatest weapons is prayer. James 5:16 says that the prayer of a righteous person availeth much; it has great power. Philippians 4:6 says to be careful for nothing, but in everything, by prayer and supplication, with Thanksgiving, let your requests be made known unto God. The weapons He has given us are mighty; they fight and work on our behalf and bring victory.

Abba, thank You for equipping us with Your powerful weapons we need to win the wars and tear down strongholds, in Yeshua's powerful name, amen.

November 30

Joel 2:25

And I will restore to you the years that the locust hath eaten, the cankerworm, and the caterpillar, and the palmerworm, my great army which I sent among you.

This verse is one of the words the Lord gave to me when He rescued me from the death of my addiction. After the enemy had devoured pretty much **all** of my life, left me desolate and broken, empty and alone, with absolutely no hope, God met me at my worst and saved me. Not only did He save my life, but He restored it too, and not only did He restore it, but He also multiplied it a hundred-fold and left me speechless.

Twenty-seven years ago, when He met me and gave me this verse, I never imagined what His restoration project would look like and never imagined being where I am today. When He says He will restore the years the locust and cankerworm had eaten, hold on tight, because He meant it, and it will blow you away; it surely did for me. I am blessed beyond measure, living in a place I never dreamed I would be, with a beautiful family that exceeds my greatest desire and an extraordinary, incredible, unbelievable, spectacular, and miraculous God that is the center of it all and holds it all together. That is way beyond anything I could ever ask, think, and it is far surpassing what I deserved. All I know is He is a God of His Word, and He doesn't do anything small.

Thank You, Lord, for Your amazing and awesome hand of res-toration that returns years of the enemy's devastation. You are beyond good, Lord, in Yeshua's name, amen.

December 1

Ezekiel 12:2

Son of man, thou dwellest in the midst of a rebellious house, which have eyes to see, and see not; they have ears to hear, and hear not: for they are a rebellious house.

The Lord says rebellion is as the sin of witchcraft in 1 Samuel 15:23. His children, the house of Israel, was rebellious and disobedient. They didn't want to hear or follow God's words; they didn't want to see His ways. It's not that they couldn't understand them or were confused; they were rebellious and closed their ears and eyes to them. They deliberately choose disobedience and defiance.

Witchcraft is the practice of magic, the using of spells, communicating with unfamiliar spirits, the devil, which is what the pagan nations did that His people chose to follow. They chose that over obedience to Him. We must be careful what we open our eyes and ears to; opening them to the wrong thing will cause them to be closed to the truth.

Abba, help us to hear and see Your words and way so we don't become deceived by the err and become a rebellious people, in Yeshua's name, amen.

December 2

John 5:44

How can ye believe, which receive honour one of another, and seek not the honour that cometh from God only?

Yeshua came seeking not the honor of men, nor did He have the honor of man; man was too busy seeking and giving honor to man instead of seeking and giving it to the only important one. That is what He was telling them here. The honor of man means nothing, only the honor that cometh from the Father alone. That is what we should be seeking and doing, giving Him alone that honor that only He deserves.

They would believe a man coming in His own name over Yeshua coming in the Father's name. They would honor that man's word over Yeshua's, the only truth, the one deserving of being heard and believed. His words are truth and are the Father's Words, the only one from which honor cometh and are deserving of honor.

Abba, help us to always be careful to give and seek honor from the only one it's due, You, Lord, in Yeshua's name, amen.

December 3

Psalm 145:8

The Lord is gracious, and full of compassion; slow to anger, and of great mercy.

Mercy is getting what we don't deserve and not getting what we do deserve. God's mercy is beyond our comprehension. His love is so vast and unconditional. His compassion is genuine and true; at our worst, He sent His son to die so that we may be saved, grace that abounds far beyond what our minds can conceive.

He is patient and longsuffering, that we may come to know Him, have eternity with Him, and not perish. He is such a good, good Father, full of mercy and grace that we don't deserve and can't understand. He is so worthy of all our adoration and praise.

Thank You, Abba, for being patient and slow to anger, giving us a chance to get it right. Thank You for Your mercy and grace that allows us to come to know You, our Creator, our King, the lover of our soul. You are perfect and beautiful in all Your ways, in Your Son Yeshua's perfect name, amen.

December 4

Daniel 6:3

Then this Daniel was preferred above the presidents and princes, because an excellent spirit was in him; and the king thought to set him over the whole realm.

Daniel was favored because of the excellent spirit he had in him. What does it mean to have an excellent spirit? In verse four, it states that the presidents and princes could find no fault nor error in him, that he was a faithful man.

Webster's Dictionary's definition of *excellent* is: "eminently good, first class, superior."[53]

Daniel must have been a pretty upright guy, always doing the right to be preferred above the presidents and princes. Can that be said about us? We may find favor in our circumstances and with others if we choose to walk circumspectly, upright, and with an excellent spirit as Daniel did.

Abba, help us to have a spirit of excellence, to walk by it and do what's right always, that others may see You in us, and we may experience Your favor, in Yeshua's name, amen.

December 5

Matthew 22:37–40

37) Jesus said unto him, thou shalt love the Lord thy God with all thy heart, and with all thy soul, and with all thy mind. 38) This is the first and great commandment. 39) And the second is like unto it, Thou shalt love thy neighbor as thyself. 40) On these two commandments hang all the law and the prophets.

I Love how this verse does nothing but confirm His Word and commandments. If we love Abba with all our hearts, souls, and minds, we will listen, follow, and obey **all** He has said. If we love our neighbors as ourselves, we will fulfill the rest; we'll honor our parents and we won't steal, murder, covet, or commit adultery. We will keep all His commands by keeping these two; they **all** hang from these. It's such a beautiful thing and so perfectly orchestrated.

Abba, Your ways are perfect and never changing. Help us to truly grasp that and walk by every word that proceeds out of Your mouth, for it is **life**! In Your precious Son Yeshua's name, we ask this, amen.

December 6

Judges 3:4

And they were to prove Israel by them, to know whether they would hearken unto the commandments of the LORD, which He commanded their fathers by the hand of Moses.

God will send others into our lives to prove us. He will allow situations to be present before us to see what we will do, which way we will go, or how we will respond. Will we remain faithful and obedient, trusting, believing, and following His truth? Or will we get caught up and distracted by the flashing lights, fun, and deceiving appearances of evil?

Will we become a cotton-pickin' Israelite (as I would call myself consistently) in the wilderness, constantly doubting and being led astray, going around the mountain over and over? Or will we believe His commands are good, true, and right and are for our good to be obedient and follow them so we can reach the Promised Land? I know I'm tired of going around that mountain and learning the hard way; how about you? The brick wall hurts, but obedience brings blessing.

Father, help us to fully realize that disobedience brings Your curses, wrath, and discipline that is painful and to know that we can spare ourselves from that by walking in obedience to Your commands, which bring blessing and life, in Yeshua's name, amen.

December 7

1 Corinthians 5:11

But now I have written unto you not to keep company, if any man that is called a brother be a fornicator, or covetous, or an idolater, or a railer, or a drunkard, or an extortioner; with such an one no not to eat.

We are instructed to be separate from sin and those choosing to live in it. We are not to associate or sit and fellowship with those who oppose God and sin and go against His Word. Notice here He's saying if any of them are called a brother, part of the family, those who know the Word, if they're sinning and not living by and being obedient to the Lord and His Word, then we are not to keep company with them.

Continuing to keep company with them will not only taint us but falsely lead us to believe our doings are accepted or ignored. We must stand and be separate and not partake in any kind of way. Taking a **bold** stand will show them their sin is noticed and unacceptable. Though this might be extremely difficult in some circumstances, we **must** be obedient to the Word.

Lord, help us to always stand for You and Your Word, even in the face of those who choose to go against it, even when it's the ones closest to us. Give us Your strength to be separate and remain pure for You. It's in Your Son Yeshua's holy name, we ask this, amen.

December 8

1 Thessalonians 5:6–8

6) Therefore let us not sleep, as do others; but let us watch and be sober. 7) For they that sleep in the night; and they that be drunken are drunken in the night. 8) But let us, who are of the day, be sober, putting on the breastplate of faith and love; and for an helmet, the hope of salvation.

This one has always been a hard one for me to learn and change. I have always been more prone to the night, being up all night and sleeping all day. If we're awake in the night, then to be alert and awake in the day isn't likely. Over and over again, He has been showing me in His Word, where it says, "RISE EARLY, AND THEY ROSE EARLY." There is something about sleeping in the night and rising early, rested, and ready to face and handle the day we've been gifted. Life is fragile and fleeting, and we're not promised tomorrow, so we must remain sober and prepared to fully meet and accomplish the tasks that He sets before us each and every day, covered in His armor.

I am a work in progress, learning this most essential truth, and I am beyond grateful for His words of teaching so I may learn to walk in them and honor Him.

Abba, help us to know all Your words are our very life and help us to learn to live and walk by them all, for every word that proceeds out of Your mouth is wisdom and for our good, in Yeshua's powerful name, amen.

December 9

Psalm 24:3–4

3) Who shall ascend into the hill of the LORD? or who shall stand in His Holy place? 4) He that hath clean hands, and a pure heart; who hath not lifted up his soul unto vanity, nor sworn deceitfully.

If we are to ascend that mountain and stand in the Holy Place with the Father, then we must get our hearts right. It says here about those with clean hands and pure hearts who have not lifted up his soul unto vanity. The definition of *pure* is: "free of any contaminants, not mixed or adulterated with any other substance or material."[54] The definition for *clean* is: "morally uncontaminated, pure, and innocent."[55] We must examine our hearts and ask the Lord to come and remove anything that may have tainted it. Ask Him to search our hearts and show us anything that shouldn't be there so we can surrender it to Him and seek forgiveness.

We must also be careful to not be entangled or enticed by *vanity*, which is defined as "falsehood, evil, idolatry,"[56] but to morally keep our hearts and minds innocent and free from all the worldly garbage that so easily wants to flood our hearts and minds and keep us from being able to stand in His Holy Place.

Lord, please wash and cleanse us, removing any impurities that may be in us. Help us to have pure hearts and clean hands, innocent and free from any contaminants, that we may ascend into Your holy mountain and stand in Your Holy Place. In Your presence, there is fullness of joy, renewing of strength, and all that we need to live. It truly is the most beautiful and powerful place to be, compared to no other, in Yeshua's name, amen.

December 10

Joel 2:1

Blow ye the trumpet in Zion, and sound an alarm in my holy mountain: let all the inhabitants of the land tremble: for the day of the LORD cometh, for it is nigh at hand.

I remember singing this song growing up, and it was always sung in an upbeat, kind of rejoicing way. To my own lack of knowledge and spending time in His Word, I never truly knew the meaning behind it. Wow, what a difference it makes picking up the Word for ourselves, reading, understanding, and knowing it in its proper context.

It wasn't meant to be a joyous triumphant alarm. It was meant to warn the people of pending judgment coming. In Joel 2:11, it says, "For the day of the LORD is great and very terrible; and who can abide it?" God's judgment is coming; the trumpet needed to be blown and the alarm sounded. God's people needed to be warned. Verse twelve states, "Therefore also now, saith the LORD, turn ye even to me with all your heart, and with fasting, and with weeping, and with mourning." This is a solemn, serious, and powerful warning; judgment is coming, and it's time to wake up and get yourself ready, people of the LORD.

It may be that same time today! Are we awake and ready?

Jehovah, please help us to see, hear, understand, and know what You're saying so we can be ready and stand a post when it's time, that we may take knowing Your heart seriously so we can be prepared to sound Your trump when You say, in Yeshua's holy and precious name, amen.

December 11

Joel 2:21

Fear not, O land; be glad and rejoice: for the LORD will do great things.

This is the follow-up from the word yesterday about taking God at His Word, sounding the alarm, and heeding it. It is so perfect for the day we live in. In verses sixteen and seventeen, they are being instructed to gather all the people, elders, children, babies, bridegroom from his chambers (in ancient Jewish custom, a bridegroom was to stay in his chamber before the wedding until called by the father; these verses are showing the seriousness of the matter by calling the bridegroom out), and the bride from her closet. It goes on to say, "Let the priests and ministers of the LORD weep saying; SPARE thy people O LORD, and give not thine heritage to reproach," and because of their obedience, the Lord had pity on His people and spared them.

He then tells them to **fear not**, **be glad,** and **rejoice**. They listened and acted, and He responded and moved. Now it's time to be happy and sing with joy for God had chosen to spare them. They heard what He was saying, understood it, and willingly obeyed and followed it. May we be a people that does the same.

Abba, You are such a good, just, and faithful Father. When we repent and turn back to You, You change everything, move on our behalf, and cause us to rejoice and be glad. Thank You, Lord, for having mercy on us. In Yeshua's name, we pray this, amen.

December 12

Joshua 22:5

But take diligent heed to do the commandment and the law, which Moses the servant of the LORD charged you, to love the LORD your God, and to walk in all his ways, and to keep his commandments, and to cleave unto him, and to serve him with all your heart and with all your soul.

In doing this lies nothing but the Father's best; His love, blessings, peace and goodness, and fullness of joy. All He has asked and commanded is for our good and protection. He knows what we don't, and He sees what we can't, so why wouldn't we just trust and follow Him?

Why would we choose not to hear, believe, and pay attention to the one who has given everything life? He's a wonderful and good Father, and His ways are perfect. He perfectly and deeply loves us and has a beautiful future with Him awaiting us, overflowing with His goodness and blessing. Why would we choose anything else?

Father, help us to see Your ways are good and perfect, help us to listen and follow them all the days of our lives, never doubting but clinging to You with all that we are, knowing You are who You say You are. In Your Son Yeshua's beautiful name, we ask this, amen.

December 13

Obadiah 1:15

For the day of the LORD is near upon all the heathen: as thou hast done, it shall be done unto thee: thy reward shall return upon thine own head.

Here is confirmation that man will reap what he sows. What the land of Edom had done to Israel, God's children, it would be done back to them. The day of the Lord is a scary day for those who don't know Him.

When we walk through life trying to defy who He is, denying He is who He says He is and the power He holds, and doing our own agenda and way consistently, we will abruptly come to the end of ourselves and find out we were wrong.

We are far better off acknowledging who He is, getting to know Him, drawing closer to Him, walking and living by His words, and reaping what is good than waiting until it's too late and reaping the judgment of our err.

Abba, help us to know You, to do what is right and true so when it comes back upon our own heads, it's a blessing and not a curse, in Yeshua's name, amen.

December 14

Ephesians 5:18–20

18) And be not drunk with wine, wherein is excess; but be filled with the Spirit; 19) Speaking to yourselves in psalms and hymns and spiritual songs, singing and making melody in your heart to the Lord; 20) Giving thanks always for all things unto God and the Father in the name of our Lord Jesus Christ.

Giving thanks, singing melodies of praise to the Lord, and speaking His Word over ourselves will do more and make us feel better than anything else the world has to offer. Being full of His Spirit is better than any drunk or high the world and all it holds can give.

True joy, peace, and contentment comes from the Lord alone, and praising Him and singing hymns to Him truly makes the heart glad. It conquers fear, dissolves depression, eases pain, and lightens darkness. Anything else we try is only a temporary fix but praising and thanking Him in and for all things, speaking and continually making melody in our hearts unto the King of kings is the answer and solution to anything and everything we face here on earth. Singing His Word at all times has the power to change circumstances and situations and causes us to walk in freedom and victory with unending joy.

Lord, please come and fill us with Your Spirit that we may walk in the fruits of it, having true freedom to live and walk victoriously, in Yeshua's wonderful name, amen.

December 15

Isaiah 26:3

Thou wilt keep him in perfect peace, whose mind is stayed on thee: because he trusteth in thee.

To have our minds stayed on Him means we have our thoughts fixed on Him and everything about Him. *Stayed* means "to remain in a specified state or position," according to the dictionary, so we are to stay fixed and remain in that position, without wandering or tossing to and fro. The Hebrew word for *stayed* is *Sâmak*, meaning "to take hold of, bear up, establish, stand fast."[57] We must establish Him and all He is in our thoughts and minds. Take hold of Him and His Word, bear it up, and stand fast in it, trusting in Him in all things if we want to be kept in perfect peace.

Perfect peace sounds magnificent to me, but that means we must keep our minds "stayed" amid all things, the storms, trials, losses, confusion, hurt, good times, and the bad. We play a part! We must believe, trust Him, and keep our minds stayed and fixed on Abba if we want to be kept and held in this perfect peace—peace that surpasses understanding; that's complete and doesn't compare to anything else. Oh, it just sounds so beautiful and something I definitely want to seek to obtain.

Abba, help us to train our minds to be "stayed" on You in and through all circumstances, to fix our thoughts on things above and on all You are so we can know Your true and perfect peace, in Yeshua's holy, beautiful, and powerful name, amen.

December 16

Micah 6:8

He hath shewed thee, O man, what is good; and what doth the LORD require of thee, but to do justly, and to love mercy, and to walk humbly with thy God?

Three things the Lord requires of us: do justly, this incorporates much, but in the simplest of terms, it means do the right thing always, live righteously, and be righteous in all thy ways. To love mercy—the Lord is so merciful to us. Without His mercy, we would be hopeless. He wants us to be merciful as He is, to love being kind, rare, and showing favor to those who might not deserve it. To mercifully help those who are lost or have erred find and walk in His path and ways. Then, last but not least, to walk humbly with Him; we deserve nothing. We are sinners saved by grace, made righteous only through the blood of Yeshua. We must always remember that and walk humbly with the Lord. Yeshua, being perfect, walked humbly before the Father in all His ways as an example for us. He came to serve and not to be served. We must learn from His example and walk humbly always. These are the three simple things that are the very fibers of being a self-sacrificing child of God that incorporates the whole essence of who we are to be. It is simple yet so profound.

Abba, help these three things become engrained in us that we may do what You require of us and be that selfless child of Yours as Yeshua was. It's in Your Son Yeshua's precious name, we ask this, amen.

December 17

John 4:24

God is a Spirit: and they that worship Him must worship him in spirit and in truth.

What an eye-opening revelation this was for me as I sat with Abba this morning. Some days can be rough for me as I sit and cry, wondering where I am, where He's taking me, what He is doing, is He even here with me, and have I turned off in the wrong direction, heading away from Him? All the whats, whys, hows, and where questions surround me. Well, today was one of those moments, and as I was reading in Isaiah 46:4, God was saying to His children, the house of Jacob, all the remnants of the house of Israel, which includes us, that He would carry them, us. He made us and will bear, carry, and deliver us till our hairs are gray.

He began to remind me of the time, just a few years ago, how He called me to bow before Him at a Wednesday night youth service. "Do you want all I have for you?" He asked. "Then bow before Me!" I fought it for a week until, finally, the next week, I fell to my knees. Long story short, I had been praying, seeking, and continually asking Him to draw me closer and take me deeper. That night on my knees, He gave me a vision. He was calling my name, reaching for my hand, picking me up by it, and drawing me to follow Him. So much has changed since that day. Good changes, lonely changes, confusing moments, but today, through all this, He revealed to me that I have known Him in Spirit and worshiped Him in Spirit, but now, I'm learning to know and worship Him in truth. Wow, what an overwhelming and powerful moment it was. See, I haven't learned the truth of His Word, how to walk in it, and worship in it, and I am learning the process. He is teaching me. We must worship Him in both Spirit and truth. Worshiping Him in Spirit can be amazing and is beautiful, but worshiping Him in truth takes truly getting to know Him and digging deep. It takes work but is powerful beyond words when you do.

Abba, help us to worship You as Your Word says, to go deep into all You are so we can know Your truth and worship You in both Spirit and truth, in Yeshua's holy and precious name, amen.

December 18

Nahum 1:7

The LORD is good, a strong hold in the day of trouble; and he knoweth them that trust in Him.

One thing I find so awesome with the Lord is that in the middle of His judgment, in the middle of His fierce indignation, He sends a word of hope to those who are His and trust in Him. He consistently reminds us that He is our defender. He will recompense our enemy, and no matter what we may have to go through, He will be there with us. He knows those who are His and will protect, defend, and keep them in and through all circumstances.

It's so reassuring in this day and age that we are in, where everything is so divided and uncertain that we have this certainty in Him. We have this promise, this vision of hope, and this assurance that He knows us and will protect and keep us in and through all the chaos going on, in the midst of His judgment taking place, as it was here in Nineveh, in the midst of whatever storm may be raging. He alone is our stronghold in that day of trouble, and He alone will hold and keep His own, those who trust in Him.

Father, help us to turn to You with our whole being, to run into Your arms and find rest under the shadow of Your wing, for You are our shelter and stronghold in all things, always, and help us daily in the midst of it all to know and walk in that. In Yeshua's powerful name, we ask this, amen.

December 19

Matthew 4:4

But He answered and said, It is written, Man shall not live by bread alone, but by every word that proceedeth out of the mouth of God.

His Word is our real nourishment, the true bread we need to live by and make it through this life. Our physical man will weaken, wither, and die without nourishment. What makes us think our spiritual man won't do the same? His words are the bread and nourishment our souls needed to live. His words are life, and they bring life. They are powerful, for at His Word, the world was formed, the sun shone, and the waters parted. Storms cease at His word; the winds and waves calm, mountains move, and lives change.

If we live and walk by His words, our lives will transform in front of our eyes. We will feel weights lifted and see steps laid out in front of us with His voice and words saying, "This is the way; walk ye in it." He is the true bread that we need to navigate and be victorious in this life. When you pick up the Word of God, imagine it being your favorite food ever; the juiciest steak because it is the best protein man could have; the most mouth-watering salad because it is the most important nutrient our souls need; and the most delicious dessert you could sink your teeth in because its promises are sweeter than the best sugars and honey.

Lord, help us to make Your Word our daily bread. Help us to begin to live and walk by every word You have spoken in it. Help us to just feed on it and receive all the nourishment it has to offer, knowing it is what truly brings life to us. In Yeshua's mighty name, we ask this, amen.

December 20

Hosea 6:6

For I desired mercy, and not sacrifice; and the knowledge of God more than burnt offerings.

Yes, the sacrifices were important. The Bible says the burnt offerings were a sweet savor to God, but without the heart change, they meant nothing. We can offer sacrifices of praise and offerings of time and money, but unless we do it with right and pure hearts, He doesn't want them. Outward rituals and actions are empty and in vain if our inwardness is not changed, purified, and right before Him. Above all else, He wants and desires our hearts.

The heart condition has always been the problem. Many good people in the world do good acts and deeds but whose hearts don't know Him, those who have denied the knowledge of His Word and truth, whose pride keeps them from humbly seeking His mercy, and who think their good works will save them and are above or better than obedience. God doesn't want all that. He only desires for us to know Him, His Word, and to humbly submit ourselves to it and obey it. If we do that alone, we become a vessel of honor to Him that He can use for His glory and not our own.

Help , Abba, to know You fully, to know Your Word and truth and to follow and obey it above all else, in Yeshua's name, amen.

December 21

Philippians 4:4

Rejoice in the Lord alway: and again I say, Rejoice.

Rejoice always, it says; not just in the good times, when you're happy or when you're feeling it, not when the sun is shining and the warm breeze is blowing on your face, but in the dark times as well. In the times of heavy downpour, in the worst of storms, when the boat is tossing to and fro, and you just don't know if you're going to stay afloat, when the pain cuts like a knife, the loss leaves you broken and speechless, and when it's completely unimaginable, rejoice in the Lord. Rejoice, knowing He is your stay, shelter, holds your every moment, and works **all** things for good to those who love Him and are called according to His purpose. Know He will never leave or forsake you, His promises are true, and He will cause the sun to shine down on you again.

He is a good, good Father and is worthy of our praise. Even when it's hard and we're broken, we can still rejoice in who He is and the promises He has made. Rejoice in the Lord always, and again I say rejoice.

Lord, help us to truly learn how to walk out the words in this passage in the midst of and through all things, every circumstance, and each situation in our lives, always, in Yeshua's holy, mighty, and beautiful name, amen.

December 22

Habakkuk 2:14

For the earth shall be filled with the knowledge of the glory of the LORD, as the waters cover the sea.

No matter what, when all is said and done, the **glory** of the LORD will **fill** the earth, and all will see Him and know He alone is the one and only true God. They will see that all the idols and false gods the enemy has deceived them into worshiping are just that, false, lifeless, and without the ability to do or change anything.

The LORD alone will reign, and all will come to the knowledge of His sovereignty and see His glory. Some will be joyous and in awe, sorrowful and disbelief, in awaited anticipation, and some dumbfounded and angry. All will see that He alone is LORD of **all**. There is nothing more beautiful, powerful, piercing, and brilliant than Him in all His glory.

Abba, help us to come to know You so intimately that we expectantly await and want nothing more than for the knowledge of Your glory to surround us and fill this earth as the waters cover the sea, in Yeshua's holy and precious name, amen.

December 23

Mark 9:23

Jesus said unto him, if thou canst believe, all things are possible to him that believeth.

Whether Yeshua's words here were directed toward the disciples who could not cast the dumb spirit out of the boy, or the father who watched his boy suffer his whole life, one thing is true, they all needed to hear it. Today, we need to hear Yeshua's words here just as much as the disciples and the father of the boy did then. We must not become a faithless generation, but we must stand strong and firm in our faith, believing in our hearts and knowing beyond a shadow of a doubt that absolutely nothing is impossible with our God.

If we trust and believe, we will see mountains move and miracles happen in Abba's perfect time. We will see the impossible become possible, and we will see that it will be as God says and **not** as man says. I personally have experienced this in my life—the impossible becoming possible—more than once, and all I can say is, **God is good** and **never** doubt what He can do. **All things** are **possible** to him who believes.

Lord, help us to know Your Word is true and all things are possible, no matter how hard, horrible, or impossible they look, and help our unbelief that may be hidden so You can move, in Yeshua's name, amen.

December 24

Romans 12:12

Rejoicing in hope, patient in tribulation; continuing instant in prayer.

These words are so on-time in every season and for such a time as this. Our world is seeing unprecedented times; division, moral decay, stress, and hardships all around, not including the individual struggles or storms we may be facing, whether it be illness or financial or relational losses; the weights of any of this can become overbearing. Paul here tries to give us some basic but important foundational instructions to guide us through this journey of life.

There are three wise and powerful truths that will help, strengthen, and keep us in and through all that may be raging on around us. Rejoice in the middle of the pain, uncertainty, and struggles because we have a hope in the Lord who is an anchor for us. Be patient in tribulation, in the tough moments, and the trying times, knowing and believing our Lord is faithful to meet us and never let us go. Remain constant in prayer as it is our most powerful weapon, always knowing the fervent prayer of a righteous man availeth much. These three simple but profound instructions can keep us living in Abba's peace and joy, standing firm and never wavering.

Father, help us to walk in and hold deeply to these three foundational principles so we can always rejoice, standing patient and firm, with our eye fixed on You, our only hope, in Yeshua's powerful and beautiful name, amen.

December 25

Haggai 2:5

According to the word that I covenanted with you when ye came out of Egypt, so my Spirit remaineth among you: fear ye not.

Wow, **fear not**—some of the most powerful and important yet so often difficult two words to live by. The Lord tells us over and over again throughout time to **fear no**t. If we truly believe He is who He says He is, then we can rest in each step we take and every moment we face, knowing **He's got it al**l.

It doesn't mean we become slothful or complacent when we're trusting and not fearing, but actually quite the opposite. It means we can be like Yeshua and the apostles, becoming mighty forces, boldly walking, and proclaiming His Word and truth. We can stand firm in it and not waver as we let our light shine bright in the darkness that's growing by the day, **not fearing** what man or the enemy can do to us. **Fear not** when the nations come up against you, the war's wage around you, and they speak evil of you to destroy and harm you. **Fear not** when the giants stand before you, the waves try to overtake you, and the council delivers you up. **Fear not**, be bold, stand firm, and know **who** fights and wins the battles, who the ultimate victor is.

Help us, Lord, to live in peace, free from the bondage of fear in every situation in our lives, standing boldly, always proclaiming Your Word of truth to the world, in Yeshua's name, amen.

December 26

1 John 2:3–4

3) And hereby we do know that we know him, if we keep his commandments. 4) He that saith, I know him, and keepeth not his commandments, is a liar, and the truth is not in him.

If we walk outside of His commands but continue to say we know Him, we are liars. That's a pretty harsh, not-so-loving truth that can be a bit hard to swallow; nonetheless, it's true. If we know Him, we **will keep His commands** because we **love Him** and **know how good** and **perfect He is**. If one is walking by His commands, then we know they know Him. Let me make it clear, I'm not talking about the commands of men here, like some might, but I'm talking about **His** commands, **Elohim**, the **Lord our God, Creator** of **all things**.

Yeshua came and followed His commands perfectly and then told us to follow Him. Are we being honest with ourselves, and do we truly know Him? Do we follow His instructions and commands and have the truth in us? Is His truth in us? How much clearer can it get? It may be time to truly examine ourselves, learn His commands, be sure we are following them, and be sure we truly **know Him**. There is **no other** way to **life**; outside of it, we are all just dead men walking.

Abba, please write Your Word and commands on our hearts that we may truly know and follow them all the days of our lives, that the truth be in us and we **not** be liars, in Yeshua's powerful name, amen.

December 27

Zechariah 1:3

Therefore say thou unto them, Thus saith the LORD of hosts; Turn ye unto me, saith the LORD of hosts, and I will turn unto you, saith the LORD of hosts.

All we have to do is turn to Him when we're fallen, hurt, have gone astray, slipped, and lost; all we need to do is turn to Him, and He will turn to us. We don't need to continue to trudge through all the garbage, sit and wallow in all the pain of bad choices, or be hopeless and walk through this life aimlessly; we just need to **turn**. I know at times it can seem so hard, literally seeming impossible; trust me when I say I was there, but it's not. If we just take the one step turning ourselves toward Him, He will be right there, turned to us.

We don't have to buy the enemy's lies that we've done too much wrong, too far away, or fallen too low; there is **nothing** that will stop the Lord from being there for us if we just **turn**. When we do, He will be right there, take our hand, and walk through everything with us from that moment forward. I was at the bottom of bottoms, the end of my life. I couldn't live another day like I was when I turned to Him in a last-ditch effort of hope, and there He was, meeting me right where I was. He took all my pain and garbage and has never left me since. **All we have to do is turn.**

Abba, help us to turn to You, even if it takes the very last ounce of strength we have, knowing You will be right there and will carry us until You've renewed our strength, and then You will walk with us for the remainder of our days, in Your Son Yeshua's precious and most powerful name, amen.

December 28

Jeremiah 4:3–4

3) For thus saith the LORD to the men of Judah and Jerusalem, Break up your fallow ground, and so not among thorns. 4) Circumcise yourselves to the LORD, and take away the foreskins of your heart, ye men of Judah and inhabitants of Jerusalem: lest my fury come forth like fire, and burn that none can quench it, because of the evil of your doings.

Israel had gotten involved in all the things they shouldn't have; they had turned away from the Father, and their hearts had become hardened. In chapter three, the Lord, on numerous times, called them backsliding children and told them that if they returned to Him and put away all their abominations, He would save, deliver them, and heal them and their land. He tells them in this verse to "break up your fallow ground"; their hearts had become so hardened by sin. If you've ever experienced farming or gardening, the ground before planting season is dry, hard, full of weeds, and in need of plowing, rototilling, and breaking up before the seed can go into it, or the seed won't fare well.

God used these words specifically to give them a vivid image of their hearts. They needed to break up the cement ground, rip out all the weeds, thorns, and roots, and cut away all the dead old garbage sin from their hearts, or God's judgment and fury would come and devour them like a wildfire because their evildoings were so great. His Word says there is nothing new under the sun, and history just repeats itself (Eccles. 1:9). I think this word was not just for then but is also so timely for right now in our world. I think it is powerful and so true and real for the day in which we live. We need radical change and to start breaking up some fallow ground and make way for the King of Glory to come and have His way.

Abba, help us to start the gruesome task of breaking up the fallow ground in our own hearts first, our gardens, towns, country, and world, so You can come and heal us and our land and plant Your harvest of the fruits of Your kingdom, in Yeshua's name, amen.

December 29

Matthew 3:10

And now also the axe is laid unto the root of the trees: therefore every tree which bringeth not forth good fruit is hewn down, and cast into the fire.

John the Baptist was preparing and making the way for the Messiah. He was telling the people to repent for the kingdom of heaven was at hand. Repent and be baptized, cutting away and burying all the old and dead so they could walk uprightly, producing fruit for the Lord. He warned them that all who didn't would be like non producing trees and would be cut down and thrown into the fire. That's a powerful word picture.

On our property, we do a lot of harvesting of dead trees, and to relate a life to being non producing and dead like one of the trees here and having to be cut down and cast into the fire makes it become a little more literal and extremely sobering. It's so important that when we repent, are baptized, and turn from our sinful ways that we start digging in and growing in the Lord. We become filled with His Word and truth, so our lives begin to develop good fruit. We then must continue to go deeper and dig in more and more, so we never become stagnant and stop bearing good fruit for Him. We grow in His image and likeness day by day from glory to glory until the day we meet our Savior face to face and are welcomed in to spend all eternity with Him and the Father; it doesn't get much more glorious that.

Lord, help us to become planted, rooted, and grounded in Your truth that we produce only good fruit for You always, in every thought, word and deed, Father, in Yeshua's name, amen.

December 30

Zephaniah 2:3

Seek ye the LORD, all ye meek of the earth, which have wrought his judgment; seek righteousness, seek meekness: it may be ye shall be hid in the day of the LORD'S anger.

Judgment was coming to the earth to God's people and the enemies of God's people. God's people had been taking on the ways of the pagan nations around them, worshiping their gods, and walking in their rituals and beliefs. Our God is a jealous God and will only tolerate sin and disobedience for so long. The coming judgment was sure and at the very door, but when judgment comes on the wicked and sinful, there is also God's mercy and protection that comes on the repentant and righteous.

Zephaniah is pleading with the people to seek the LORD, righteousness, and mercy, and in the day of God's great wrath and judgment you may be hidden and saved from it. Today is a time like this again, and we need to seek the LORD with all we are so we may be found as His remnant, hidden and protected under the shadow of His wing.

Abba, help us to run far from the compromise of sin that so easily wants to turn our hearts from You and help us to run wholeheartedly to You, seeking You with all we are so we may be saved on that day. In Yeshua's powerful name, we ask this, amen.

December 31

Mark 12:42–43

42) And there came a certain poor widow, and she threw in two mites, which make a farthing. 43) And He called unto him His disciples, and saith unto them, Verily I say unto you, That this poor widow hath cast more in, than all they which have cast into the treasury.

While all the others casted from their abundance, Yeshua said this poor widow casted from her want. She gave all she had, trusting and believing who holds her tomorrow. Her gift was greater than all the other gifts. She gave from her heart **all** she had. Not only was she trusting and believing, but she must have been truly devoted to the Lord and the furtherance of His kingdom to give the last of her living to the Temple.

I often used to stop and ask myself what I would have done. Would I have maybe only given one? Would I have debated it for a while? There have been times in my life where I've had much and times, like in my addiction days, when I had nothing. I have now learned through both that nothing beats giving, even when there's not much to give. Just do it with a grateful heart, trusting and believing, then watch God increase it beyond what you can imagine. Giving out of our want will produce a true joy that no one can take away and will definitely reach the ears of the Almighty, just as this widow reached Yeshua's.

Abba, help us to give with the kind of heart this woman gave, whether we have much or little. Help us to give genuinely from the depth of our hearts, in Yeshua's name, amen.

ACKNOWLEDGEMENTS

I first want to give ALL praise and thanks to my Lord and Savior for saving my life. For delivering me from addiction and the path of destruction I was walking in. For restoring all the canker worm had eaten and destroyed, above and beyond all I could ever imagine. Thank you for holding my every moment, Abba, for walking with me always and for never leaving me alone. You are truly my everything, my King, and the Rock upon which I stand always.

I want to thank my husband, who saw something in me when no one else did, who loved me through the rough times, believed in me through my failures, encouraged me when I wanted to give up, and prayed for me through it all. You are my knight in shining armor and my biggest blessing, and I thank the Lord for sending you to me. Your love and support has made this all possible.

Thank you to my daughter Bethany for giving me journal after journal and encouraging me to write. Thank you as well for your hard work you put in designing and painting the cover of this book. It is absolutely beautiful and exactly what I envisioned for it.

Thank you to my daughter Hannah for taking time and drawing my monthly pictures for the book. I love having that extra touch on the pages of this book. They are perfect and everything I desired them to be.

Thank you to my daughter-in-law Rachel, who's really just a daughter, for helping me with my book summary and my bio I was struggling with. You are so good and such a blessing always.

Thank you to my son-in-law Miles, who once again is just a son, for taking time out of your day to come over and use your photography skills to do the difficult job of capturing a headshot of me for the back cover and making it look good. You're amazing.

A huge thank you to all my kids, James and Rachel, Jeremy and Amanda, Miles and Bethany, and Hannah, for loving me, encouraging me always, and seeing me through to this point. You are all huge miracles and blessings I don't deserve, and I thank the Lord for you. You are my most precious gifts.

A thank you to my Uncle Ted, who is no longer with us today. He has through all his amazing achievements inspired me to press on for the Lord. He lived his life loud and proud for the Lord, being the President of World Vision, Editorial Director and General Manager of Zondervan Publishing House, writing and publishing more than fifty books, and being the Executive Director of Youth for Christ. His example taught me all things are possible through the Lord, to run the race and never give up.

I want to remember my Aunt Ruth, who was a selfless woman, giving herself to a life of missionary work in Laos, taking me in as a troubled teen, and loving me and teaching me the qualities of a godly woman, leading me by the beautiful example she was.

My parents, who raised me to know the Father, gave me my name in hopes that I would live it out for Him and prayed for me nonstop, believing He would lead me to the life He purposed for me all along.

My Uncle Guen, who sat on the floor in my closet with me when I tried to end my life. I remember him praying with me, talking to me, and helping me see my life was worth something and I was precious in the Father's eyes.

My Aunt Frieda, who faithfully prayed for me daily and poured the Word of the Lord into me when everyone else gave up on me. She still welcomed me open armed.

I want to give a **big** thank you to Todd Bullington from Xulon Press, who from minute one made me feel like Xulon Press was not just a publishing company but a family that I was a part of. The love of the Father just flowed out of him each time we spoke, and I felt like he was a brother I had known all my life. In those times I couldn't see this book coming to fruition, he would help me see the end result and encourage me to keep pressing on.

I want to give a **huge** thank you to Courtney Maile, who truly was sent from the Lord especially for me. What a gift and miracle she was. When I was ready to give up and walk away from this book Abba had called me to, He sent her. She sat with me for hours on the phone, walking me through everything I struggled with and didn't understand. She took this manuscript and polished it to the point of shining. I believe Abba knew I was at my end with this and sent me this **amazing, talented, patient, and sweet** woman to come alongside me and really turn this into a reality. From her amazing heart of just wanting to help me to our mutual love for Aussies, she has been a blessing beyond words. So thankful to once again feel like family because of her.

Lastly, I want to thank all of my family and friends who helped me in so many ways, supported me through this whole journey, and lifted me in prayer continually. I have been fortunate and blessed to be surrounded by some of the **best** people in the world. I love and cherish you all.

ABOUT THE AUTHOR

I grew up in a suburb outside of Detroit, Michigan. I came from a strong Christian heritage with my Grandfather being a lay minister. My Uncle Ted and Aunt Ruth Andrianoff were missionaries in Laos for a good majority of their lives. My Uncle Ted W. Engstrom was president of World Vision, head of Youth for Christ, Editorial Director and General Manager of Zondervan Publishing House, publishing over fifty books throughout his life and ministry. My parents, Don and Ruth Engstrom, worked for Youth for Christ Ministries as well, being part of the praise team. They raised me in a well-known Christian church in Detroit, MI. I played in the orchestra there, was involved in the youth group, and had a heart for the Lord. I knew right from wrong, and I knew firsthand about Abba's love, goodness, and miracle-working power. Not only did I experience it in my own life, but I witnessed it in so many lives around me as well. As I was entering my mid-teens and early adulthood, I began to struggle with insecurities, doubts, and lies of the enemy. I faced many frightening moments where I stood wiping my tear-stained cheeks, wondering how I got to this place I was in and begging for help. I spent six years on the streets of Detroit, battling a horrific addiction and being so close to death one too many times. I was in and out of treatment centers and programs, and nothing worked; I lost everything I had. I lost my home, I lost my children to the State of Michigan, I lost my family and all the friends I had.

It was finally when I was at the end of myself that I found the **grace** and **mercy** of a loving and forgiving Father. He met me as I knelt on my living room floor all alone. My husband had packed most of our belongings up and had left while I was gone on a three-day binge. I was broken, alone, and at my end; I couldn't go on one minute longer in the state I was in. I believed my heavenly Father knew that when He met me there in the middle of that living room that day and delivered me from the nightmare I was living in. Not only did He meet me and take it all away, but He threw it as far as the east is from the west, buried it in the deepest ocean, never to be remembered again, and had me rise up to walk in newness of life. He then began to restore **all** the canker worm had destroyed and eaten. He blew my mind and took my breath away with **all the amazing blessings** He had awaiting me. He restored my family and caused my husband, my knight in shining armor, to see me as Abba Himself saw me, not as the garbage I was. He returned to me my precious children and **blessed** me with two more miracle babies. He has also blessed me with eight cherished grandbabies and has surrounded me with amazing friends I call family and a beautiful family I call friends. He took all the ashes and garbage of my life and turned it into **beauty**, leaving me in **awe** and **wonder**. I have fallen and continue to fall so deeply in love with a Daddy who just wanted to shower His love on me all along. Now, thirty years later, He's called me to share that **love, faithfulness,** and **goodness** of His with others in this 365-day devotional with a passage from His Holy Scriptures, personal testimonies, and so much more. My prayer is that when you open this book up and begin to soak in the reading for the day, you will be **blessed** beyond measure. That you will experience an **amazing** and **never changing** Abba who loves you more than anything you could imagine and is waiting to spend precious moments with you. May Yah **bless you** as you spend **Daily Moments with Abba**.

Note: You will find throughout the text the original Hebrew names for God and Jesus, being Yah and Yeshua.

Endnotes

1 *Oxford Languages,* s.v. "Good."

2 *Oxford Languages,* s.v. "Proper." *Dictionary.com,* s.v. "Proper."

3 *Lexico.com, s.v.* "Qualities." *Dictionary.com,* s.v. "Qualities." *Oxford Languages,* s.v. "Qualities."

4 Chris Christian, "Living Sacrifice," recorded 1985, *Mirror of Your Heart,* Home Sweet Home Records.

5 Justin Rizzo, "Tree," recorded 2008, *Found Faithful,* Forerunner Music.

6 Oxford Languages, s.v. "Perfect."

7 *Strong's Concordance*, s.v. "Perfect," "Tâmîym," "Teleios," "Telos," E-Sword.net.

8 Randy Scruggs, "Sanctuary," recorded 1995, *Acoustic Worship.*

9 *Strong's Concordance*, s.v. "Still," E-Sword.net.

10 *Strong's Concordance*, s.v. "Seek," E-Sword.net.

11 *Strong's Concordance*, s.v. "Seek," E-Sword.net.

12 *Strong's Concordance*, s.v. "Seek," E-Sword.net.

13 *Strong's Concordance*, s.v. "Babblings," E-Sword.net.

14 *Strong's Concordance*, s.v. "Oppositions," E-Sword.net.

15 *Strong's Concordance*, s.v. "Follow," E-Sword.net.

16 *Strong's Concordance*, s.v. "Jot," E-Sword.net.

17 *Strong's Concordance*, s.v. "Spue," E-Sword.net. *Merriam-Webster Dictionary,* s.v. "Spue." *Dictionary.com,* s.v. "Spue."

18 *Merriam-Webster Dictionary,* s.v. "Remember." *Strong's Concordance*, s.v. "Remember," E-Sword.net.

19 *Strong's Concordance*, s.v. "Evil," E-Sword.net.

20 *Strong's Concordance*, s.v. "Communications," E-Sword.net.

21 *Strong's Concordance*, s.v. "Corrupt," E-Sword.net.

22 *Strong's Concordance*, s.v. "Good," E-Sword.net.

23 *Strong's Concordance*, s.v. "Manners," E-Sword.net.

24 *Strong's Concordance*, s.v. "Violence," E-Sword.net.

25 *Strong's Concordance*, s.v. "Rend," E-Sword.net.

26 *Strong's Concordance*, s.v. "Stranger," E-Sword.net.

27 Jesus Culture, "You Won't Relent," recorded 2008, *Your Love Never Fails,* Jesus Culture Music.
28 *Oxford Languages,* s.v. "Humble."
29 *Oxford Languages,* s.v. "Gentle."
30 *Oxford Languages,* s.v. "Patient."
31 *Webster's New World Dictionary,* 2nd College ed. (Warner Books, 1984), s.v. "Devour."
32 *Strong's Concordance,* s.v. "Keep," "Phulasso," E-Sword.net.
33 *Strong's Concordance,* s.v. "Hear," E-Sword.net.
34 *Strong's Concordance,* s.v. "Fear," E-Sword.net.
35 *Strong's Concordance,* s.v. "Direct," E-Sword.net.
36 *Strong's Concordance,* s.v. "Abased," "Tapeinoo," E-Sword.net.
37 *Oxford Languages,* s.v. "Exceeding."
38 *Strong's Concordance,* s.v. "Dwell," "Yaw-shab," E-Sword.net.
39 *Strong's Concordance,* s.v. "Holy,"àylos/hagios," E-Sword.net.
40 *Strong's Concordance,* s.v. "Conversation," "àvaotpoqń," E-Sword.net.
41 *Strong's Concordance,* s.v. "Abomination," E-Sword.net.
42 *Dictionary.com,* s.v. "Blessed." *Oxford Advanced Learner's Dictionary,* s.v. "Blessed." *Lexico.com, s.v.* "Blessed."
43 *Oxford Languages,* s.v. "Gracious." *Strong's Concordance,* s.v. "Gracious," E-Sword.net.
44 *Strong's Concordance,* s.v. "Honor," E-Sword.net.
45 *Oxford Languages,* s.v. "Virtuous." *Strong's Concordance,* s.v. "Virtuous," E-Sword.net.
46 *Strong's Concordance,* s.v. "Perceive," "Take," E-Sword.net.
47 *Oxford Languages,* s.v. "Envy." *Strong's Concordance,* s.v. "Envy," E-Sword.net.
48 *Strong's Concordance,* s.v. "Babe," Biblehub.com.
49 *Oxford Languages,* s.v. "Suckling."
50 *Strong's Concordance,* s.v. "Shield," E-Sword.net. *Dictionary.com,* s.v. "Shield."
51 *Oxford Languages,* s.v. "Steadfast."
52 *Wiktionary,* s.v. "Unmovable," Definitions.net.
53 *Merriam-Webster Dictionary,* s.v. "Excellent."
54 *Oxford Languages,* s.v. "Pure."
55 *Oxford Languages,* s.v. "Clean."

56 *Strong's Concordance*, s.v. "Vanity," Biblehub.com. *Strong's Concordance*, s.v. "Vanity," E-Sword.net.
57 *Oxford Languages,* s.v. "Stayed." *Strong's Concordance*, s.v. "Stayed," "Sâmak," E-Sword.net.

CPSIA information can be obtained
at www.ICGtesting.com
Printed in the USA
LVHW082019210222
711654LV00003B/135

9 781662 842979